JOHN HUSTON

Maker of Magic

Books by Stuart Kaminsky

Don Siegel
Clint Eastwood
American Film Genres
Ingmar Bergman: Essays in Criticism
    (with Joseph F. Hill)
Bullet for a Star (novel)
John Huston: Maker of Magic

JOHN HUSTON

Maker of Magic

STUART KAMINSKY

Illustrated with photographs

HOUGHTON MIFFLIN COMPANY BOSTON 1978

Library of Congress Cataloging in Publication Data

Kaminsky, Stuart
   John Huston, maker of magic.
   "Filmography": p.
   Bibliography: p.
   Includes index.
   1. Huston, John, 1906–   2. Moving-picture produc-
ers and directors—United States—Biography. I. Title
PN1998.A3H795   791.43′0233′0924 [B] 77-17017
ISBN 0-395-25716-6

Printed in the United States of America

W 10 9 8 7 6 5 4 3 2

To Toby

Acknowledgments

MANY PEOPLE have contributed to this book.

For providing material, photographs and ideas, I would like to thank, particularly, John Huston and Gladys Hill, William Wyler, Edith Head, Eli Wallach, and Gregory Peck.

Vital suggestions, interview material, and additional photographs were provided by Jim Hillier of The British Film Institute, Fred MacDonald, Gene Phillips, Karl Stange, and Hap Kindem.

Two sources particularly helpful in providing me with prints of John Huston's films for study were Films, Inc., and Universal 16.

Additional thanks go to Merle Kaminsky, who helped me to organize this book, to Daphne Ehrlich, and Jeffrey C. Smith, who spent great time and effort in editing the book, and to Dominick Abel, for arranging for me to have this opportunity to put my thoughts about John Huston's work into book form.

Finally, thanks must be given to three people who spent dozens of hours on research to provide the basic historical data for this book. The three are Charles Derry, Leo Kaminsky, and Aaron Lipstadt.

Foreword

WRITING THIS BOOK about John Huston has proved to be a pleasure, but at times a difficult one. I should have anticipated the trouble I would have tracking down and dealing with the elusive and enigmatic director-actor. I knew the pleasure would come in reconsidering his work and spending hundreds of hours reviewing such films as *The Maltese Falcon, The Treasure of the Sierra Madre, Reflections in a Golden Eye, Fat City,* and *The Man Who Would Be King.*

In the five years I have been teaching film history and criticism at the university level, I have found myself returning constantly to John Huston's films for examples and out of a deep love and respect for the films. As each new film came out, I became more fascinated with the enigma of John Huston. I had some ideas about his artistic interests and development in the films, but I wanted to look at them more carefully and in chronological order and to examine them against the history of his life.

The first task was to contact John Huston and his assistant-partner-friend Gladys Hill, a task that proved more difficult than I had anticipated. I finally traced them by mail to Puerto Vallarta, Mexico, where Huston lives when he is at work on a project. Gladys Hill informed me that they were working on a screenplay for Ernest Hemingway's *Across the River and into the Trees,* that John Huston did not like to give interviews in Mexico, and that he did not like to answer questions sent to him by mail. She did add that he would be happy to talk on the phone or that a meeting could be arranged some time after the script was written. I opted for the latter.

As weeks turned to months and I moved forward on my writing, I contacted Hill and Huston again. I was informed that the project was taking longer than anticipated, but that a meeting would be set up. Meanwhile, as an act of good faith, they sent me the names of people I might wish to contact and some very valuable photographic material, particularly a personal photograph of Huston with Hemingway taken in 1955.

Since I knew Huston was moving around the United States acting in various films, I again contacted the duo, indicating that the book was almost finished, that a year had passed, and that I would go anywhere to get the interview. Patience was again advised. I am still waiting for that elusive interview.

Actually, I have had two meetings with John Huston. One took place in Beverly Hills in the summer of 1972. I was doing research for a book on director Don Siegel and had accompanied Siegel to a meeting at the American Film Institute. Huston was the last to arrive. Tall, stately, dressed in black, he made a grand entrance down a flight of marble stairs. In a gathering that included Gregory Peck, Ricardo Montalban, and dozens of famous actors and directors, John Huston was noticed. I had the impression that he had not choreographed the entrance. It was simply natural for him to be "on" all the time. He seemed to be acting, playing John Huston and doing a damn good job of it. Even the simple act of getting coffee and cookies was a performance of pursed lips, careful inspection, and reflection. His introduction to me and his coffee-table conversation took on the air of tremendous moment and import. His pregnant pauses, even when the subject didn't merit it, drew attention and respect.

My next encounter with him was at a similar function and the show was repeated.

In neither encounter did I tell the man what I thought of his work. All film directors and actors are beseiged by praise and well-wishers. About 3 or 4 percent actually do think the actor or director is "great" or their "favorite." Knowing this, I was reluctant to tell him that I knew all of his films well. People are always saying such things, often without having seen or even having been aware of half of the work of the creator being confronted. I wanted to tell Huston that there wasn't a film of his I didn't like and respect, even those films he has himself denounced. I wanted to tell him that I had spent hours on horizontal editors examining his films frame by frame, that I had used sequences from *Sinful Davey* as models of filmmaking, that my favorite film in the world is the neglected *The List of Adrian Messen-*

ger, that there are a handful of his films that so move me that no matter how many times I see them, I am unable to speak for several minutes after the lights go on. I wanted to tell him that I had unconsciously memorized scenes from his work and have found myself silently saying familiar dialogue with the characters as I watched.

I've studied Huston's films carefully and watched him move from the ironic humor of *The Maltese Falcon,* through the tough morality of *San Pietro,* to the sentimentality of *The Treasure of the Sierra Madre* and *The African Queen,* to the bitter sadness of *Fat City* and *Reflections in a Golden Eye,* to the youthful nostalgia of *The Life and Times of Judge Roy Bean* and *The Man Who Would Be King.*

I have wanted to tell him what his work has meant to me and, perhaps, millions of others. I have taken the opportunity to do so in the following pages.

STUART KAMINSKY
Evanston, Illinois
1977

Contents

Acknowledgments   vii

Foreword   ix

1. In the Shadow of the Father   1

2. Adventures of a Young Man   13

3. The Bird   19

4. Southern Discomfort   27

5. At War   37

6. Amigos   47

7. The Animal with Its Shell Off   59

8. A Left-Handed Form of Human Endeavor   69

9. Crippled Epic   75

10. The Rumpot and the Queen   83

11. The Dwarf and the Devil   91

12. The White Rubber Whale   101

13. The Nun and the Geisha   111

14. Return to Africa   119

15. The Fit and the Misfit   129

16. Freud and the Foxes   139

17. Actor   149

18. Defrocked   155

19. The Bible   161

20. Spies and Voyeurs   171

21. Love and Death in Europe   179

22. A Pug, a Legend and a Spy   187

23. The King   197

   Filmography   207

   Bibliography   223

   Index   227

Illustrations

following page 78

Walter and John Huston about 1937
John Huston shakes his father's hand on the set of *The Maltese Falcon*
Huston and Humphrey Bogart on location in Mexico
A scene from *The Treasure of the Sierra Madre*
Walter and John Huston at the Academy Awards in 1949
A Christmas party during the shooting of *The Asphalt Jungle*
Huston and Louis Calhern
Huston rehearses a scene from *The Red Badge of Courage*
Richard Basehart and Gregory Peck in a scene from *Moby Dick*
Marlon Brando and Elizabeth Taylor in *Reflections in a Golden Eye*
Ernest Hemingway and John Huston
Lillian Gish and Audrey Hepburn in *The Unforgiven*
Anthony Huston and his father watch a rehearsal
Huston directs Montgomery Clift in *Freud*
Huston directs daughter, Anjelica, in a scene from *A Walk with Love and Death*
Anjelica Huston and Assaf Dayan in a scene from *A Walk with Love and Death*
John Huston with Orson Welles
A group of spies in *The Kremlin Letter*
A bearded Huston directs a shot in *The Mackintosh Man*
Stacy Keach as a washed-up boxer and Jeff Bridges in *Fat City*
Paul Newman as Judge Roy Bean in *The Life and Times of Judge Roy Bean*
Doghmi Larbi as Ootah in *The Man Who Would Be King*
John Huston at work
John Huston at a fox hunt in Ireland

JOHN HUSTON

Maker of Magic

CHAPTER I

In the Shadow of the Father

JOHN MARCELLUS HUSTON was born in Nevada, Missouri, a small town near the Kansas-Missouri border, on August 5, 1906.

At the time of his birth, both Huston's father and mother were probably wondering what they were doing in Nevada. Walter Huston had left an unpromising career on the stage to take a post as Nevada's engineer in charge of power and light. His wife, the former Rhea Gore, had been a successful New York City newspaperwoman when they married.

There is not much documented material available about John Huston's beginnings. Huston himself has told many stories about his life and that of his parents — stories that may or may not be true. Huston's love of fantasy and storytelling must be counted as much an element in his account of his biography as in his work.

For example, he has claimed that the family path led to Nevada because Rhea's father, a professional gambler, won the town in a poker game. When Huston became an important director, Warner Brothers issued a biographical release on him, a practice that studios continue to follow for stars and directors today. In the release, he is quoted as saying about Nevada, "And here was grandfather with a whole town belonging to him. It was nothing much, of course, hardly a whistle stop, but Dad took over as Chief Engineer."

At other times, Huston has claimed his grandfather won Weatherford, Texas, where the family later moved. Neither town's records contain evidence that this story is true.

Chief Engineer Walter Houghston was born in Toronto, Canada, on April 6, 1884, the son of Elizabeth McGibbon Houghston and Robert Houghston. Walter Houghston's grandfather had come to the United States in 1840 from Ireland. More than 100 years later, Great-Grandson John was to reverse the immigration and become an Irish citizen.

During his teens, Robert Houghston had moved to Canada, married a Scottish immigrant, Elizabeth McGibbon, and started a construction and contracting company that grew and prospered.

When Walter Houghston was born, he seemed destined for an engineering career and a place in the family business. As a boy he was sent to the Landdown School in Toronto. When he graduated at seventeen, he took a job as a hardware-store clerk but was persuaded by his family to return to school to study engineering. After a few months of study, he began attending classes in the dramatics department of the Toronto College of Music, and his engineering classes were ignored.

At the age of eighteen, with a few months of stage training behind him, Houghston tried out for and got a small role in a Toronto play. The lanky six-footer was hooked and joined a road company without bothering to let anyone know that he was dropping out of his engineering studies.

Houghston went on the road with the play in the United States and Canada and shortened his name to Huston. When the company played New York three years after he joined it, he decided to try for Broadway.

With a naturally resonant voice, a hearty laugh, and growing confidence, the twenty-one-year-old would-be actor landed a role in a play called *In Convict Stripes.*

Within a few months of his arrival in New York, Huston met Rhea Gore, a tough, practical newspaperwoman who loved horses, travel, and gambling, the last a trait she apparently had acquired from her father.

The honeymoon was brief. Rhea kept writing, and Walter moved on to a role in Richard Mansfield's production of *Julius Caesar.* The problem with the role was that Huston had only one line — which he could not remember. He was promptly fired and found that he couldn't get another acting job on Broadway. Unwilling to give up the stage, he turned to vaudeville and road-show acting jobs. None of the roles amounted to much, and his career seemed to be dying before it had even begun. In addition, both Walter and Rhea were beginning to worry about their uncertain income and the high cost of living in New York. The solution, they decided, was a radical change in life-style.

Walter agreed to give up the stage and devote himself to engineering, the career he had been avoiding since he was old enough to know what it meant. Rhea agreed to drop her profession and be a housewife. By exaggerating his engineering credentials, Walter got the job in Nevada, Missouri.

According to John Huston's writer-friend James Agee in a 1950 *Life* magazine article,* Walter never really gave up his love for the stage. As soon as John was old enough to listen, his father would put aside his correspondence-school engineering course and perform for the willing audience of one. When he was barely two years old, John would find himself seated at a kitchen table, his feet well off the ground, while his father would sing, tell gags, and dance for him.

The boy became a tryout audience for sketches and songs that Huston dreamed of performing one day before New York audiences. John returned his father's crooked smile and listened for hours to early versions of such original compositions as "Why Bring That Up?" and "I Haven't Got the Do-Re-Mi."

John might have had an uneventful boyhood in Missouri if it hadn't been for an incident that sent the family traveling. In his studio biography, John reported that fires were infrequent in the small town, so when one occurred it was an important event. One night such an event took place, and Walter, his mind possibly on a new vaudeville song, turned the town water supply off instead of increasing the flow to fight the fire. "Seems," said John, "there was a fire, and dad got mixed up in the intricacies of valves, water pressure, and gauges and the rest of it." John's recollection was that the mistake led to half the town's being burned down and the Huston family on the road in search of employment.

From Nevada, they moved to Weatherford, Texas, and from Weatherford to St. Louis, Missouri, in search of an electrical power plant Huston could call home. John's preschool memories were of moving between Midwestern and Southwestern towns.

Walter's engineering failures strained his marriage. In 1909 he met a young actress named Bayonne Whipple. He left his wife and went

*The article, entitled "Undirectable Director," was published on September 18 and is included in *Agee on Film*.
Complete sources for textual references throughout can be found in the Bibliography.

back to vaudeville. Four years later, in 1913, Walter and Rhea were divorced and Walter married his vaudeville partner. For fifteen years Whipple and Huston remained a song-and-dance team. Meanwhile, Rhea returned to her journalism career and proved to be a highly successful writer, first in California and later in New York. Eventually she married a vice president of the Northern Pacific Railroad.

John was three years old when his parents separated and spent his childhood shuttling from one to the other. With his father, John lived in a world of near poverty, tall stories, and fantasy. "I was six when I first saw Dad do his act," Huston told Lillian Ross in 1949 for her book, *Picture.* "Dad played a house painter, come to paint a lady's house. There was a picture of her husband behind the front door. The husband's face would begin to make faces, and then this big head would shove through the door with electric lights for eyes. And I'd roar and Dad would sing."

When John was with his mother, the situation was reversed: money, good living, and a philosophy of living for the moment. "I traveled a great deal with each of my parents," Huston said in a *Newsweek* interview in 1956. "From overnight fleabags with Dad to spacious hotels with Mother. She was crazy about playing the ponies. She taught me that money's for spending, and to hell with the odds." Huston recalled a time when he and his mother pooled their last ten dollars on a ten-to-one shot in a horse race and won. He remembered as well the more down-to-earth aspects of living with Rhea. One Easter morning, annoyed at his impatience to be up and around looking for painted eggs, she told him, "Look here, there is no Easter bunny. I put the eggs there. I dyed those eggs. I stayed up last night to hide them."

A number of Huston's friends and associates have suggested that his cynical attitude and lack of faith in his fellow man spring from the uncertainty he experienced as a small child.

From time to time his mother would place him in a private school, but frequently, when she was in the money, they traveled around the country.

At the age of twelve, while staying in a private school, John became seriously ill. The illness was diagnosed as an enlarged heart and a kidney ailment. Rhea put him in a private sanitarium, where he was watched carefully and told that he had to be protected and cautious for the rest of his life.

"I haven't the slightest doubt," he later said to Agee, "that if things had gone on like that I'd have died inside a few more months."

Agee was convinced, according to his *Life* article, that this was the most significant point in Huston's life. Huston told Agee that in the sanitarium he became a shy, frightened child. One night he decided to test his fear. When everyone was asleep, he got out of bed, took his clothes off, and ran to a stream that flowed through the sanitarium grounds. Without hesitating, the lean, pale boy dived into the water and let the current carry him over a steep, stony waterfall. When he stepped out of the water, apparently still among the living, he repeated the dive into the water and over the falls.

"The first few times," Huston told Agee, "it scared the living hell out of me, but I realized — instinctively anyhow — it was exactly fear I had to get over." Night after night Huston repeated his diving and ride over the falls. However, he continued to play the invalid until he was spotted by a sanitarium employee. When the boy informed the staff members that he had been doing the same thing for many nights, there was a radical change in his diagnosis and he was pronounced healthy.

According to Agee, "The traits revealed in this incident are central and permanent in Huston's character. Risk, not to say recklessness, are virtual reflexes in him. Action, and the most vivid possible use of the immediate present, were his personal salvation; they have remained lifelong habits. Because action also is the natural language of the screen and the instant present is its tense, Huston is a born popular artist."

Released from the sanitarium, John was sent to a California military school on the condition that he not participate in physical activity. At the end of the school year, he went to New York to visit his father, who was still in vaudeville. Away from California and memories of the sanitarium and restriction, thirteen-year-old John threw off the last vestiges of invalidism. He would never again think of himself as sickly or allow himself to be treated as if he were ill.

John returned to California to attend Lincoln Heights High School in Los Angeles but after two years quit school at the age of fifteen determined to become a professional boxer.

"I went to Lincoln Heights High School," Huston told Gideon Bachmann in a 1965 interview for *Film Quarterly*, "because of the boxing. The school was in a rather poor area of town, and my family was much better off than most of the other kids in the school; it took me nearly an hour to get there by streetcar. Three world champions came from our group at the school."

"I always felt constrained in the presence of too many severe rules," said Huston of his short academic life, perhaps remembering the sanitarium and military school. "They distress me. I like the sense of freedom."

In addition to escaping from rules, Huston told Bachmann, "boxing enabled me to travel up and down the Pacific Coast. That had a lot to do with my going into it. I hated staying put in one place, but after getting the broken beak [in a boxing match] it occurred to me that a kid as skinny as I was couldn't last much longer in the racket. We'd box in little towns all up and down and they'd pay us sometimes in watches or goods; we were amateurs then. And later we'd get perhaps fifty dollars."

Huston has told various interviewers that he won twenty-three out of twenty-five fights and was briefly Amateur Lightweight Boxing Champion of California. In his first published short story, "Fool," Huston described himself as a boxer:

> I was tall with long arms, and I knew how to keep them out. I was naturally a straight hitter, right from the start when I had my fights at grammar school. I developed a short jab in my left that was almost automatic. It would work without my thinking of it. The blow was not hard, you understand, but it was stinging and cutting, and it used to make them first mad and then disheartened.

"The best I did," Huston later recalled of his boxing career, "was a semi-windup with Bobby West, a Frisco boy."

With his nose permanently flattened, Huston quit the ring and accepted his mother's invitation to join her on a world tour. When the tour was over, he was eighteen and the year was 1924. His father had recently moved from vaudeville to the legitimate theater, and he invited his son to come to New York. John accepted, with some idea of continuing to box. Walter had been noticed by a producer, Brock Pemberton, who had cast him in the title role of the Broadway play *Mister Pitt.* The play opened on January 19, 1924, and was an immediate hit. *Theatre Magazine* wrote that "Huston has made one of the conspicuous hits of this season and given one of its most beautiful performances." *Mister Pitt* was followed by a far less successful play,

The Easy Mark. From that, in November of 1924, Walter Huston went to the role of Ephraim Cabot in Eugene O'Neill's *Desire Under the Elms.*

It was during the successful run of this play that John joined his father in New York. "I didn't get to know him [John] well until he came to New York to live with me," Walter recalled in a 1948 interview with Dan Fowler in *Look* magazine. "I knew he'd done some boxing, but didn't know he'd been state champion. He got me into a ring, and pretty soon I knew I'd made a mistake and something had to be done. So I put everything I had into one Sunday punch and knocked him out. 'That was pretty good, Pop,' he said when he came around. 'Let's try that again.' "

During this period, John decided to follow his father's path and become an actor. Throughout his life, John Huston was to move from his mother's profession, writing, to his father's, acting, and find his greatest success in a profession that combined the two, directing.

Remembering his father in *Desire Under the Elms,* Huston remarked in a *Close-Up* magazine interview in 1958, "My old man was the greatest actor I ever knew. He was able to strike right at the heart, something you can't learn in any dramatic school; it would come out magnified in depth on the stage or screen.

"It wasn't imitating a model's gestures. Something was born and it was all new, and if he played a newspaperman, it wasn't just one man — he became all newspapermen, the archetype. He had that. I admired my father very much. He had a great effect on my attitude to life. Father didn't encourage me with words but by example. He was a great influence on me but I don't think he ever gave me any advice. It was always through what he did, and I would imitate him."

Thirty-four years after *Desire Under the Elms* first played on Broadway, someone commented to Huston that he often stood and moved like his father. According to the *Close-Up* article, Huston immediately rose and gave a near-perfect imitation of one of his father's speeches from that play.

John moved to New York in the twenties — to what he called the "sporty" life on MacDougal Street in Greenwich Village — and began looking for work as an actor. While looking, he met his upstairs neighbor, another would-be actor named Sam Jaffe, who was later to have a distinguished Broadway and film career including the title role in *Gunga Din* and memorable roles as the Emperor in *The*

Scarlet Express, a Tibetan in *Lost Horizon,* and a Jewish servant in *Ben Hur.* He also played Dr. Zorba for four years in the *Ben Casey* television series. Huston and Jaffe were to become close friends, a friendship John did not forget when he became a director. He gave Jaffe roles in *The Asphalt Jungle* and *The Barbarian and the Geisha.*

Huston's interest in horses, one of his mother's passions, began to develop even in the crowded city. He wanted a horse. On his nineteenth birthday, Sam Jaffe brought him one, and John rode in the park when he wasn't looking for jobs. "Sam," Huston told Lillian Ross, "the kindest, most retiring guy in the world, had gone out and bought the oldest, saddest, most worn-out gray mare. It was all wonderful. The best birthday I ever had."

Huston's passion for horses merged with another lifelong interest, art. Wherever he was to go, he would endlessly draw pictures of horses. His interest in art gradually became a passion itself and led eventually to his assembling an impressive collection of French Impressionist paintings. One of his favorite painters was Toulouse-Lautrec, about whom Huston would make a movie, *Moulin Rouge.*

At the age of nineteen, Huston did get an opportunity to act. With some help from his father, in 1925 John received the lead in a small New York production of Sherwood Anderson's *The Triumph of the Egg.*

In the same year, Huston appeared in Matcher Hughes's *Ruint* with the Princetown Players in Greenwich Village. Sam Jaffe was also in the cast. Huston played a rich man who stops in a backwoods community, seduces a young girl, and is run out of town. He recalls the experience without enthusiasm, describing the play in his Warner Brothers biography as "a little thing Kenneth Macgowan was doing down in Greenwich Village. I didn't like it much."

With no other roles in sight, Huston spent more and more time riding his old horse in the park. He laid out whatever money he could get on riding lessons with a German man name Hattie Weldon. He also took time out to marry a girl he had known in high school and who had come to New York to join him. His marriage to Dorothy Harvey lasted less than a year and ended in divorce when he decided to enlist in the Mexican army.

This occurred one afternoon when Weldon was visited by a Mexican cavalry officer. John was present, and when the officer saw him ride, he offered the young man a commission in the Mexican army. Huston accepted.

His stated reason for joining the Mexican cavalry was logical, if somewhat immature. Why pay for horses if you can be in the army and get them free?

For two years, the six-foot-two, rail-thin lieutenant got to ride his beloved horse. When he eventually left the cavalry, he had learned Spanish, become an expert horseman, and developed a love for Mexico.

Huston has frequently described those days with affection. He tells of officers driving around in Pierce-Arrows, drinking champagne, playing poker in brothels, and winding up in somebody's hotel room for Mexican roulette. In this game, according to Huston, when someone won a big pot, the group would turn out the lights, cock a loaded pistol, and throw it into the air. The pistol would go off when it hit the ceiling. Then the men would turn the lights back on to see who was dead. If the winner survived, he could keep the money. If not, the others split even.

As bizarre as this anecdote is, enough incidents have arisen throughout Huston's life to make it difficult to dismiss such stories as simply tall tales.

During his odd hours in Mexico, Huston had written a play, *Frankie and Johnny,* which the artist Covarrubias illustrated. He had also written a number of stories about what he knew best, gambling, horses, and boxing. When, at the age of twenty-one, the young lieutenant went to New York City to perform in a horse show at Madison Square Garden with his cavalry troop, he decided he wanted to become a successful writer, and did not return to Mexico.

For over a year, John divided his time between writing, horses, and women. In the time he had been gone, his father had expanded his reputation as a leading American actor. In 1925, Walter had starred in *The Fountain;* in 1926 in *Kongo.* After John's return, Walter's reputation grew with *Elmer the Great* in 1928 and *The Commodore Marries* in 1929. Walter read "Fool" and showed it to writer Ring Lardner. Lardner in turn showed the story to H. L. Mencken, editor of *The American Mercury,* then the leading literary publication in the United States. Mencken liked the story and ran it in the March 1929 issue of the magazine.

The five-page story is narrated by a young boxer, clearly Huston, who agrees to fight against a vastly superior boxer, a friend. The fight is staged in a Los Angeles arena called Madison Square Gardens. Only blacks attend. The friend allows the narrator to beat him, and the winner feels like a fool. (The resemblance between Victor du Lara, the losing fighter, in the story and the Mexican boxer in Huston's film *Fat City* is striking.) In recalling his own boxing experience, Huston told Rosemary Lord in *Transatlantic Review,* "I remember there was one place called Madison Square Gardens and it was on Central Avenue which was a black community. They used to make up posters for the fight and pick out names. They'd say, that's gonna be your name. If you had red hair, you'd be Red O'Reilly, something like that. I remember fighting there one night under two different names."

Some important themes that were to remain with Huston throughout his career are apparent in this early story. Two people are brought together to perform a shared act. One person suffers in the process — the defeated fighter is upset because he has to participate in a sham, a fake fight, and doesn't know how to get out of it. But he faces his suffering and loss with dignity. The protagonist-narrator, however, finds himself doing something he doesn't wish to do and doesn't know how to stop. Although the narrator wins the fight (as does Tully, the Stacy Keach character, in *Fat City*), he thinks of himself as someone who betrayed a friend.

The story ends with the defeated boxer, Victor, drawing a parallel between the match and the death of Christ:

> Listen, I believe that Christ and Judas were in cahoots. I believe it was all laid out between them. Christ told Judas in private to sell Him for thirty pieces of silver, that if the Jews thought he'd been sold for that much, had suffered on the cross all for thirty pieces of silver, then they would not want to be like Judas and would want to be like Christ. It would make them good. I believe it was all fixed.

The influence of such popular writers as Ernest Hemingway, whom Huston greatly admired, W. R. Burnett, and Ring Lardner are apparent in "Fool." Perhaps Lardner's interest in the story was, in fact, aroused by its similarity to his own work. In any case, with this first story, Huston demonstrated one of his great strengths as a writer, an ability to take outrageous dialogue and convert it to a kind of never-never world between harsh reality and fantasy, a reflection of the split in his own life.

"Fool" was followed by Huston's completion of the play *Frankie and Johnny,* which again dealt with defeat and broken relationships.

Sam Jaffe composed and arranged music for it, and *Frankie and Johnny* was performed in New York by puppets in 1929. The publishing firm of Boni and Liveright gave Huston a $500 advance to write a publishable version of it. According to William Nolan, John took his advance, hurried to Saratoga, and ran the sum into $11,000 at a crap table. Within a few days, the story goes, he had gambled his winnings away and was back in New York.

This was a low period for Huston, but he never turned to his now famous father for help. "I'm enough of a gambler to know if you're in a bad streak you just got to roll it through," he told *Newsweek* in 1956. "Not much anybody can do to help you out."

Short of money, Huston did accept his father's offer to join him in a movie. Walter had moved to Hollywood to take advantage of the coming of sound to film and his own reputation as an actor.

John's first film as an actor was a Universal Studio short called *Two Americans.* His father also appeared in the production. Through his father, John then got small roles in three films at Universal, all directed by William Wyler, who was to become the single greatest influence on Huston's directing career. The three films, all released in 1929–1930, were *Shakedown, Hell's Heroes,* and *The Storm. Hell's Heroes,* starring Charles Bickford, was Wyler's first critical success. However, following the three films, no producers signed Huston to an acting contract. To make some money, he decided to become an opera singer but had almost no success. "The less said about that, the better" is his terse comment.

In 1930, the book *Frankie and Johnny* appeared. A colorful red volume, it included Huston's play, complete with bizarre dialogue and the addition of a boxer character, plus various versions of the story of Frankie and Johnny in prose and verse. It was a commendable job of combining creative writing and solid folklore research.

Still short of money, Huston went to his mother, who got him a job working as a reporter for the New York *Graphic,* where she was employed. "I was the world's lousiest reporter," he told Agee.

After having been fired, and rehired several times (thanks to his mother's influence), he was nearing the end of a brief career as a reporter after only a few months on the job. Huston remembers without enthusiasm the time his city editor told the police he was not a *Graphic* reporter just to get him in trouble and out of his hair for a few hours. Huston finally lost his job for good when he mixed up the names of the victim and the criminal in a murder story.

In 1931, *The American Mercury* published Huston's second story, "Figures of Fighting Men." Less a story than a series of short sketches about down-and-out boxers with names such as Maxie, The Old Timer, The King, The Champion, and Ad, the three pages were a radical stylistic departure from his play and his earlier story. Huston's growing ability as a writer was clear now. One section, "The King," for example, opens with this terse paragraph:

> The Irish boy has a half-frightened look on his face. His body is tense, the muscles are flexed in his big, rigid arms, and his movements are short and jerky. King, the colored heavy, outweighs the boy nearly forty pounds, but his advanced years more than make up for it. He is old enough to be the boy's father, and there is something fatherly about the way he handles him.

The entire sketch about King and the boy is only five paragraphs long, in a style comparable to Hemingway's. Again, Huston concentrates on the defeated, the losers. Along with this piece, *The American Mercury* also published a brief autobiographical note with a self-portrait by the author. The drawing shows a long-faced young man with a mashed nose and pursed lips. The last paragraph of the autobiographical sketch says:

> My life in New York is very sporty — a continual round of the fight clubs. My taste in writers runs from Lardner to Thomas Mann and includes Joyce. Right now I am at work on two books, one a novel, the other to be called "The Gambler's Rose," and to be made up of stories of artists, composers, etc., whose names have been forgotten, or were never known — mainly fly-by-nights, who had much to do with the culture of this country and who now rest in shallow graves.

Neither of the books was ever to be completed. At the age of twenty-five, Huston received a letter from the Goldwyn Studios. On the basis of his published book, *Frankie and Johnny,* he was being offered a job as a contract writer in Hollywood. Huston packed his bag and headed for California. Now an ex-boxer, cavalry officer, actor, reporter, and playwright, he was ready for a shot at the film world.

CHAPTER 2

Adventures of a Young Man

FOR SIX MONTHS, Huston received $150 a week for doing no work at all. At the end of that period, he quit Goldwyn and got a job at Universal Studios, where his father was a star.

His first assignment was to write some dialogue for *A House Divided,* starring his father and directed by William Wyler. John B. Clymer and Dale Van Every's screenplay was based on a short story by Olive Edens called "Heart and Hand." Huston had very little to do on the film, but he did get to work with Wyler again. Huston was proud of that first effort and has pointed out that while the film, released in December 1931, was not a success in the United States, it ran for two years in a little theater on the Left Bank in Paris.

For the next year Huston was to remain close to his father and Wyler. At first glance, the tall, thin, and flamboyant Huston seems a strange companion for the small, slightly accented, and urbane Alsatian Jewish immigrant, but the mutual respect was evident.

Wyler and John Huston decided to collaborate on a film of social significance, a film about the Depression. To get a feeling for the depths of poverty, they spent a day on Skid Row in Los Angeles. Wyler recalled, "We got a lousy free dinner in a mission after we had listened to a spiel and signed a statement to the effect that we had come to Christ. Then we spent the night in a flophouse. Ten cents it cost." The planned film never materialized.

John then received co-writing credit with Tom Reed for *Law and Order,* which starred his father as Wyatt Earp and was based on a story by W. R. Burnett, who had written the highly successful *Little Caesar.* Edward Cahn directed. John also worked as dialogue writer for director Robert Florey's 1932 release, *Murders in the Rue Morgue,* which starred Bela Lugosi.

Wyler next decided to do a film version of Oliver La Farge's Pulitzer Prize–winning novel *Laughing Boy,* a tale of the degradation of Indians at the hands of whites. Huston was to do the screenplay. Wyler and Huston went to Arizona and spent a week with La Farge, followed by two weeks during which the two lived on a Navajo Reservation in Monument Valley, Arizona. "We visualized it like another *Nanook of the North,* another Robert Flaherty semidocumentary," said Wyler to biographer Axel Madsen in 1973. "But we couldn't cast it. We worked on it for months but we couldn't get it off the ground."

Back at Universal, Huston shared an office with writer Allen Rivkin, who recalls Huston vividly in his book, *Hello, Hollywood,* published in 1962. Rivkin said he especially remembers one Christmas day when he, Huston, and writer P. J. "Pinky" Wolfson got roaring drunk. Wolfson, who had an extensive gun collection, had brought a .25 to the studio and was showing off. Huston, in riding habit, was drunkenly bumping up a flight of steps on his behind, pretending the steps were a horse. Wolfson shot his .25 at a large light fixture over the stairs, which sprayed shattered glass everywhere, including the steps. When Huston reached the top of the stairs going backward, Rivkin and the others saw blood dripping from his riding pants, the seat of which had been cut to pieces. A group of people went to look for a doctor, but when they got back, Huston had disappeared. When the medical safari did locate him, he was in Wolfson's office giving a lecture on the use of firearms while he continued to bleed.

Although Rivkin was three years older than his friend, he recalls that Huston called him "kid." Rivkin discovered, however, that Huston called everyone either "kid" or "amigo."

Still twenty-five and unable to remain in one place for more than a few months, Huston quit Universal after deciding that the studio was going downhill. He took a job with Gaumont-British studios in London as a writer. The job lasted a few months and was a repeat of the Goldwyn experience — no assignments.

According to William Nolan, Huston refused to send a plea for help to his parents. Instead, he sang on street corners in London for pennies and slept in Hyde Park at night. Gradually, still bumming, Huston made his way to Paris, where he lived for a year and a half. While there, he sometimes sketched tourists at outdoor cafés for a few cents a portrait. As his French improved and he managed to gather some money, he began to study art, particularly oil painting.

The need to wander struck again and Huston gathered enough money to make his way back to New York City in 1932. From New York he sent his father a telegram: "Understand you have signed a contract to make twelve pictures a year for ten years. When do you plan to practice acting?" Once back in New York, with his mother's support he got a job as an editor of the *Mid-Week Pictorial* magazine, New York's first picture magazine. The job was fine, but neither the young editor nor the magazine survived long. Within months, Huston, now twenty-seven, decided to "head for Chicago and another crack at acting."

The year was 1933, the president was Roosevelt, and the WPA was supporting theater projects in various cities. In Chicago, Huston played the title role in *Abe Lincoln in Illinois.* The play had been adapted by Howard Koch, who would later become a director and screenwriter but who is recognized primarily as the producer of such films as *The Manchurian Candidate* and *The Odd Couple.* Three years earlier, Walter Huston had played Lincoln in D. W. Griffith's *Abraham Lincoln.* The family physique made the two men natural choices for the roles.

During the run of the play, Huston met an Irish girl, Leslie Black. Fifteen minutes after their meeting, Huston proposed. She did not say yes immediately. Meanwhile, he continued to act in the theater. In Chicago, he played Lincoln again in *Lonely Man,* a drama dealing with Lincoln's reincarnation as a liberal professor in a small college and as a labor union lawyer. The play, a WPA Federal Theater Project, ran for more than two months. In a review of the play in the Chicago *Tribune,* critic Charles Collins wrote, "John Huston, son of Walter Huston, the stage and film star, plays the character with poise and skill."

During this period, Huston also wrote two unproduced plays: *Shadows Pursuing,* from a story by Hugh Walpole, and *Storm Child,* an original play co-written with R. F. Morris, Jr.

Making his way to Hollywood again, Huston, now thirty-one, was still having trouble finding himself. One of the people who remembers him from this period was Henry Blanke, the Warner Brothers producer, who was later to produce two of John's most critically acclaimed films as a director, *The Maltese Falcon* and *The Treasure of the Sierra Madre.* Blanke told Agee that he remembered Huston at this time as "just a drunken boy; hopelessly immature. You'd see him at every party, wearing bangs, with a monkey on his shoulder. Charming. Very talented but without an ounce of discipline in his make-up."

An important change came in 1937. Leslie Black finally accepted Huston's proposal, and, with her help, he determined to pursue a serious career as a writer. Blanke was to tell James Agee that he felt Leslie set her husband the standards and incentives which brought his abilities into focus.

Early in 1938 Huston became a contract writer at Warner Brothers. While Leslie Huston's influence may have helped to focus his talents, two events of significance in that year may have affected his attitude. First, his mother died. Later that same year, his father was married a third time, to actress Nan Sunderland.

John's first assignment was to co-write *Jezebel.* The film was directed by Wyler, with Blanke as associated producer and Bette Davis as star. Davis won the Academy Award for best actress for her performance. Next Huston was one of the writers on William Dieterle's *Juarez,* with Blanke as associate producer to Hal Wallis. The film starred Paul Muni. This was followed by a co-scripting credit with John Wexley on a gangster film, *The Amazing Dr. Clitterhouse,* directed by Anatole Litvak. While writing the screenplay, Huston met Humphrey Bogart for the first time and the two became friends, beginning a relationship that was to lead to one of the best-known director-actor teams in film history. Others in the film were Edward G. Robinson and Claire Trevor. A decade later, Huston would team the three in his own gangster film, *Key Largo.*

Huston's writing was beginning to develop a noticeable style. "I remember when I was a kid," he told Gideon Bachmann in a 1965 interview for *Film Quarterly,* "this question of style puzzled me. I didn't know what they meant by the style of a certain writer. One day Plato's *Apology* fell into my hands. It was an accident, but it was an eye-opener for me as far as style was concerned. I understood that the words of Socrates were in keeping with the monumentality of his conceptions . . . ."

The ending of *Dr. Clitterhouse* appears to be a Huston stylistic contribution. In the film, a doctor (Robinson) joins a gang of thieves to study the criminal mind. One of the gang members (Bogart) tries to blackmail him. Robinson kills him, and his lawyer tries to get him off on a plea of insanity. Robinson vigorously protests that he is quite sane. The jury finds him innocent, declaring that no man in his right mind facing execution would maintain that he was sane. The film ends with a dumbfounded and confused Robinson on the witness stand. For 1938, this ending was audacious: a man guilty of murder was allowed to go with minimal punishment in an American film. Robinson stands as one of Huston's first villain/heroes.

Huston's memory of this period is vivid, and in 1973 he pointed out to Gene Phillips the contrast to today's system in which no studio has actors, writers, or directors under exclusive contract: "In those days, the Hollywood set-up was much different than it is now. There was an executive producer who had a number of individual producers working under him. A producer would be given a property to film and he would select from among the contract writers, directors, and actors that the studio employed those people who could handle the material that was to be made into a film.

"Screenwriters at the time were much more concerned with the perfection of their work than they are now. They were on salary: when they finished an assignment they would either be moved on to another film or let go if their work wasn't satisfactory. Hence a writer fought for the leisure to be able to polish and improve his material before it went before the cameras. The writer handed in twenty pages or so of the script at a time, not the finished product. If he got behind schedule he would be urged on. Writers and directors often had no control over their material once they had finished it.

"The writer never came on the set unless he was asked for in extraordinary circumstances. By the same token, when the director finished shooting a picture, the footage was turned over to the editor. This kind of set-up in the studio gave the creative writer and director something to fight against. These who say that there is too much freedom today in the filmmaking business may have a point."

In 1939 Huston conducted a Los Angeles workshop on screenwriting, and, with a growing reputation as a screenwriter, he decided to take a year off to become a Broadway director and playwright.

He did not, in fact, write the first play he directed, *A Passenger to Bali* by Ellis St. Joseph. Walter Huston played the Reverend Mr. Walkes, who incites the crew of a freighter out of Shanghai to mutiny. Walkes is discovered to be a fake preacher and goes down with the sinking ship. The play opened at the Ethel Barrymore Theatre on March 15, 1940, and announced a spectacular typhoon sequence. Neither the typhoon nor Walter could save the play. It closed after four performances.

Huston's second Broadway effort, which did not come until 1942, met with a bit more success. With Howard Koch, he wrote *In Time to Come.* The play consisted of a prologue taken from Woodrow Wilson's Declaration of War speech in 1917 and went on to seven key scenes in Wilson's life, including his relations with his wife, his illness, and the rise of Harding. The play concluded optimistically, as one might expect in a drama produced during World War II, with an assertion that Wilson had accomplished something that wouldn't die if men were willing to fight and believe. Produced by Otto Preminger, the play was not a box-office success, but it ran for forty performances and won the New York Drama Critics Circle award, beating out John Steinbeck's *The Moon is Down. Time* wrote: "No great shakes as a play . . . yet a vivid stage document . . ."

In 1941 Huston wrote, along with four others, the film *Sergeant York,* which was directed by Howard Hawks and starred Gary Cooper. Cooper won the Oscar and the writers were nominated for one.

High Sierra followed in 1941. Directed by Raoul Walsh and starring Bogart, the script was by Huston and W. R. Burnett from Burnett's novel.

"Once I had become established as a screenwriter at Warners," Huston told Phillips, "I got a clause put into my contract that if I stayed on there they would give me the chance to direct. I saw no great dividing line between writing and directing, although few writers had become directors at the time — Preston Sturges and Gar Kanin were, I believe, my only predecessors."

CHAPTER 3

The Bird

ACCORDING TO HUSTON, he and Allen Rivkin were assigned to write *The Maltese Falcon.*

"After Allen Rivkin and I finished the screenplay of *The Maltese Falcon,*" Huston told Gene Phillips in a 1973 interview for *Film Comment,* "I asked to direct it. Dashiell Hammett's book had been filmed twice before, but the previous screen adaptors didn't have the faith in the story that we did. Our script simply reduced the book to a screenplay, without any fancy additions of our own."

According to Rivkin, Huston came into his office one afternoon and said, "Kid, [Jack] Warner says if I can get a good screenplay out of this Dash Hammett thing, he'll let me direct it."

According to Rivkin, he read the book and agreed with Huston that the first film versions of the novel had not stuck with the Hammett text. Huston suggested that before they begin writing, a secretary should recopy the book, setting it up in shots, scenes, and dialogue. Rivkin agreed and a secretary was assigned.

"About a week later John ambled into my office, looking very puzzled," Rivkin recalled. " 'Goddamndest thing happened, kid,' he said, giving each word a close-up. My eyes asked what. 'Something maybe you didn't know,' he said. 'Everything those secretaries do, a copy's got to go to the department. This *Maltese* thing our secretary was doing, that went there, too.' "

According to both Huston and Rivkin, Jack Warner saw the secretary's copy, liked it, called Huston, and told him to start shooting the picture within a week.

The year was 1941 and John Huston, at the age of thirty-five, had officially become a movie director.

Important technical and sequential as well as plot and character differences exist in the two versions of the story. For instance, Hammett's original novel was written and set in 1928–1929. The Huston script is clearly updated to 1940. Also, the conclusion of Hammett's novel is quite different from the conclusion of Huston's film. The film ends with Bogart as Sam Spade, watching Brigid O'Shaughnessy's face disappear downward through the prisonlike bars of the elevator in his apartment building. Hammett's novel ends with Spade back in his office, where he puts his arm around the waist of his secretary, Effie, and she pulls away from him in confusion over the fact that he has turned Brigid in. The novel's last few lines indicate that Spade will have to deal with Iva Archer, who has come to see him again.

It also seems strange that Rivkin and Huston should so firmly denounce the 1931 script. In fact, this version of *The Maltese Falcon,* directed by Roy Del Ruth, contains very little dialogue that is not in the original novel. Scenes in both the Del Ruth and Huston versions of the film are the same, sometimes word for word. There are marked differences, but they are as much or more in lighting, setting, character development, and direction than in the story.

In the 1931 version, for example, Spade (Ricardo Cortez) is a well-to-do detective with a large office and well-appointed apartment. His dress is early thirties stylish and he is given to wearing velvet smoking jackets in his apartment. Bebe Daniels is a more vulnerable Miss Wonderly (alias Brigid) than Mary Astor. Many differences exist, not primarily in the dialogue but in how Huston has the dialogue delivered. For Del Ruth, Spade is converted to a classical, elegant detective in the Sherlock Holmes–Philo Vance tradition. For Huston, Spade is an archetypal hard-boiled eye on the edge of society and in constant danger of a beating by the police.

There are even specific shots in the earlier version repeated in the 1941 film which imply that Huston in fact saw the Del Ruth film. For example, one well-known shot in Huston's version involved placing the camera on the floor below Kasper Gutman (Sydney Greenstreet) to make him look even fatter and larger than he was. The shot exists in the 1931 version in which Gutman was played by Dudley Digges, who was not nearly as fat as Greenstreet, so the view is not nearly as remarkable.

The point is not made to detract from Huston's achievement but to indicate that the change in the two versions was less in the dialogue and story than in how each director imagined the same dialogue and story and brought them to the screen. Huston's tough version emphasizes the marginal existence of Spade, his cynicism, commitment to principle, near-madness, and enjoyment of irony. Huston further suggests an admiration for those who can accept defeat. Another important element of the Huston version is his emphasis on the world of lies and masks through which Spade must move, masks that Spade must penetrate to get to the truth while he himself is proving to be a master at deception.

The second version of the Hammett novel had been the 1936 *Satan Met a Lady,* directed by William Dieterle and starring Bette Davis and Warren William, who was not called Spade in the film. Significantly, Henry Blanke, who was producer on Huston's film, was also producer of this version. *Satan Met a Lady* bore little resemblance to the Hammett novel. The basic story was converted into a light screwball comedy with Arthur Treacher as the villain and Marie Wilson as the detective's secretary.

When the Huston script was finished, George Raft was assigned to star in it, but, Huston told Gene Phillips, Raft turned down the film because "he didn't want to work with a director who was a newcomer." Bogart, who liked Huston and the work he had done on *High Sierra,* was happy to get the role of Spade. Huston was also given Sydney Greenstreet, a sixty-one-year-old stage actor who had just completed a successful tour with the Lunts. *Falcon* was Greenstreet's first film.

Huston set to work with little time for preparation. "I made drawings," he says. "I wanted to be very sure. I was uncertain of myself as far as the camera was concerned and I wanted to be sure not to fumble, not to get lost in the mechanical aspects of the film. So I made drawings of every set-up, but didn't show the drawings to anyone. I discovered that about half the time the actors themselves automatically fell into the drawings, which were, in fact, set-up designs. But another quarter of the time they did something better than I had thought of myself."

When it came time to begin shooting, Huston recalls that "everyone was leaning over backwards to help me. They were very kind. The crew and the cameraman were very good to me, but I knew pretty well what I was doing. I'd gone to great pains, sketched out each set-up. I'd drawn not just each scene, but each cut as well.

"Warner Brothers was indulgent with me, and I was allowed to work with the editor to some extent after shooting was finished and with the composer. Ever since, I have made it a point to involve myself in the making of a film from the pre-production work right through to the end of post-production work. Even when I have made a picture from a screenplay written by another writer, I have worked with him."

Mary Astor found the role of Brigid particularly challenging and later said she would have preferred her Oscar for *Falcon* instead of *The Great Lie,* which was also released in 1941. Huston had required that she and all cast members read the book to get an understanding of the character.

"First of all," Astor remembers in *A Life on Film,* "Brigid was a congenital liar, and slightly psychopathic. And that kind of liar wears the face of truth, although they send out all sorts of signals that they are lying. There is an unstable quality to them like nitro. One of the tip-offs is they can't help breathing rather rapidly. So I hyperventilated before going into most of the scenes."

Astor confirmed that every shot was on paper. "It was highly limited, almost stylized," she said. "We never took our time with a scene." Speed and efficiency would eventually bring the film to completion in two months at a cost of less than $300,000.

Astor remembers that Greenstreet was particularly nervous in his first film and in spite of his more than thirty-four years of stage acting, asked her to hold his hand and reassure him before his first scene.

Huston's plan was to rehearse a scene after discussing it with the cast and then shoot it in a minimal number of takes when possible. He wasn't, however, above shooting a shot many times as a gag.

"Dad said he wanted to appear in every film I directed, for luck," John recalls. For his first part in one of his son's films, Walter was given the walk-on role of Captain Jacobi, who staggers into Spade's office, mumbles something about a bird, and drops dead.

The scene was easy and should have taken no more than half an hour or so. John kept having his father stagger in, repeat the line, and fall over. Eventually, Walter began to grumble. After more than ten takes, John dismissed his father.

The next morning he looked at the scene on film and it was fine, but he had Mary Astor call Walter and pretend to be a studio secretary. Astor, who had known Walter for years and starred with him in the film version of *Dodsworth,* disguised her voice. She explains: "When Walter answered, I told him that Mr. Huston was sorry, but that we'd have to retake the sequence that afternoon, something had happened to the film in the lab. I held the receiver from my ear and everybody could hear Walter yelling, 'You tell my son to get another actor or go to hell. He made me take twenty falls, and I'm sore all over, and I'm not about to take twenty more, or even one.' "

Peter Lorre remembered another on-the-set practical joke. Huston thought up an act for each cast member to go into when guests were brought on the set. The idea was that each act would so embarrass or enrage the unwelcome visitors brought by the publicity department that they would quickly depart.

When a group of women came to watch the shooting one day, Huston signaled Bogart and Greenstreet. Bogart began to scream at Greenstreet, claiming that his co-actor was a fat incompetent, had made a mistake, and upstaged him. When Bogart was near fake apoplexy, Huston pretended to try to calm him down, but Bogart kept up a steady stream of name-calling until the women left.

To get rid of another group, Lorre went into Astor's portable dressing room. Huston sat the women visitors right next to it, telling them they would have good seats. Lorre immediately came out of the room with a silly smile on his face as he zipped up his pants and Astor waved to him from the doorway.

Huston eventually directed Bogart in six movies.

He said of Bogart in an NBC radio interview following the actor's death in 1957, "The better I got to know him, the more I admired him. He was a very serious man about his work. He took great pride in being an actor. The face that he presented to the world was quite a different one than the one that those who knew him truly well knew. In society, at Hollywood parties, he assumed the role of gadfly and tormentor of the fat cats. This gave a misunderstanding to those who only saw him on those occasions. They thought of him as rowdy, bawdy and gaudy. In truth, he was a very sincere, deeply humble and faithful man, faithful to his work, his friends and finally, his family.

"I took Bogey to many places in the world and some of them were hardships. Well Bogey didn't like that at all. Bogey gave the air of being an adventurer, but really he loved being at home. But he was wonderful to be with . . . He would never know his lines when he came to the set and in rehearsals he would learn them, and they would have a spontaneity that was remarkable."

When *The Maltese Falcon* was completed, the studio wanted to call it *The Gent from Frisco,* but no one felt strongly enough to make the change. In fact, no one at Warner Brothers seemed to feel strongly about the picture at all. It was released with the least publicity of any of the studio's films that year.

The reaction to the film, however, quickly changed the minds of Jack Warner and his brothers. For instance, in the New York *Herald Tribune,* Howard Barnes wrote, "Thanks to John Huston's expert adaptation and cagey direction, few punches have been pulled in reproducing the intolerable suspense and excitement of a classic in its field. It is hard to say whether Huston the adapter, or Huston the fledgling director, is more responsible for this triumph. In any case, it is a knockout job of cinematic melodrama."

The film itself opens with the credits appearing over the falcon statue, which casts a shadow into the depth of the frame. This is followed by a printed commentary over the image about the falcon's history. A shot of San Francisco showing the Golden Gate Bridge establishes location and we move to the Spade and Archer sign on the window of the office. The shadow letters "Spade and Archer" appear on the office floor throughout the opening scene. Spade and Archer share the same office, are inextricably linked, and, as we discover, even share Archer's wife, Iva (Gladys George). Huston quickly establishes the link between the two men so that later, when Spade denounces Brigid for Archer's murder, we understand that it has nothing to do with Spade's like or dislike of his partner.

"When a man's partner is killed," says Spade, "he's supposed to do something about it. It doesn't make any difference what you thought of him. He was your partner and you're supposed to do something about it. Then it happens we were in the detective business. Well, when one of your organization gets killed it's bad business to let the killer get away with it."

To emphasize the constriction of investigation, Huston frequently limits the space Spade has to move in. Spade's office is small, as is his apartment. In fact, in a departure from convention, Huston chose to build some of his sets with ceilings. The more usual procedure during that period of filmmaking was not to show the ceiling so that lights could be placed above and the camera could be free to move upward.

As a personal touch, there are several specific references to horses in the décor. In Spade's apartment there are photographs and drawings of horses. In Gutman's hotel room there is a statue on the mantelpiece of a horse and rider.

The relationship between people and horses is a natural one for Huston to make. When asked once about what makes a star, Huston quickly replied, "In certain instances it stands out all over the individual, just as it stands out in certain horses now and then. You look at an animal and you know it is top class. It's the same with certain persons . . . with a Humphrey Bogart . . . there's no mistaking that quality when you see it any more than there is a chance of mistaking the looks of a great horse in the paddock."

Huston also explored his style of framing with *The Maltese Falcon*. Following his sketches, he set up shots like the canvases of paintings he had studied. Specifically, Huston showed an interest in characters appearing in the foreground of a shot, with their faces often covering half the screen. Frequently, too, the person whose face half fills the screen is not talking, but listening. The reaction thus becomes more important than the person who is speaking or moving.

Huston's first film presented situations he would return to again and again. Spade is the obsessed professional, a man who will adhere to pride and dedication to principle unto death. Women are a threat, temptations that can only sway the hero from his professional commitment. They may be willfully trying to deceive as Brigid and Iva, or they may, as in later Huston films, be the unwitting cause of the protagonist's defeat or near-defeat.

Protagonists in Huston films frequently take risks, gamble with their lives as Huston had done with his in the waterfall. Spade constantly taunts the mad Wilmer (Elisha Cook, Jr.), even using Huston's favorite phrase, "kid," to goad him. The taunting is potentially dangerous, but Spade, as played by Bogart, enjoys it.

As Huston was to develop, the image of the ill-fated group that begins with *Falcon* was to emerge more strongly. Gutman, Cairo (Lorre), Wilmer, and Brigid are part of an alliance of greed. They distrust each other but also respect each other. Spade refuses to join the group and survives. The others don't. Huston was to increasingly develop the idea that such groups are doomed families, the survivors of which must learn to accept defeat with grace and dignity.

The idea of appreciating expert deception also emerges in *Falcon*. Bogart's admiration for Brigid's ability to lie is part of his love for her. "You're good, you're real good," he says with a smile after a particular hyperventilating lie. In contrast, Spade is scornful of Iva because her lies are so transparent. A Huston hero, like Huston, appreciates wit, intelligence, and a good performance even if it is from a consummate villain.

When the first successful run of *The Maltese Falcon* was nearing completion, Warner Brothers announced that Huston would direct a sequel with the same cast, but it was never made.

Bogart so respected Huston and his Sam Spade role that he continued to look for a script to recapture the feeling that established him as a cult figure. A few years before his death, Bogart announced that he had purchased a book to be adapted into a film for him and his wife, Lauren Bacall. "We might do it," he told a radio interviewer, "in association with John Huston and do it abroad. Its setting is in France and Spain. It's a little on the order of *The Maltese Falcon.*"

It was Bogart who began to call Huston "The Monster." "I like to work with John," he said. "The Monster is stimulating. Offbeat kind of mind. Off center. He's brilliant and unpredictable. Never dull. When I work with John, I think about acting."

The Maltese Falcon, a box-office smash, also received an Academy Award nomination as best picture of the year. With his initial success, The Monster's reputation began to grow. He was noted by columnists for his hard drinking, his chain smoking of small and large cigars, and, gradually, for one of the world's most bizarre wardrobes.

At thirty-six, he was ready to take on the world. His next project, he decided, would be a serious melodrama, the kind his mentor, Willy Wyler, did. In fact, with the strength of his first film's success behind him, he would get the actress who had been in some of Wyler's biggest recent hits, including the one he had co-written, *Jezebel.* Bette Davis, he decided, would be his next star.

CHAPTER 4

Southern Discomfort

DURING THE FILMING of *The Maltese Falcon,* Huston earned another nickname besides The Monster. The crew named him "The Great Unpressed" because of his uncanny ability to make even brand-new clothes look rumpled moments after he put them on. With a handful of nicknames and a successful first film behind him, Huston was an aging boy wonder in 1942 when he and Howard Koch settled down to prepare a screenplay based on Ellen Glasgow's Pulitzer Prize–winning novel, *In This Our Life.*

Huston divided his time between writing and the sketch pad. As he had done for *The Maltese Falcon,* he made hundreds of drawings to cover scenes and shots for *In This Our Life.** He not only drew pictures of the sets, he sketched the people as well. When he completed the sketches, he had the art department at Warner Brothers prepare miniature sets. On these scale models, he made his final plans for the scenes.

In shooting *In This Our Life,* Huston had a cast that included Bette Davis, Olivia de Havilland, George Brent, Dennis Morgan, and two of the studio's top character actors, Frank Craven and Charles Coburn.

A reporter from the *New York Times* who was visiting the set noted that "The Great Unpressed is not addicted to retakes. First he rehearses his cast until they satisfy him; then he has the sound man and the photographer and the electrician rehearse, too. Then he shoots his scene. It's usually good the first time, purely because by

---

*Other directors have also been known to make sketches of individual shots. Alfred Hitchcock, who started his career as a cartoonist, did this, as did Norman McLeod, who began as an animator, then directed such films as *Horse Feathers* and *Topper.*

not attempting to rush anybody, he has people better prepared for the crucial moment."

The reporter also noted that Huston's face was an ever-changing mask and that the director was constantly "grimacing, grinning or otherwise disarranging the normal cast of his features . . . he hops all over the set while staging his scenes and then slumps down to watch the rehearsal with an extended siege of lip-pursing and leg-crossing."

The film deals with the Timberlake sisters, Stanley and Roy, who are played by Davis and de Havilland. Stanley steals Roy's husband, Peter (Morgan), and they run away, but Stanley eventually drives him to suicide. She returns home under the protection of Uncle William (Coburn), who has stolen the family business from the girls' father (Craven). Uncle William clearly has sexual thoughts about Stanley, and she leads the old man on. Stanley next makes a play to regain Craig, her old boyfriend (Brent), who is now in love with Roy, but he rejects her. In her fury, she accidentally but recklessly hits and kills a child with her car. Stanley attempts to blame a young black man, Parry (Ernest Anderson), for the crime, but her accusation falls apart when a bartender (played in his "good luck" role by Walter Huston) swears that he saw Stanley with her car on the night she said Parry had taken it. Stanley hurries to Uncle William for protection, but he has discovered he is dying and fails to respond to her. In a dash from the police, Stanley is killed in her car.

There are several elements in the story that clearly attracted Huston, who was free to select almost any project he wished. First, the story has distinct biographical references. A marriage breaks up when a more glamorous woman takes the husband away with her to another town. The highly pragmatic abandoned sister pulls her life together and comes into her own. Superficially, the story has elements of the breakup of Huston's own family, the departure of his father and the assertion of his mother's personality.

The resolution of the film can, to some extent, be seen as a fantasy solution to Huston's own childhood problems, a solution involving punishment of the father who leaves the home and punishment of the woman who takes the father. To explore the analysis, if the George Brent character is seen as the surrogate for the abandoned child, he is left at the end of the film with the surrogate mother.

When the film appeared, it failed to live up to the box office or critical promise that the studio and Huston expected.

Newsweek said Ernest Anderson "played eloquently," but added that "his part lifts the otherwise low dramatic level of the picture."

Seventeen years after the film's release, Eugene Archer in *Film Culture* reexamined Huston's second directorial effort and observed that it does, indeed, struggle for social comment. He added that "the subtler implications of the theme are subordinate to a conventionally melodramatic plot." Archer also singles out Anderson's performance, calling it "persuasive," but he adds that "Charles Coburn's perceptive performance as the partriarchal head of the family . . . establishes a background for the drama which succeeds in explaining much of the protagonists' motivations."

When viewed as a familiar melodrama, which it is, *In This Our Life* is all the things the critics said it was. What the critics may have failed to observe, was that Huston, like Wyler, had attempted to establish a visual style related to the telling of the tale. No film is simply a story. It is a story in images, with actors, sets, and a camera that can move, distort, and lie.

There is, for example, a scene on the stairway of the Timberlake house.* The father is in the foreground and a woman is on the stairway. The father mistakes Roy for Stanley in the shadows. Roy steps down the stairs and out of the shadow both literally and figuratively to announce that she plans to be hard and practical instead of docile as she has been up to that point.

Another example occurs in the living room of the Timberlake house, where Huston sets up a visual tableau with the father and mother in the foreground. On the left Roy, about to enter, is framed in a doorway. On the right stands Craig, balancing her in the frame. To further underscore the balance and the relationship between them, Craig announces casually that he plans to buy a red tie to match Roy's new red hat.

In scene after scene, Huston sets up a variety of visual relationships between characters who barely move. A change in camera angle puts a different character in the foreground and rearranges the balance of the room to indicate which character has dominance in the conversation and what the alliances are. It is Stanley who constantly breaks the tableaux, just as she has broken up the home. At one point, in fact, she announces that she doesn't want to go to the

---

*Stairway scenes have always been Wyler trademarks. Perhaps the single best known scene in *The Little Foxes* involves Bette Davis on a stairway in the background while in the foreground Herbert Marshall dies in close-up.

opera: "I'd have to keep still at the opera and I'd rather do anything than keep still."

Examples of the union of style and content are numerous and reflect, perhaps, not only Wyler's influence but Huston's training in painting.

In This Our Life can also be examined for parallels to *The Maltese Falcon.* For one thing, Huston's father is crucial in the turning point of both films. In *The Maltese Falcon,* he appears to hand the bird to Spade. In *In This Our Life,* he exists to thwart the injustice planned by Stanley and sends the police on the chase that results in her death. There is a personal irony in Walter's appearance. He is seen as a bartender who is listening to a fight on the radio and is disturbed by Stanley, who comes in and turns on the jukebox. Were it not for drawing attention to herself by violating the boxing match, which is sacred to the younger Huston, she would not have been remembered. Walter is even given a prophetic line in his small role when he mutters as she leaves, "I hope she breaks her neck," which is, indeed, what she eventually does.

Another connection to *The Maltese Falcon* was in the casting of Lee Patrick, who played Spade's secretary, Effie, in the role of Davis' only friend in *In This Our Life.* In both films, the Patrick character befriends and trusts the female character who proves to be evil and guilty.

Characteristically, both films are about the dissolution of a group. In *The Maltese Falcon,* the group was an ironic and false family. In *In This Our Life,* it is a literal family. In both films, a weak husband (Archer in *The Maltese Falcon,* Peter in *In This Our Life*) dies as a result of pursuing an evil woman. In both films, the man (Bogart, Brent) who loves the evil woman rejects her and eventually survives, though he must suffer emotionally from casting her out.

Faced with the financial failure of *In This Our Life,* Huston wanted something sure-fire for his next project. "I don't make pictures for myself," said Huston. "I do believe that if I like a film, others will like it too. I make films with the intention that they be seen. I make a picture for others. It's not just a personal satisfaction I'm seeking. On the other hand I don't try to imagine the reactions or figure out, ahead of time, the minds of others. It's hard enough for me to understand my own mind and to understand myself. I couldn't possibly speculate on what fifty million people might like or not like. I can only hope that among those fifty million there are enough who resemble me in taste."

Warner Brothers and Huston returned to Bogart, Astor, and Greenstreet for his next film, an effort, clearly, to capitalize on the success of *The Maltese Falcon*. They obtained the rights to Robert Carson's serial "Aloha Means Goodbye," which had appeared in the *Saturday Evening Post*. Richard Macaulay was assigned as writer on the project, to be named *Across the Pacific*.

According to Mary Astor, the main problem with *Across the Pacific* was the lack of story. The film was, she said, "too timely. We began filming about a week or ten days before Pearl Harbor. Since much of the plot concerned a ship sailing for Honolulu and thwarting the plans of the Japs to blow up Pearl Harbor, there was considerable rewriting to do, so we had to close the picture down. It was kind of a creepy feeling, to have been talking about the plans of the Japanese in the picture, and have them practically blueprint our script."

There was some consideration of shelving the picture because of scripting problems, but after a month's delay, shooting began again.

Huston's problem was compounded when the government wanted to ship Japanese-American members of his cast to internment camps in California. He and the studio protested to the government, which resulted in a temporary restraint. However, a number of the people in the film who played Japanese spies were interned the moment the film shooting ended.

Astor remembered one incident that particularly touched her. One afternoon a Nisei actor in the film showed her how her name would look in Japanese. He was explaining and drawing the details of the characters when someone ran up shouting happily that the United States had just bombed Tokyo. The actor, whose family lived in Tokyo, did not lift his head when the announcement came but kept talking about the meaning of the Japanese characters.

The most missed *Falcon* actor was Lorre, who had developed a close friendship with the cast members, especially Greenstreet, with whom he would appear in several later films, including *Three Strangers, The Mask of Dimitrios,* and *The Verdict.*

One afternoon Lorre came to the set dressed as a waiter. With Huston in on the gag, Lorre replaced the actor who played the waiter in the Astor-Greenstreet scene. The cameras rolled, and Lorre proceeded to confuse Greenstreet, who was not supposed to look at the waiter. He pulled the coffee cup from Greenstreet's hand while the portly actor tried to ignore him and go on with the scene. The joke ended when Lorre leaned over to kiss Astor's neck as Huston roared with laughter.

One problem in shooting resulted from the authenticity of the studio set. Much of the film takes place on a boat, and Huston arranged for the set to roll gently, supporting it with hydraulic lifts. This worked constantly and almost unnoticeably until members of the cast began to get seasick on dry land on the Warner Brothers back lot.

Shooting was nearing completion when Huston received a parcel. He put it aside, not realizing that the package contained his shipping orders. Eventually he got a phone call from Washington asking why he hadn't reported. Huston, at thirty-six, had been drafted into the Army Special Services to serve as a filmmaker.

In less than a day, Huston hammered out a wild scene with Bogart and Astor trapped in a plantation in Panama by Greenstreet. He even had Bogart tied up and about to be killed. Huston said he purposely did this as a joke on whoever took over direction of the film.

Director Vincent Sherman, who had joined Warner Brothers in 1939 and directed Bogart in *All Through the Night,* got the thankless job of ending the film. He gathered some studio writers and came up with a last-minute escape for Bogart and Astor, ending with Bogart's destruction of a Japanese plane that is about to take off and bomb the Panama Canal.

Questioned about the ending, Sherman responded, "Listen, if you ask me we were lucky to get the bastard out of there at all."

Montage sequences in the film were directed by Don Siegel, who would later become a director himself with such films as *Dirty Harry* and *The Shootist.* For Siegel, montage had originally "meant simply editing, but it had come to mean any series of quick cuts in brief takes to indicate the passage of time or rapid action."

Siegel remembers Huston as a hardworking writer/director off the set who became a performer when he directed scenes with actors and often lost himself in their performances when he was on the set.

Although his part of the film was ended, Huston managed to do some work for Warner Brothers, after he had reported for duty, while waiting for his orders to go overseas. He worked on the script for Raoul Walsh's *Background to Danger,* which was released the next year, 1943, starring George Raft and Peter Lorre.

When *Across the Pacific* was released, it met with reasonably good box-office revenue and lightly affirmative reviews.

Looking back at the film in 1959, Eugene Archer praised Huston's "gift for atmosphere detail," citing the montage sequence of a ship's departure in fog. Unfortunately, unknown to Archer, the sequence was directed by Don Siegel and not Huston. Archer concluded that "the film emerges as a minor but workmanlike directorial exercise within a conventional suspense format."

An examination of the film itself reveals much about Huston's development.

The film deals with a group of people, all of whom are hiding behind masks, pretending to be what they are not. The four principals in the film, Bogart, Astor, Greenstreet, and Victor Sen Yung, all turn out to be liars. Bogart pretends he is a deserter from the air force but is revealed as a government agent. Astor pretends she is a peanut-brittle salesperson on a pleasure trip to Los Angeles, but she is really on the way to see her father, who is a prisoner in his own plantation. Greenstreet pretends to be a sociologist going to the Philippines but is actually a Japanese spy heading for Panama. Sen Yung pretends to be a young, slang-throwing Nisei but is, like Greenstreet, a Japanese spy. A number of the other characters, in fact, turn out to be something other than what they represent themselves as being.

The idea of the fragmenting group is also explored again. The members joke with each other, have respect for each other, but ultimately do not trust each other, and with good reason.

Strangely, there are few examples of the visual style Huston had been developing. The use of characters in the foreground, with actions at various levels, is relatively absent from the film. Perhaps the reason was the haste with which it was put together to get a Huston success into the theaters.

There are, however, specific echoes of both *The Maltese Falcon* and elements that Huston was to develop in later films. Bogart refers to Astor as both "precious" and "Angel," recalling his relationship to her in the previous film. One bit of dialogue, in fact, is drawn almost verbatim from *Falcon.* After Astor has told a lie, Bogart

smiles and says, "You're good, Angel. You're very, very good."
There is also a scene between Bogart and Greenstreet very much like
the hotel room scene in *Falcon*. Both times, instead of praising
Bogart's willingness to talk, Greenstreet praises his frankness.

There is one sequence that bears comparison with a later Huston
film, *The Barbarian and the Geisha*. In *Across the Pacific,* a judo
demonstration is held on the deck of the boat. Rick (Bogart) is asked
to throw a punch at Joe (Sen Yung). He is reluctant to hurt him but
agrees, and finds himself thrown by the smaller man. Astor laughs
at Rick's humiliation. Rick accepts defeat gracefully. Precisely the
same thing happens almost sixteen years later in *Barbarian,* when
John Wayne as Townsend Harris, America's ambassador to Japan,
beats up a giant and then is defeated by a tiny, laughing Japanese
judo expert. Townsend accepts the humiliation gracefully. Huston
clearly admires his characters, particularly the males, for their ability
to take defeat gracefully.

Huston himself had suffered a similar mishap. At a party, the
former boxer and Errol Flynn were confronting each other in an
argument. They stepped outside, where Huston, with his experience,
expected to flatten Flynn. To his surprise, it was Huston who ended
up on the ground. Flynn, who had done some boxing himself and
displayed his ability when he played Jim Corbett in *Gentleman Jim,*
continued to knock Huston down each time the director got up.

Eventually, Flynn shook his head and sighed. The battered Huston looked up at him and began to roar with laughter. Soon Flynn
joined him. After helping Huston up, actor and director returned to
the party and became friends. Eventually, Huston was to cast Flynn
in a key role in *The Roots of Heaven* at the very moment the actor's
career was in deep trouble.

There is a curious scene in *Across the Pacific* in which Sydney
Greenstreet equates judo with brotherhood and Freemasonry. The
mysterious unifying possibilities of Freemasonry were to be brought
up in later Huston films, particularly *The Man Who Would Be King,*
in which it becomes a central concern.

In another unusual sequence, Bogart goes to a Japanese theater in
Panama to meet an informant. The Japanese audience is laughing at
the comedy, which Bogart does not understand. The informant is
killed while the audience is laughing, and Bogart is surrounded by
the spies. He leaps to the stage, disrupting the film inside the film.

The harmony between the audience in the film and what is happening on the screen is broken when the murder takes place and Bogart destroys the illusion the audience had been under. This was not an original idea with Huston. Several of Fritz Lang's films, especially the 1928 *Spies,* contain similar scenes, as does Hitchcock's 1942 film, *Saboteur.*

It was to be seven years before Huston would make another feature film. As a farewell irony that Huston appreciated, his first assignment for the United States Army was across the Pacific, in the Aleutian Islands.

CHAPTER 5

At War

LIEUTENANT JOHN HUSTON'S first assignment was to make a film about the most distant battle area of the war, the Aleutian Islands in the North Pacific.

Huston gathered a six-man crew that included cinematographers Lieutenant Ray Scott and Lieutenant Jules Buck. Scott had earlier shot and directed a film on China called *Kukan,* which the *New York Times* called "one of the noteworthy film documents of this war." Buck was to remain with Huston throughout the war and then move to England, where he became a producer.

The Huston crew spent six months on the island of Adak in the Aleutians starting in August of 1942. Adak was being used by the United States as a base for bomber attacks against Attu and Kiska islands.

Adak is a large, barren, cold, tundra-covered, and windswept island. Using 16mm color film (later blown up to 35mm for theatrical purposes), the Huston crew documented the building of the bomber base under almost impossible weather conditions. The film crew then went on fifteen bomber missions against the Japanese-held islands.

At one point, the plane Huston was in crash-landed and barely missed destruction. In another flight, a burst of fire from a Japanese plane killed the bomber gunner less than three feet from Huston.

Report from the Aleutians was released in July 1943 as part of the documentary series *Why We Fight* produced by the War Department. Narration of the film written by John Huston was read by Walter Huston, who served as the voice in several films in the series by different directors who had been drafted, including Frank Capra and Anatole Litvak. Music for the forty-seven-minute film was written by Dmitri Tiomkin.

When *Report from the Aleutians* opened at the Rialto in New York, the *New York Times* said Huston "has directed the film with the same terseness that marked his Hollywood films." The *Times* cited particular scenes as outstanding: "Here are the clusters of tents on the deceptive tundra, the smoke curling upward, then swept horizontal by the unending wind; here are the bulldozers pushing through the sludge to build airports almost overnight; here are the men with their muffler beards often joshing like little boys over a batch of mail from home. And here too are the planes going out on missions from fields partially inundated in seepage and sea water, and those same planes sometimes bringing back their dead."

The *Times* concluded by calling the film "one of the war's outstanding records of what our men are doing. It is furthermore an honest record."

Huston was promoted to captain and told to report to England. "I was sent to England," Huston told Robert Hughes in a 1960 interview, "where there was an attempt to make a report on the American and British, the Allied task force landings and the fighting in North Africa . . . I think the way this arose was that President Roosevelt asked to see the film that existed on the North African landing, and there wasn't any."

Apparently Anatole Litvak had been the only American member of the crew at the landing. He had put the film on his boat and gone ashore. While he was on shore, the boat was sunk. There was no footage of the landing.

The Americans' embarrassment was extreme. The landing film was supposed to be a joint production of the English and Americans and be supervised by Frank Capra. The English provided their film, which Huston described as "swell footage," but the American film was in the sea.

To cover the Americans' humiliation, Huston was assigned to re-create the invasion. He asked for the help of Jack Chennault, son of Air Force General Claire Chennault, to authenticate the film. Jack had been in charge of fighter plane support in the Aleutians. "Jack came over with his squadron," says Huston, "and, oh, he put on glorious air battles over Orlando, Florida . . . then we shot ground forces out in California." For this, they used canvas tanks.

The War Department eventually edited the film, but it was never released.

Huston recalled that the Americans withheld their faked footage from the British until the final version was put together and it was too late for them to protest. He says, "It was a hell of a dirty trick we played on the English."

Huston went back to England while Capra was editing *Report from the Aleutians* and met novelist Eric Ambler, who was a British officer. Ambler, author of *The Mask of Dimitrios* and *Journey Into Fear,* was assigned as a writer to work on British documentary war films.

When Huston was assigned to Italy to make a film using the Army Signal Corps to explain why U.S. progress was so slow, Ambler received permission to join his crew.

Huston, with Buck and Ambler, decided to concentrate on the upcoming battle for the 700-year-old town of San Pietro. This, Huston told Robert Hughes, "was the first battle of the Liri valley, and the reason we settled on that was simply because we were held there for so long. The story of the 36th Texas Infantry Division and the Liri valley just grew out of a military situation."

Huston wrote narration and script for *The Battle of San Pietro* in pencil each night after he and his crew had spent a day shooting. Buck remembers, "We couldn't really plan ahead too much, because we would sometimes get pinned down for half a day ducking what the Nazis threw at us."

Every night Huston would try to figure out what he had shot and what the military strategy had been. After that, he would try to assess the success and failure of each day and operation. He wrote sequences showing maps, a pointer, and other visual devices to explain the battle into the script.

Later, when the film was completed, the War Department chose General Mark Clark to appear in an introduction. Huston told Hughes that Clark "wasn't the most popular general that ever lived . . . They wanted Clark to say something that would take three or four minutes on the screen, and so I wrote something explaining the principle of the Italian campaign . . . I was surprised, rather aghast, when the film of Clark arrived, and he had memorized the damn speech."

A general in the U.S. Army had, in fact, accepted John Huston's military explanation of the Italian campaign and the battle of San Pietro.

As in the Aleutians, Huston and his crew again found themselves dealing with bad weather and risking their lives. He recalls one wintry day early in 1944 near San Pietro. A few days before United States troops were to move into the town, Army Intelligence reported that it had been evacuated. Huston, Buck, and Ambler headed for the town.

The director remembers passing by the bodies of hundreds of dead Americans and Germans on the walk to San Pietro. Eleven hundred American fatalities were eventually to be reported for the battle to take the town.

"We got to the base of a hill," recalled Huston in the Hughes interview. "On top of the hill was San Pietro . . . I had fallen, taken a dive someplace, and sprained an ankle; I had a walking stick, and I'm sure this saved our lives because the Germans still had San Pietro; and here we came marching right up to San Pietro. Our Intelligence was mistaken. But the Germans didn't fire on us until we paused down by the wall below the town. We were standing there trying to decide what to do when they opened fire on us. They threw two mortar shells in; and they made so much dust that we were able to run under cover of that dust."

With further Intelligence information, the trio returned cautiously to the town three days later to find it empty, but they had to take cover when both the Americans and the Germans, thinking the other side now held what remained of the town, started to shell the ruins. The people of San Pietro had departed and hidden during the campaign. Huston, Buck, and Ambler were alone in sitting out the shelling.

The town was almost reduced to nonexistence by the bombings, as the opening of Huston's film shows.

The false reports so enraged Huston that, sprained ankle and all, he ran to Intelligence headquarters and up five flights of stairs to throw a few good punches at the officer who had given him the false information. However, he was so out of breath by the time he reached the top of the stairway that he cooled off and hobbled back down again and toward the war.

Agee reported in *The Nation* that "in Italy during the shooting of *San Pietro*, his [Huston's] simian curiosity about literally everything made him the beau ideal of the contrivers of booby traps; time and again he was spared an arm, leg or skull only by the grace of God and the horrified vigilance of his friend Lieutenant Jules Buck. He sauntered through mine fields where plain man feared to tread."

The next step was to edit the footage and create a finished film. "We edited the film in Hollywood," Buck remembers, "finishing sometime around late summer (August, perhaps) 1944."

Huston was in for a shock when his editing was finally completed. "When I put the film together," he told Phillips, "it was described as anti-war by the brass at the Pentagon. The picture was shelved until General George C. Marshall saw it, because it was thought the film would discourage men who were going to go into combat. Marshall felt, however, that it should be used as a training film to show men what was in store for them in combat. There were some cuts, but I believe they were justified. For example, some of the soldiers with whom I had spoken during the making of the film had been subsequently killed in action. I had used their voices over later shots of their dead bodies covered with blankets, and it was thought that this would have upset their families should they see the film."

In his initial struggle with the War Department to have the film shown, Huston was told by one general that the picture was pacifist, against war. Huston responded, "Well, sir, whenever I make a picture that's *for* war — why I hope you take me out and shoot me."

Huston's planned version of *San Pietro* was about 50 minutes long. With the cuts, it ran about 32 minutes. The final version included a narration written and spoken by Huston himself and music by Tiomkin.

Eventually, a third edited version of the film was made, eliminating Clark and cutting the film back to less than twenty minutes for showing on an army-sponsored television show, "The Big Picture."

On viewing *San Pietro*, it is easy to see why the War Department might have some reservations about it. Clearly, Huston had not made the film out of hatred for the war, although he was fervently anti-Nazi and had no reservations about killing them. "My God," he says. "Nobody ever wanted to kill Germans more than I did. Or to see them killed. I thought it was anti-war to stop Hitler."

However, the film is filled with bitter irony about war's destruction, especially the destruction of young children and architecture. Huston's films, in general, are remarkably devoid of children. *San Pietro*, however, concludes with a series of emotionally charged images of children posing for, laughing at, and being cautious about the camera.

While Huston's voice tells us of the points of interest in San Pietro, we see shots of the rubble where such points once existed. When he mentions an individual "building, not for himself alone, but for future generations," we see the body of a dead woman.

Huston's voice and narration in this film were precursors to his use of himself as narrator in such later films as *Freud* and *The Bible*. In fact, the narration itself has distinct Biblical echoes with lines like "many fields lay fallow" and "ahead lay more rivers, towns, a thousand more."

Huston makes every move of the forces and every tank's advance precise and clear in words and on the map. He repeats the numbers of the hills "1205" and "950" slowly, solemnly over and over again until they begin to take on the importance that they clearly had for Huston and the men who fought and died there.

At one point, Huston's voice announces that "enlisted men came forward to serve as leaders." The theme arises again in *The Red Badge of Courage* and more recently in the discussion between Peachy and Dravot in *The Man Who Would Be King*. Huston's view of courage and facing death with dignity emerges in a number of his films during and after the war and appears to be strongly influenced by his experience.

There is also a disturbing and typical Huston shot in the film. The camera, placed low, reveals the head of a dead soldier in the foreground at the right filling a quarter of the frame. His dead eyes seem to be looking up at the advancing comrades we see moving toward him and toward San Pietro.

The film opens with a painting of Saint Peter, patron saint of the town, and closes with a religious procession and a cut to a statue of Saint Peter. There is no comment in the narrative of how Huston views the role of religion, but it is clear that he wishes to frame his film with it.

For a man with no religious training and nothing to say overtly about God, Huston has chosen at a number of points in his career to examine the failure of religion to respond to man's needs and to demonstrate his distrust of clerics as dangerous masqueraders.

The religious images of San Pietro begin an interesting continuum of the failure of religion when joined with Huston's treatment of the subject in such films as *The Night of the Iguana, The List of Adrian Messenger, The Bible,* and *The Man Who Would Be King.*

Agee, writing in *The Nation,* said that "no war film I have seen has been quite so attentive to the heaviness of casualties, and to the number of yards gained or lost, in such an action; none has so levelly watched and implied what it meant, in such full and complex terms — in military terms; in terms of the men who were doing the fighting; in terms of the villagers; and of their village; and of the surrounding country; and of the natural world; and of human existence and hope."

Time said *San Pietro* "is in every respect as good a war film as any that has been made; in some respects it is the best."

The War Department promoted John Huston to major and gave him the Legion of Merit.

Huston's last army film was *Let There Be Light.* It was shot at the Mason General Hospital on Long Island, New York, at the request of the War Department. With the war coming to a close, they wanted, according to Huston, "a film to show industry that nervous and emotional casualties were not lunatics; because at that time these men weren't getting jobs."

To make the film, Huston was given the services of Stanley Cortez. The brother of actor Ricardo Cortez, Stanley had been a cinematographer since the silent days and had recently worked on *The Magnificent Ambersons* and *Since You Went Away.* Tiomkin again did the music and Walter Huston delivered the narration written by his son.

However, there was one major difference between this and the other Huston-directed films. It is the only one that has never been released.

When the War Department announced that they would not release it, Huston said that he was shocked. "It seemed to me to be a wonderfully hopeful and even inspiring film. And I take no credit for all this, because all I did was to stand by and tell the cameramen when to grind, and later put the thing together . . . It was banned because, I believe, the War Department felt it was too strong medicine. This is only my opinion, but it's the only opinion that stands up under scrutiny."

The War Department announced that the film would not be released for "legal" reasons.

Agee's comment in *The Nation* was that "the War Department has mumbled a number of reasons why it has been withheld; the glaring obvious reason has not been mentioned: that any sane human being who saw the film would join the armed services, if at all, with a straight face and a painfully maturing mind."

The finished film runs forty-five minutes and is a study of methods of mental therapy developed to rehabilitate victims of psychoneuroses resulting from combat.

Although the film is not available, a copy of Huston's script can be found in *Film: Book 2: Films of Peace and War,* edited by Robert Hughes.

Let There Be Light opens with John Huston's prologue stating that about 20 percent of all battle casualties in the American army during the Second World War were of a neuropsychiatric nature.

"The special treatment methods shown in this film, such as hypnosis and narco-synthesis, have been particularly successful in acute cases, such as battle neurosis," according to the film's narration. "Equal success is not to be expected when dealing with peacetime neuroses which are usually of a chronic nature."

The prologue then indicates that no scenes in the film were staged. Indeed, three hidden cameras were used to record the patients.

"While making *Let There Be Light,*" Huston told Phillips, "I had the benefit of a quick course in psychiatry by constantly asking Army psychiatrists questions about various aspects of what they were doing. The figure of Freud began to emerge, and that was the beginning of my later film about Freud."

Some who have seen the film have criticized the quick recovery through hypnosis and the miracle cures of the various drugs in the film.

To this Huston responds, "Well, there is certainly some point to that. We try to explain in the film's commentary that these men have not undergone a complete recovery from all the ills that they have ever had. Some of them of course came into the army with hidden neuroses, hidden so far as the medical examiner was concerned; but I think it is fairly true that these men were put back into as good shape as they were when they had come in. And of course they had undergone terrible emotional experiences.

"Certainly you can't expect to reach an original trauma, the original cause of neurosis, in any six weeks' time. That's a matter of years, and it's not done by hypnosis or sodium-pentothal or -amytal, or any of those drugs, in a few sessions."

One of the few to see the film was Archer Winston of the *New York Post,* who wrote: "It's so great a picture, so inspiring medically and humanly, so tremendously graphic as a movie penetration of basic fears . . . that they just don't know what to do with it . . . Seeing it,

I felt as if I had never before witnessed emotion on the screen so stripped of extraneous self-consciousness."

Several years after the war, Huston obtained permission to have *Let There Be Light* shown at the Museum of Modern Art. When the film was ready to be screened by a small group, military policemen arrived and seized it.

In 1947, *Let There Be Light* was remade using actors in the roles of the patients. This commercial version was called *Shades of Grey* and John Huston wanted nothing to do with it.

The year 1945 marked an end of the war, and it also marked the end of something else for Huston, his second marriage. Olivia de Havilland, his heroine in *In This Our Life,* announced that she and Huston were in love and would be married. De Havilland claimed that Huston pursued her relentlessly, but apparently nothing permanent ever came of it except that Leslie Black Huston divorced her husband before 1945 ended.

John met actress Evelyn Keyes in June of 1946. A star at Columbia, Evelyn had recently been divorced from director Charles Vidor.

The twenty-seven-year-old actress had known Walter Huston and toured with him on a bond-selling tour during World War II. The elder Huston had talked constantly about his son, and when the war ended, she met John at a party.

According to James Robert Parish and Lennard DeCarl, three weeks after their meeting, John took Evelyn to Romanoff's for dinner and asked her to marry him. When she agreed, Huston sent restauranteur Mike Romanoff to Huston's home to dredge his pool. John remembered that someone had dropped a wedding ring in it recently. Romanoff found the ring and John chartered a plane. Stunt flyer Paul Mantz flew them to a justice of the peace and served as witness along with a taxi driver when the wedding took place at 3:30 A.M.

CHAPTER 6

Amigos

WHEN HE LEFT the army, Huston touched up a screenplay of *Three Strangers,* which he had written in 1942 with Howard Koch. Huston's idea was to make the film another vehicle for Bogart, Astor, and Greenstreet. Before he could begin shooting, though, he found himself involved with directing a play, Jean Paul Sartre's *No Exit,* and the film was assigned to director Jean Negulesco, with Lorre, Greenstreet, and Geraldine Fitzgerald in the leads.

Huston also did some work during this period with Anthony Veiller on *The Killers,* based on Ernest Hemingway's short story. Although Huston received no credit for the screenplay, which was directed by Robert Siodmak, there are several clear Huston interests in the film. The mysterious Swede, played by Burt Lancaster, turns out to be a boxer who gamely battles with a broken hand, loses, falls in love with a woman, Ava Gardner, who betrays him, and joins a gang at her urging. As in most Huston films, the initial group effort, a robbery, is successful, but, as with other Huston groups, success is followed by a breakdown of faith among the gang members, who kill each other off.

Huston's version of *No Exit* opened in November of 1946 at New York City's Biltmore Theatre. It marked the introduction of Sartre's drama to the United States. The concept of man's acceptance of the meaninglessness of existence and his reliance on himself did not turn out to be very popular. *No Exit* closed after thirty-one performances. In spite of its public failure, the play was a critical success, earning praise especially from *Saturday Review* and *Time.* It also won the New York Drama Critics Circle award as the best foreign play of the year.

According to Huston, in spite of the good reviews, the critics did not really know what the play had been about. "They thought," he told Gene Phillips "that it was a French love triangle instead of a rather strongly philosophic work."

Back in Hollywood, Huston quickly reestablished himself as the industry's resident bad man.

"He's a First Class Character with a busted nose, cadaverous frame, stooped shoulders, rubber face and berserk hair — all adding up to his nickname 'Double Ugly,'" wrote Dan Fowler in *Look* magazine. "His uninhibited behavior pattern delights even hardened experts in the art of self-publicity. Not since John Barrymore has anybody handed the acting colony such outrageous subject matter for after-dinner conversation."

The Double Ugly Great Unpressed Monster's exploits included walking up to Joan Crawford at one party, smearing her rouge down her face with his thumbs, and telling her loudly, "You wear too much make-up."

At another party, he purposely maneuvered Bogart and producer Sam Spiegel into a series of arguments, bating them to the point where both men were ready to throw punches at each other.

Visiting a friend, he taught the young child in the house how to cut up the rug with a scissors and hit the furniture with a hammer.

According to Fowler, "Once Huston started home to dress for director Lewis Milestone's Christmas Eve Party — strictly a black-tie event — but stopped off en route at Bogart's. As usual, he lost all track of time. And since his meetings with Bogart were robust events highlighted by living room football and wrestling matches, Huston arrived at the Milestones' at midnight in tweeds, his coat torn and his face bloody."

At this point in his career, when he was forty-one, Huston plunged into another film project. In 1936, Huston had read a new novel, set in Mexico. From time to time he had talked to friends about this book, *The Treasure of the Sierra Madre,* by B. Traven, and how it reminded him of his days in the Mexican cavalry.

Warner Brothers, the studio where Huston was employed, owned the rights to the novel and planned to film it during World War II. Henry Blanke knew of Huston's affection for the work and managed to keep the film from production until his return. Now Huston was back and ready.

The Treasure of the Sierra Madre, published in 1935, presented a primary difficulty for John Huston as both writer and director. Like Traven's other work, it contains a high level of unusual dialogue. "Traven's unique," Huston told interviewer Philip K. Scheuer in 1948, "a combination of Conrad and Dreiser, if you can imagine such a thing. His people speak no known language, or English, at any rate, like none I've ever heard."

The dialogue of the novel might, on first reading, appear to be undeliverable in "realist" terms. For example, here the old man, Howard, is ridiculing his two partners, Dobbs and Curtin, for not recognizing the gold they are standing on:

> Well, tell my old gra'mother. I have burdened myself with a couple of fine lodgers, two very elegant bedfellers who kick at the first drop of rain and crawl under mother's petticoat when thunder rumbles. My, my, what great prospectors a driller and a tool-dresser can make! Drilling a hole with a half a hundred Mexican peons around to lend you hands and feet! I still can do that after a two days' spree you bet. Two guys! Two guys reading in the magazines about crossing a lazy river up in Alaska and now going prospecting on their own.

The style removes the monologue from the natural. However, it is exactly this challenge of surreal dialogue that probably intrigued Huston, himself a teller of tall tales, accomplished writer, and lover of the bizarre. It is the same kind of challenge met by Huston in 1975 in his adaptation of Kipling's *The Man Who Would Be King,* in which he retains the very dialogue of the original story, which, on reading, might appear to be the most difficult, especially the encounter with Kipling in his office when Dravot and Peacy discuss their trip and their pact.

As already mentioned, a great deal of the dialogue of *Treasure* is taken from the novel, especially scenes with Howard, Dobbs, and Curtin. Most of the film was shot in Mexico, and it appears that Traven was present and served as consultant. It is necessary to qualify this because Traven, who guarded his identity carefully, never admitted who he was. He lived alone in Mexico and refused to have photographs taken or to grant interviews. Huston read the novel shortly after it appeared and followed his interest by contacting Traven's agent. During World War II, Huston corresponded with Traven. In 1946, he wrote the author indicating that he was ready to shoot the film version of the book. Traven then sent the director a twenty-page statement that included suggestions about set construction and lighting. Huston asked to meet with Traven, but the reluctant author would guarantee nothing. While Huston was waiting at the Reforma Hotel in Mexico City one morning, a thin little man with gray hair handed Huston a card introducing himself as H. Croves, a translator from Acapulco. Croves had a note from Traven indicating that he was the author's representative. Convinced that Croves was, in fact, the shy Traven, Huston hired him as technical adviser for shooting in Mexico. Croves was present for all the shooting and did, indeed, make many suggestions that Huston accepted.* However, much of Traven's own concept is clearly altered.

For example, a primary concern of Traven's work in general is Bolshevism. Traven's sympathy with Bolshevik principles and his anti-Catholicism are evident in the novel. However, in the film version, all such references have been removed.

The novel, like the film, opens in Tampico, but Traven's novel devotes a number of pages to the Hotel Oso Negro and its inhabitants. Traven uses the hotel as a socialist microcosm of the human condition, a hierarchy to show how the lowest members of society can function and protect themselves. Huston's film includes two relatively brief sequences in the hotel, which is presented quite differently from the description in the novel. In the novel, a group of men are in a small, hot, and dirty room during their conversation. In the film the room is large with dozens of beds. Traven is concerned about the conditions of life of the men. Clearly, Huston's concerns are not with Traven's social issues, but with the character of his protagonists.

A number of other specific differences between novel and film help in understanding Huston's attitudes.

In the novel, after Curtin and Dobbs have been cheated out of their wages by McCormick, they find him in a bar. Cornered and outnumbered, he gives in and pays them without a battle. In the film, a brutal fight takes place, with McCormick very nearly beating the two partners, whom he gets partially drunk. In the film, bleeding and unable to see, McCormick pays the two men as he lies stunned on the floor. Again, Huston's interest in the human interaction and the battle

---

*Traven's pose as Croves was recently confirmed by Traven's wife in the introduction to the (1976) edition of *The Bridge in the Jungle.*

takes precedence over Traven's interest in showing McCormick as an exploiting capitalist. Huston admires McCormick's decision to fight, and also uses the scene to bring Dobbs and Curtin closer together.

As another example, in the novel, Lacaud, the stranger who tries to become a partner, tells a bloody story about bandits who a week or so before his arrival robbed a train. The graphic tale involves the murder of women and children. In Huston's film, the robbery is shown with Dobbs, Curtin, and Howard on the train helping to fight off the bandits and getting their first glimpse of Gold Hat, the bandit who will eventually kill Dobbs. There are only four passengers killed, according to the conductor, and we see none of them. Again, Huston has taken a strange tale in the novel that does not directly involve the trio and has converted it to a presentation involving the humanized reaction and interaction of his principals. Huston's concern is their reaction to the train robbery attempt, not the social system that led to the robbery and the slaughter of innocents. Gold Hat becomes, in the film, a precise villain, encountered three magical times — on the train, at the campsite, and near the town when he kills Dobbs in the Traven novel.

In the film Cody, the intruder, is killed in the battle on the mountain with Gold Hat and his gang. In Traven's novel, the comparable character, Lacaud, is presented as half-mad. He is not killed by the bandits, but is left behind to work the mine when the others leave. Cody's death gives the three partners in Huston's version an opportunity to show their varying attitudes toward death and responsibility.

In Huston's film, Cody's past is revealed when, after his death, Howard and Curtin read a letter and look in his wallet to discover that he has a fruit orchard in Texas and a wife and child. Traven gives nothing of Lacaud's past. Again, Huston specifies character and reduces abstraction. He makes the situation as concrete as possible and moves away from those aspects that might be considered metaphorical or even surreal. In a sense, Traven's novel can be read as a Kafka-like allegory while Huston's film version more closely resembles a film by Ernest Hemingway. This is not to say straightforward adventure is a general trend in Huston. It is not found in such films as *Reflections in a Golden Eye* or *A Walk with Love and Death,* but in his films of adventure, Huston clearly moves away from the overt presentation of metaphor. In this sense, Huston's work, in general, can be divided between art films of metaphor and meaning and adventure films that disdain metaphor.

Returning to the comparison of novel and film, which illustrates choices made and their meaning, Traven indicates throughout the novel a firm respect for the quick justice of the Mexican soldiers who are hunting the bandits. At three points in the novel, we are presented with scenes of resolute bravery by the soldiers, whom Traven sees as instruments of a struggling socialist system. Huston gives us no individual soldier and only a brief sequence of a single firing squad.

The conclusion of the film is also radically different from that of Traven's novel in which the wounded Curtin says nothing about returning to the United States. In fact, it is quite probable that he will take Howard's offer to join him as an assistant medicine man. The difference may be seen as representing the attitudes of two different creators. Traven lived in Mexico, chose Mexico, and did not return to the United States. Huston, whose affection for Mexico is clear, nevertheless returned to his country, the United States, and his family, as does Curtin in his film when he leaves Howard.

In both novel and film, Howard says to Curtin:

> Yes, my boy, even you will take off your hat when you see how much respected I am there. Only the day before yesterday they wanted to make me their legislature, the whole legislature. I don't know what they mean by that but I figure it must be the greatest honor they can bestow.

As a footnote to the issue of adaptation, it is particularly interesting to note that Traven's novel has a number of specific references to movies, all of which have been removed from Huston's film.

For example, in the novel Dobbs and Howard talk about taking their money and starting a movie house in Tampico, with Howard as business manager and Dobbs as artistic manager. At the end of the novel, Curtin and Howard find two bags of gold left (they find none in the film) and discuss and reject the idea of starting a movie theater.

In the siege by bandits at the campsite, one of the miners wishes that he were in a movie so that he could be rescued, and he is indeed rescued. When the bandits leave, Howard doesn't think it is a trick and announces, "They would have to be awfully good movie actors to play a trick like that so perfectly." In the film version, the word "movie" is not in Howard's statement.

This, perhaps, is further indication of Huston's moving away from overt metaphor in the film. Traven frequently refers to the action of his novel as a kind of dream or movie. Huston does his best to move away from that idea.

While the attitude toward material on the part of novelist and filmmaker may have been different, there is no doubt that Huston respected the novel and relied heavily upon it. The difference was in (a) what he selected to use and (b) how he viewed and presented it. As with any work, adaptations by two different directors would almost certainly be radically different.

Some of the most frequently cited sequences in the film are, in fact, taken from the novel. For example, Dobbs gets a series of handouts from a white-suited man in Tampico (played by John Huston), who finally says, "From now on you have to make it through life without my assistance."

Also in the novel are the trip to the mountain, most of Howard's dialogue, the trip back by Dobbs and Curtin and Dobbs's shooting of Curtin, the murder of Dobbs, and the hysterical and cathartic laughter of Howard at the end.

A primary similarity between the novelist and director is their attitudes toward their three protagonists.

Dobbs is frequently described by reviewers as a moral brute and a madman, but clearly he is a highly contradictory character until his crackup. He is initially generous and willing to share his cash, and he rather nobly throws away the gold Curtin offers him to pay back the extra money he put up to finance the trip. Later, it is Dobbs who agrees to help Howard refill the "wounded" mountain they've dug into. Howard, the doctor/father (indeed John Huston's real father, Walter), constantly warns that gold is a potential disease. He is aware of it and protects himself, and Curtin learns to do so, but even Curtin has a moment of hesitation when he almost leaves Dobbs in the mine after a collapse. It is Dobbs who succumbs to the disease, but he is not viewed as evil by Traven or Huston or, for that matter, by Howard.

Huston's interest in the characters is shown in the way he shoots. *Treasure* is a constant reorganization of the three partners in a single frame. The nature of the partnership is referred to in dialogue

— the word "partner" is repeated by each of the trio frequently, an occurrence not as evident in the novel. The partnership is also explored visually. For example, in the hotel when the three decide to become mining partners, Dobbs and Curtin shake hands. We see only their clasped hands in the frame with the seated Howard between them looking uncertainly from one to the other, implying his skepticism about the partnership.

As he did in his earlier films, Huston frequently places one character in the foreground of a shot with action going on behind him. There is a constant visual emphasis on the relationship of the three men, a relationship that is commented on in the novel, but obviously cannot be shown in the same way in the film.

Huston employs a variety of other techniques that cannot be used in the novel. For example, the principals frequently lie down and talk. When a character in the film lies down, he generally speaks more honestly than when he is standing. There is a potential relationship to couch, dream, and confession. In the novel the author can say that a man is lying down, but he cannot show the immediate visual effect of this position on the man's words or the reactions of the other characters. In the film, the image is constantly evident and becomes part of our perception of dialogue and events.

Huston also emphasizes Dobbs's deterioration and animalism through make-up and movement, also impossible in a novel. Twice in the film Dobbs resents being called an animal or compared to an animal. His first resentful reaction occurs when he believes Curtin has called him a "hog" about the money. It is at that point that Dobbs throws away the gold Curtin offers him, to prove he is a civilized human. Later, when the intruder implies that Dobbs is "uncivilized," Dobbs hits him.

However, in the film, we watch Dobbs's clothing deteriorate, his beard grow, and his body move closer to the ground as Huston emphasizes his growing inversion. Several times he straightens himself out to emphasize his humanness, only to crouch forward or rest on his heels moments later.

As a final example in this comparison of novel and film, look at the very end of each. Traven's novel concludes with Howard getting on his horse. The last line is "No sooner was he seated in the saddle than the Indians shouted, whipped their ponies into action, and hurried back home." The implication of the last word of the novel, "home," is one of resolution and potential peace.

But Huston's film ends with an ironic shot. Curtin will sell the burros and head for Texas and an uncertain future. Howard will remain with the Indians as a revered medicine man. A storm is coming and the last shot is of an empty gold bag against a dry cactus. The partnership is dissolved and the man who had been introduced as the principal character, Dobbs, is dead.

Curtin has hopes of creating some family roots and Howard has a kingdom, but Huston sees the wish for wealth as an empty bag blowing on the thorns of a desert cactus.

*

The Treasure of the Sierra Madre has become the archetypal Huston film for several reasons. One is that it is a clear examination of the exploration of the quest. As in many Huston films to come (and *The Maltese Falcon* to some extent, before it), the director was to examine a small group of people on a quest, usually for wealth. Generally, the members of the group accomplish their initial goal: they obtain the money or the treasure. Once having attained it, however, potential power often becomes too much for the individuals to handle. Human greed, weakness, or obsession destroys their victory.

This is remarkably true of *Treasure, The Asphalt Jungle, Beat the Devil, The Kremlin Letter,* and *The Man Who Would Be King.* In all of these films, however, Huston does not simply examine greed and present a moral statement about it. He examines the disintegration or change within the individual who has to learn to cope with the specter of wealth or power and the erosion of the fragile group or couple when chance, greed, envy, or obsession intrudes.

Treasure is not a moral statement by Huston but an examination of characters under pressure, characters who fall apart when least expected to and rise to noble reactions when no reason is given to believe they will. Like the soldiers in *Let There Be Light,* actions and reactions of Huston characters are often unpredictable. Like Huston himself, his characters are capable of sudden movement from total compassion to extreme selfishness and apparent cruelty.

To make *The Treasure of the Sierra Madre,* Huston convinced Warner Brothers to let him shoot on location in Mexico for ten weeks. In the army he had grown accustomed to location work and now felt comfortable with it. "Locationing? Nothing to it," he said, "The only time it's tough to make pictures on location is when someone is shooting at you." The request to shoot on location was a radical one for Warners, but they approved it when producer Henry Blanke put himself on the line with Jack Warner.

In his search for the concrete in making the film, Huston went to the extreme of shooting exteriors in San José de Purua, an isolated village 140 miles north of Mexico City.

Humphrey Bogart, who played Dobbs, told Joe Hyams, "John wanted everything perfect. If he saw a nearby mountain that could serve for photographic purposes, that mountain was not good; too easy to reach. If we could get to a location site without fording a couple of streams and walking through snake-infested areas in the scorching sun, then it wasn't quite right."

Huston's other stars included his father and cowboy actor Tim Holt as Curtin. Originally, John Garfield had been announced to play Curtin but the actor's last-minute change of mind forced the replacement.

To play Howard, the old man, Huston insisted that his sixty-two-year-old father remove his dentures. Walter, accustomed to suffering indignities from his son, complied, but without enthusiasm. "The director is always the father figure on the set, so I suppose," John told Gene Phillips, "that while the film was being made, I was my father's father figure."

After finishing her role in Columbia's *The Jolson Story,* John's wife, Evelyn, visited the Mexican location and noticed a fourteen-year-old boy who had attached himself to the cast and crew. The boy, Pablo Abarran, slept under station wagons at night and hustled Cokes for the cast during the day. Evelyn felt sorry for him.

When location shooting ended, Huston called Evelyn in Hollywood, where she was working opposite Dick Powell in *Johnny O'-Clock,* to announce a surprise: he had legally adopted the boy and renamed him Pablo Huston. Pablo was from that time on to remain close to Huston, and, eventually, when the director moved to Ireland, Pablo would marry an Irish girl and settle in that country.

Huston got along well with his cast and crew in Mexico, but at the end of location work he decided that some extra scenes had to be shot. This caused Bogart to miss a Honolulu yacht race that he wanted to enter.

"We had a terrible row and were sore as hell at each other for days," Huston recalled in an NBC radio tribute to Bogart. "Then we had a few drinks of an ancient tequila laced with Scotch, and anger melted into understanding and sympathy."

Warner Brothers had some difficulty deciding what to do with the strange film that had cost them $2,800,000 to make, so they began by promoting it as a Western. To further support the opening of the film, the studio distributed treasure maps showing the locations of the action in the film for display in theater lobbies.

The studio also pointed out in their promotional material that the flophouse where Howard meets Curtin and Dobbs was a studio set constructed from drawings John Huston had done based on his memory of such places during the time he had been in the Mexican army.

Time called the film "one of the best things Hollywood has done since it learned to talk . . . Walter Huston's performance is his best job in a lifetime of acting."

Crowther in the *New York Times* wrote that "Huston has shaped a searching drama of the collision of civilization's vicious greeds with the instinct for self-preservation in an environment where all the barriers are down."

Agee and *Newsweek* also praised the film, but there was some antagonism. John McCarten in *The New Yorker* said the film could be reduced to the idea that greed does not pay. He went on to say that "even if the premise is granted, the film's methods of elaborating on it are certainly something less than beguiling."

When the mixed reviews filtered in, Holt vowed to go back to Westerns and Huston plunged into his next project, but his work was disrupted when the Academy Awards for 1948 were announced. For the first time, a father-and-son team won the awards, John as best director, Walter as best supporting actor. Bogart was nominated but was nosed out as best actor by Laurence Olivier in *Hamlet.* In addition, *Treasure* won Huston the New York Film Critics award for best direction and the best director's award from *Film Daily.* Composer Max Steiner also won a Venice Film Festival award for *Treasure.*

Huston held an Oscar celebration at his recently purchased San Fernando Valley ranch and appeared with what became his almost constant companion, a monkey named Liberty, which clung to his shoulder. For other playmates, Huston gradually obtained a white German shepherd, Paulette, named for Paulette Goddard, who was a friend of Evelyn's, a fox terrier named Jenny for Jennifer Jones, and a burro named Socrates.

With Liberty around his neck, John began a football game with a writer and producer. The game was played in mud with a genuine Ming vase for the ball. Henry Blanke and Lauren Bacall served as referees. All players wore tuxedoes. The producer broke two ribs, and Ida Lupino, who joined the game, sprained her back.

Huston may have been a sober father during the making of a film, but he turned into an uncontrolled child at other times. "That's John," said Walter to *Look*'s Dan Fowler. "I called him 'that wild Indian' . . . but I always knew he had something special."

CHAPTER 7

The Animal with Its Shell Off

JOHN HUSTON had begun shooting *Key Largo* before he received the Oscar for *The Treasure of the Sierra Madre*. *Key Largo* was apparently not a project he selected but one he was convinced to do by Warner Brothers producer Jerry Wald. Wald, reported to be the model for Budd Schulberg's protagonist-villain in *What Makes Sammy Run?*, convinced Huston that he had a great play to be converted to an even greater film. The producer, who had recently had two critical, commercial, and Oscar-winning successes, *Mildred Pierce* and *Johnny Belinda,* had little trouble convincing Huston that he should direct the film. However, when Huston actually received a copy of the property he was to work on, he was enraged.

Maxwell Anderson's blank-verse play *Key Largo,* written before World War II, was about a disillusioned Spanish-American War veteran returning to the United States. The stage version, with Paul Muni, had been only a moderate success, and the reviewers and public had found the play heavy-handed.

Huston and Richard Brooks began to rewrite the Anderson play. Brooks had previously written *Brute Force* and *Crossfire* (the latter from his own novel), both of which were brought to the screen, and was to become producer-writer-director for such films as *Lord Jim* and *In Cold Blood*. When they completed their rewrite, Huston and Brooks had radically changed the Anderson play.

Jerry Wald was barred by Huston from the set when shooting began, but Wald didn't care. He had obtained a top director and a cast that included Edward G. Robinson, Bogart, Lionel Barrymore, Claire Trevor, Lauren Bacall, Thomas Gomez, and Marc Lawrence.

In the Huston-Brooks script, Frank McCloud (Bogart) is a returning World War II veteran, a major — like John Huston — who goes to visit the widow (Bacall) and father (Barrymore) of one of his troops. McCloud and the family find themselves held prisoners by a group of gangsters led by Johnny Rocco, played by Robinson in a resurrection of his character of Rico in *Little Caesar*. The major refuses to fight, refusing to spread more blood until Rocco gives him no choice when he kills a policeman and two American Indians. With the help of Rocco's girlfriend (Trevor) and the widow, McCloud kills Rocco and five of the gangsters. Clearly Huston and Brooks had added a lot of action to Anderson's dialogue-heavy play.

In a 1948 *Time* interview, Huston said about his film: "Rocco was supposed to represent a sort of evil flower of reaction. In other words we are headed for the same kind of world we had before, even down to the gang lords . . . There is great talk of the good old days and Prohibition; in other words, return to the old order . . . I tried to make all the characters old-fashioned (the gangster's moll is out of the twenties), to brand them as familiar figures, and to suggest they were ready to take over again."

After *Key Largo* was finished, the usually laudatory Agee wrote in *The Nation,* "I rather doubt . . . whether gangsters can be made to represent all that he meant them to — practically everything that is fundamentally wrong with post-war America."

Several critics were fascinated by the first shot of Rocco in the film: Robinson sitting in a bathtub with a cigar in his mouth. "I wanted to get a look at the animal with its shell off," Huston told *Time.* Agee called the shot "one of the most powerful and efficient 'first entrances' of a character on record" and referred to Robinson's "bestial lolling in the bathtub."

The film also contains a scene that won an Academy Award for Claire Trevor as Gaye Dawn, Rocco's girlfriend. A former singer, the boozy Gaye is goaded into singing "Moanin' Low." Rocco wants to make fun of her in front of his gang and the prisoners. She doesn't want to sing, but he forces her to and her pathetic trek through the song, from beginning to end, is painful and embarrassing.

When it came time to shoot the scene, Trevor had a cold and worried about singing. Actually, she could sing quite well. "Don't worry," Huston is quoted as saying in a Warner Brothers publicity story issued in 1948. "You're playing the part of a throaty, has-been singer. The sniffles will be perfect." He further instructed her to sing the entire song off-key.

To get Trevor to look as pathetic as possible, Huston told her, "You're the kind of drunken dame whose elbows are always a little too big, your voice is a little too loud, you're a little too polite. You're very sad, very resigned." He then showed her how to lean against the bar in a way that caught her fancy, and she repeated it several times in the film.

At another point, to get a particularly pained expression from Lauren Bacall, Huston walked up to her and twisted her arm.

The director was particularly interested in a storm sequence in which Rocco becomes afraid of the elements. To make the storm's destruction as spontaneous as possible, Huston rigged a variety of special effects and shots with Robert Burks, later to become Alfred Hitchcock's cameraman. In one shot, for instance, a gangster played by Dan Seymour stands behind a bar with a row of shot glasses tied to his fingers, which are hidden from the camera's view. As the scene progresses, Seymour pulls one finger and then another, sending the glasses mysteriously flying.

The climax of the film takes place on the yacht owned by the widow and her father. For luck, Huston used Bogart's own yacht, the *Santana*. The name of the boat is clearly visible in several shots and became the name of Bogart's own production company. It was the same boat that was to have been in the yacht race Huston and Bogart argued about after finishing *The Treasure of the Sierra Madre*.

The cameraman was Karl Freund, who had worked on such German films as *The Last Laugh* and *Metropolis* and had won an Academy Award for his work on *The Good Earth* in 1937. The German films had received worldwide attention for their elaborate camera movement, and *Key Largo* contains a great deal more, perhaps, than any other Huston film.

Not as striking as the camera movement are Huston's changes in dialogue. There is one specific comic reference to the director's analogy between people and good horses. When asked who he is after hearing a horse race on the radio, McCloud introduces himself by bloodline as "Frank McCloud by Frank out of Ellen."

Huston said Jack Warner agreed that when the film was completed, nothing important would be cut. When he saw the release print, however, he was irate. What he considered the strongest and thematically most necessary speeches in the film were cut. "Why goddammit," Huston shouted, "they cut the very gizzard out of it."

According to Huston, the studio removed an important motivating scene after Rocco kills the deputy. In this scene McCloud justifies his nonresistance, the only time he clearly does so. The deletion made McCloud's motivation unclear.

Although the reviews were generally good, Huston retained some resentment toward the studio.

Key Largo appears to reflect some of Huston's growing political interests, and McCloud bears resemblance to the Huston who returned from the war and found the unpleasantness unchanged in spite of the men he had seen die. At one point in the film, McCloud actually starts to talk about his war experiences: "Once outside San Pietro . . ." and then he stops.

Allusions to home-grown Hitlers are evident, and the film includes frequent references to Rocco as a would-be Fascist dictator. "He was more than a king," McCloud explains sarcastically, "he was an Emperor." The potential dictator accepts this as a compliment. At one point the following exchange takes place:

MCCLOUD: He knows what he wants. He wants more.

ROCCO (beaming with satisfaction): Yeah, more.

MCCLOUD: And I wanted a world in which there was no place for Johnny Rocco.

Rocco has a resemblance to the then recently deported gangster Lucky Luciano, and the likeness was noted by reviewers. But the film is not simply a statement against organized crime, it is an attempt on Huston's part to make Rocco represent the evils he had cited in the *Time* interview. As Agee said, the burden of this message was perhaps too much for one character to carry.

Angry with Warner Brothers over their cutting of his film, Huston left the studio in 1948 and founded Horizon Films with Sam Spiegel and his wartime partner Jules Buck, who had worked on *San Pietro.* Perhaps partly in retaliation, Warner Brothers released *The Treasure of the Sierra Madre* and *Key Largo* across the country in a double bill without mentioning Huston's name in its promotion ads.

It was now 1949 and the House Un-American Activities Committee was angrily ferreting out "Communists."

Huston's belief in personal freedom dates back to his own movement away from formal schooling and his unwillingness to accept other people's views of his responsibilities. He has invariably stood behind the underdog as a matter of principle.

For example, though he himself had faced literal death in the war, he publicly defended actor Lew Ayres's right to be a conscientious objector. He also served as a sponsor of third-party presidential candidate Henry Wallace in the 1948 campaign.

Although his career as an independent director had just begun and there had been a sudden drop in film attendance due to the advent of television, the forty-three-year-old Huston again put himself on the line.

He and his friend William Wyler were among those who spoke out against the Hollywood blacklist, which included such people as Dalton Trumbo, Herbert J. Biberman, and Abraham Polonsky. Huston and Wyler went so far as to label the investigation of communism in film an "obscenity."

Huston, Wyler, and screenwriter Philip Dunne organized the Committee for the First Amendment to combat the House Un-American Activities Committee. With Bogart, Bacall, and other Committee members, Huston signed a petition and sent it to the House committee. Other signers included writer Norman Corwin, Henry Fonda, Ava Gardner, Paulette Goddard, Benny Goodman, Van Heflin, Katharine Hepburn, John Houseman, Myrna Loy, Burgess Meredith, Gregory Peck, Barry Sullivan, Cornel Wilde, and Billy Wilder. The petition said, in part, that the people who signed it were "disgusted and outraged by the House Un-American Activities Committee's" attack on the motion-picture industry. Huston, Bogart, and Bacall went to Washington to present the petition and also to put together a radio broadcast attacking the committee.

Twenty-eight members of Huston's committee, including Huston, actually testified before the House committee. Those testifying included Bogart, Bacall, Ira Gershwin, Sterling Hayden, Gene Kelly, Huston's wife, Evelyn, Danny Kaye, and Jane Wyatt. At a time when motion picture careers were being destroyed as fast as the committee could call witnesses, Huston was risking a great deal.

Among the signers of the petition was actor John Garfield, who was suddenly put under pressure by the House committee. Under advice from his counsel, he gave one of the committee members, J. Parnell Thomas of New Jersey, a statement of loyalty to the United States government and a denial of association with Communists. Garfield had left Warner Brothers to start the Roberts Company after HUAC pressure began, but despite his denial of Communist ties, he was unable to raise funds for production.

Working out of the MGM lot, Horizon Films had just announced plans for a new film that was to star Gene Kelly and Jennifer Jones. It was to be based on part of a Robert Sylvester novel, *Rough Sketch,* about 1930s Cuban revolutionaries.

The casting of Kelly proved to be only a rumor. Huston approached Garfield about starring in the film. Because the HUAC was defaming some of his past and present associates, Garfield had few offers. Having missed the chance to work with Huston on *Treasure,* Garfield jumped at the offer of *Rough Sketch.* He contended that the film would be a political allegory addressed to the House Un-American Activities Committee.

The film, as written by Huston and Peter Viertel, tells the tale of Cuban-American revolutionary Fenner (Garfield), who recruits a band of dedicated Cubans, including China Valdes (Jennifer Jones). Together they dig a tunnel from the cellar of China's home to a nearby cemetery. Fenner's plan is to blow up the Cuban dictator and his entire cabinet while they attend the funeral of a senator.

The plot has much in common with some of Huston's other scripts in which the protaganists are foiled by circumstance. The group begins working together solidly to dig the tunnel, but just at the moment of their victory, chance and betrayal combine to cause the death of Fenner and China and of their persecuting enemy, the policeman Ariete (Pedro Armendariz).

When the $900,000 film was released as *We Were Strangers,* both the public and the reviewers failed to see the political allegory Garfield and, apparently, Huston had intended. John McCarten in *The New Yorker* called the film a "mixture of violence, baby talk about revolution and standard romantic hokum."

The Hollywood Reporter called *We Were Strangers,* "the heaviest dish of Red theory ever served to an audience outside the Soviet Union." But the *Communist Daily Worker* called it "capitalistic propaganda."

Financially, *We Were Strangers* was Huston's first disaster. Surprisingly, *The Treasure of the Sierra Madre* in spite of its awards and reviews had failed to turn a profit. *We Were Strangers,* however, never even got a chance to climb into the black. Columbia, the distributors, took the film out of circulation soon after its release because ticket sales were so poor.

Huston's apparent seriousness about his subject didn't keep him from making some of his famous grim jokes during shooting. Once, one of Jennifer Jones's scenes was under eerie light and in the middle of fresh graves. Huston told her to dig, and her shovel unearthed a prop hand he had planted. Huston grinned as his star screamed. In honor of the trick, Jones presented the director with a full-grown female chimpanzee. Huston was delighted with the gift and described the chimp's homecoming meeting with his wife, Evelyn, to Dan Fowler: "It was like a wife meeting a mistress, you know? Both hating each other's guts but being very polite. The chimp slept with me that night, or did when she wasn't wrecking the place."

In spite of his reputation and high salary, Huston was and remained in debt for years, living off the advance on each forthcoming film. His plunge from project to project was sometimes less an act of zeal and artistry than his need to get enough money to keep living in the style to which he had become accustomed. In addition to gambling heavily, as his mother had taught him, Huston often gave away large sums to friends and spent lavishly on travel, clothes, and alimony.

The ranch was filling up with all kinds of animals, and Evelyn soon discovered that she was highly allergic to almost all of them. Finally, the Hustons abandoned the 480-acre property to the animals, but John visited them as often as he could.

John designed a home for Evelyn in Tarzana, California. "Frank Lloyd Wright, hearing about the place, once paid me a visit," Huston told *House Beautiful* in 1949. "From time to time he would pause before some architectural feature, and remark, 'Oh that's very Frank Lloyd Wright.' Wright then remarked that the ceilings were too high. 'I like low ceilings that give me a sense of shelter,' said Wright."

Huston respectfully suggested that the reason might be that Wright, at no more than five-foot-eight, was a relatively short man.

Replied Wright, looking up at Huston, "Anyone over five-ten is a weed."

Huston next announced plans for two major projects. First, he was going to take over direction of *Quo Vadis?* in Italy for MGM and then direct another film for Horizon called *Reminiscences of a Cowboy*. He also stated that he planned to travel around the world making a film for the One World Committee. The committee had chosen Huston to receive its annual flight-around-the-world award, which involved making a movie to help unite the people of the earth.

When Huston was announced as recipient of the award, several members of the committee resigned, charging that Columbia Pictures was putting up a large part of the money for the trip, possibly in the hope of breathing new life into the director's reputation and resurrecting *We Were Strangers.* Huston's partner Sam Spiegel declared that the first Huston and Columbia knew of his selection was when the committee had called him and asked if he would accept.

At the 1949 presentation Huston was introduced by Dr. Benjamin Cohen, Assistant Secretary General of the United Nations, who began the evening by announcing that Russia had just lifted the Berlin blockade. Norman Corwin then spoke, saying that the award was being given to Huston "because in his work he has advanced the cause of freedom and has founded his motion pictures upon the firm basis of the dignity of the human being regardless of race and station."

Huston responded that he accepted the award "as both a solemn obligation and a challenge, a challenge to my abilities and a challenge to my intellectual and artistic integrity." He said he was "going around the world to fashion a portrait, as true a likeness as I can of man in the aggregate, of his thoughts, desires, frustrations and fulfillments."

A little less than three years after their marriage, Evelyn announced to the press: "John is the best director and the worst husband in Hollywood." She elaborated on her allergy to fur and animals, claiming she had to share her husband with wild horses, dogs, cats, monkeys that hadn't been housebroken, goats, pigs, and a burro.

The Hustons' parting was friendly. The couple tossed a coin to see who would get a valuable set of Inca figures rather than fight over community property. Evelyn won the figures.

On February 10, 1950, Huston obtained a Mexican divorce from Evelyn. The next day he married Enrica Soma, twenty-one-year-old ballerina and model. Miss Soma was the daughter of Anthony Soma, who owned Tony's, a nightclub in New York. She had been placed under a film contract by David O. Selznick, although she had been brought to Hollywood after she had been spotted on a magazine cover by Jesse Lasky, one of the founders of Paramount Pictures.

Huston began preparation for his three projects and granted an interview to *The New Yorker* in which he outlined his plans for the good-will film. However, the *Quo Vadis?* offer fell through and Horizon was not in a financial position to proceed with *Reminiscences of a Cowboy.* As financial need was a constant, the One World trip was permanently put aside and Huston accepted MGM's offer to write and direct *The Asphalt Jungle.*

CHAPTER 8

A Left-Handed Form of Human Endeavor

HUSTON'S *Quo Vadis?* assignment fell through because Gregory Peck, who was to play the lead, had an eye infection, which meant that shooting had to be delayed. Ironically, when filming finally had to begin, Peck was replaced by Robert Taylor, as Peck's infection continued. Huston's agreement with MGM was that he would both write and direct *Quo Vadis?* with Peck, Elizabeth Taylor, and Walter Huston as Saint Peter. For his efforts, John was to receive $3000 a week.

Because of the delay, producer Arthur Hornblow, Jr., and MGM offered Huston another assignment. Studio and director amiably agreed on a screen version of W. R. Burnett's novel *The Asphalt Jungle.* Burnett had been writing for films since his novel *Little Caesar* became a best seller in the late 1920s. Huston had already received praise for his script of Burnett's *High Sierra,* and his respect for *Little Caesar* had been evident in *Key Largo.* With Ben Maddow, who had recently written *Intruder in the Dust* from the William Faulkner novel, Huston began his script.

When the writing was completed, Huston decided to cast his film with relative unknowns. His first selection was his old friend Sam Jaffe to play the role of Doc, the mastermind behind the big caper. His other choices for main roles were Sterling Hayden, who had never been in a major film; Louis Calhern; James Whitmore; Jean Hagen, who had only limited stage and film experience; the then unknown Marilyn Monroe; and Marc Lawrence, who had played Ziggy, one of the gangsters in *Key Largo.*

One reason Huston may have chosen Hayden was that the two had met when they flew to Washington the previous year to protest the Un-American Activities Committee investigations.

"When you're greeted by John Huston," Hayden said in his autobiography, *Wanderer,* "you know what it's like to be met. You step into a big corner office full of people and smoke. His feet are on his desk. The moment he sees you, he swings to his feet and cleaves the room with his eyes on you alone. You suddenly sense that simply by coming here today you have relieved this rangy man of some immense burden. You are the one man alive he wanted to see at 2 P.M. sharp."

Huston told Hayden that MGM had wanted a top-name star for the role of Dix Handley but added, "Fortunately, they're not making this picture. I am." With his eyes half closed, Huston then began to describe Dix. After the description, Huston, apologizing, said Hayden had to go through some screen tests.

Hayden in *Wanderer* remembered his test opposite Jean Hagen, whom Huston described to him as "a consummate actress." Her portrayal as Doll in *The Asphalt Jungle* and that of the brassy blonde with the lower-class voice in *Singin' in the Rain* were to be her best-remembered film roles.

Huston's comments to Hayden before the test were, "Kid, play it the way it feels best. Lie down, sit up, walk around, do any damn thing you please. Wherever you go, we'll follow. Take your time. Let me know when you're ready." After the test the director ran up to Hayden and said, "The next time somebody says you can't act, tell them to call Huston." Hayden got the part and a big break in his career.

Huston had met Marilyn Monroe before *The Asphalt Jungle.* In fact, he and John Garfield had planned to give her a screen test at Columbia during the shooting of *We Were Strangers.* Sam Spiegel convinced Huston that Horizon couldn't afford to do it, that a test would be too expensive in terms of studio time, lighting, equipment, and salaries. The test was called off. Huston, however, remembered when Monroe's name was brought up by Lucille Ryman, a former head of MGM's talent department, and arranged for her to come to Metro for *The Asphalt Jungle* test.

"I was not too surprised when she asked if she could sit on the floor," Huston told Fred Lawrence Guiles. "I'd been told that she was unusual. I told her that would be just fine. The cameras rolled and when it was over, Marilyn looked very insecure about the whole thing and asked to do it over again. I agreed, but I had already decided on the first take. The part of Angela was hers."

Huston also remembered that Monroe brought her drama coach to the test, a procedure that he could not recall happening with any previous supporting actor or actress.

In fact, Monroe had not been his first choice for the role of Angela. He had wanted Lola Albright, whom he had just seen in *Champion,* but she was tied up with another picture.

When the film was released, the director's name was just below the title. *The Asphalt Jungle* was labeled "A John Huston Film," the first time Huston had received such billing.

In *The Asphalt Jungle,* Doc, recently out of prison, wants to pull a big caper, a million-dollar jewel robbery. He goes to a small-time bookie, Cobby (Marc Lawrence), who in turn goes to Mr. Emmerich (Louis Calhern), who is deeply in debt and has a mistress (Monroe) adding to his financial woes. Emmerich and Bannerman (Brad Dexter) get Cobby to put up the money for the robbery, planning to steal the jewels from Doc's gang when the robbery is over. Doc's gang includes Dix, Gus, a hunchback driver (Whitmore), and Louis, a safecracker (Anthony Caruso). Louis is accidentally killed by a discharging gun during the robbery, and Gus is picked up by the police when Cobby talks after being beaten by a crooked cop. Dix kills Bannerman and is himself wounded when he tries to stop Emmerich and Bannerman from taking the jewels. Emmerich then commits suicide, and Doc is caught fleeing with the jewels when he pauses a minute too long to watch a young girl dancing. Dix, with his girlfriend, Doll, heads for his childhood home and his beloved horses. Weakened by a loss of blood, he staggers into the field at his old home, and the film ends as he collapses in the middle of a group of horses.

Huston added a new dimension to the gangster film with *The Asphalt Jungle:* he not only creates sympathy for the criminal but respect for the way he does his job.

The safecracker is shown as a family man who lives in a tenement. He is a readily identifiable type: an Italian husband with a houseful of kids and a hardworking wife. Thus, it is especially gratifying to the audience to see him with the gang, professionally self-confident, filling the screen as he pulls his coat back like a magician to reveal a neat lining of crowbar, nitro, drill, and extra bits. Doc works out the caper with Germanic confidence and then earns embarrassed pity when he cannot pull himself away from the opportunity to watch the young girl dance. Cobby's breakdown, in a close-up of sweat, parallels Emmerich's breakdown, which is revealed at first only by the slight letdown of his mask of social dignity and then by the shock of his suicide. The film keeps returning to screen-filling faces: Doll, with her make-up running as she sits crying at the side of the dying Dix, Gus's face and hunched back as he smiles at his beloved cat.

The love of animals is evident, as are the pitfalls of man's attraction to woman. The women in the film are not evil; it is the men's obsession with them that causes disaster.

As in past and future Huston films, a small group undertakes a task and fails. The gang members commit themselves to the task and die as the result of betrayal. Emmerich, who describes crime to his invalid wife as "nothing more than a left-handed form of human endeavor," betrays Doc and Dix from the top, while Cobby, in his fear, betrays them from below. Again, there is a climax of death and destruction that Huston characters can never evade.

The New Yorker wrote that "in the end one is tempted to regret that crime doesn't pay, because the malefactors are depicted so sympathetically."

Lighting throughout the film is low-key; dark corners abound. The audience is shown night-world rooms illuminated by naked bulbs and inhabited by squinting, sweating men. Each camera shot seems to act primarily as a frame within which an action takes place. The film has a lack of camera movement, which, combined with the lighting, gives it more the flavor of the 1930s Warner Brothers gangster films than the crisp, cold urbanity of *The Maltese Falcon* and *Key Largo.*

The Asphalt Jungle was to spawn a short-lived but highly successful film formula, the big caper as planned by sympathetic but doomed characters. One of the most famous of these films was Stanley Kubrick's *The Killing,* made in 1956 and also starring Sterling Hayden.

The Asphalt Jungle did well with the reviewers and the public in the United States and won Huston Academy Award nominations for best screenplay and best direction. In addition, he won the Screen Directors Guild award.

When Hornblow and Huston prepared to release *The Asphalt Jungle* in England, they hesitated because it was so full of American slang. At this time, American films with a lot of slang were regularly redubbed for English audiences. Gerard Fairlie, British author of the Bulldog Drummond stories, was called in as a consultant. Fairlie advised against redubbing, even though some of the words would be unintelligible to British audiences. The film was not redubbed and proved highly successful in England.

At the end of the film's shooting Huston received another award, which he always keeps with him. It was a silver tray inscribed "To John Huston, One Hell of a Guy. The Macadamized Award from all the Members of *The Asphalt Jungle.*"

Walter Huston came to Hollywood for his son's forty-fourth birthday while filming was still in progress. The party was held at Romanoff's. When Walter got back to his room at the Beverly Hills Hotel, he felt ill. Two days later, with his son at his side, Walter Huston died of heart failure at the age of sixty-six.

CHAPTER 9

Crippled Epic

"ONE OF MY favorite films, at least as I shot it, is *The Red Badge of Courage,*" John Huston told Gene Phillips in 1973. The catch is that only a handful of people has ever seen the film as Huston shot it. Huston's original conception was to shoot a lengthy epic of the Civil War. Gradually, in the course of a two-year struggle with MGM, the epic was cut to seventy-eight minutes, then to sixty-nine minutes. The final film ran slightly over an hour.

In many ways, the making of *The Red Badge of Courage* was a nightmare for John Huston, one well documented in Lillian Ross's *Picture,* which may be the best book ever written about the making of a film. Published originally as a series of *New Yorker* articles in 1952 on the making of *The Red Badge of Courage,* the book became, essentially, an early documentary novel with John Huston as central character.

In talking to Phillips about *Picture,* Huston said, "Lillian Ross . . . is extremely accurate about what went on during production. She was a fine journalist. I say this even though I myself come in for some body blows in the course of the book. So, you see, I am speaking with a certain detachment. I think that she was a little harder on the studio than perhaps was fair."

According to Huston, "There was a power struggle going on at MGM at the time: one group wanted to make the film and the other group didn't. Whoever won the battle would be in charge of the studio."

The struggle for control of MGM was between Louis B. Mayer, who was head of the studio, and Dore Schary, vice president in charge of production. Both men frequently took their case long-distance to Nicholas Schenck, president of Loew's Consolidated Enterprises, which had financial control of MGM. Schary and Mayer were in Los Angeles, while Schenk, a former amusement park owner, had his offices in New York.

The Red Badge of Courage became a key issue — if not the only issue — in the studio battle. Schary had proposed the project and supported it. Mayer was against it. To head off the battle, Mayer called in the producer of the film, Gottfried Reinhardt, and Huston to persuade them to give up the project.

"In 35 years," Ross quotes Mayer as saying, "we've had two wars — two terrible wars with millions slaughtered and whole cities destroyed. And you're going to make a picture about boys in funny caps shooting pop-guns and try to make people think this is terrible. Dave Selznick was too smart to try that. He wouldn't show you the Civil War battles in *Gone With The Wind.*"

Huston says he told Mayer "that if he was against my making the picture I wouldn't pursue it."

Bosley Crowther reports in his book on MGM, *The Lion's Share,* that Mayer changed his mind after receiving a letter from Schary. Crowther says the volatile Mayer was so moved by the letter he immediately summoned Reinhardt and Huston and said, "As a personal favor to me, won't you take this thing and make it. I may be wrong. You believe in the project, don't you? You continue to defend it, even though I am against it. I would be deeply disappointed in you if you didn't fight for it."

However, Crowther presented evidence that it wasn't simply Mayer's emotion and sense of fair play that moved him to accept the project. Apparently, Mayer had sent the script of the film to Schenck expecting him to veto it. Instead Schenck suggested that Schary be allowed to make the picture. It was evidently at that point that Mayer backed away and called Huston in. As Lillian Ross documents, however, Mayer's hostility to the undertaking returned and the film continued to be a political football in studio power struggles.

Huston was paid $4000 a week for the project. He moved ahead on preparing the script and announced that his version of the Stephen Crane novel would be "a story about the psychology of courage. It demonstrates how cowardice and courage are really composed of the same material."

"I'd approach a picture about the last war with great trepidation," he told the New York *Daily News* in 1950 in an oblique response to Mayer's fears. "But putting the action back in the Civil War gives me a chance to stand back and look at war from a distance, from the vantage point of time.

"Crane was an extraordinary genius," Huston continued. "I rank his book with the great war chronicles of Thucydides, Caesar, Tolstoy, Stendhal and Norman Mailer."

Huston was filled with plans and enthusiasm about the film. He would, he said, do much of his directing from horseback, something he had always wanted to do, and do a lot of the filming near his ranch in the San Fernando Valley so that he could be near home.

He also planned to shoot the film by a method he called "piggyback," which would allow scenes to be set up in advance by another director, Andrew Marton, so Huston's shooting would not be delayed and Marton could be working on a scene while Huston was filming another one. The piggyback idea was soon abandoned, and directing on horseback proved to be nearly impossible, though Huston did give it a try.

The director also announced that there would be no women in the film, "and there will be no references to women either." *The Treasure of the Sierra Madre,* Huston's most successful film critically to that point, had also been essentially womanless.

In his enthusiasm, Huston turned out a treatment of the novel in three days and a final shooting script in ten. Since *Badge* would eventually take almost two years to make and release, his zeal was unnecessary.

Advance estimates of the cost of the picture were $1,434,000. By the time it was completed, the cost had risen to only $1,640,000. Considering the eventual wrangling and reshooting, cutting and changing, Huston did a remarkable job of keeping close to his budget.

Before the film went into production, Huston told Goodman he was going to begin a search for the lead, Henry, the Youth, who runs from battle and then returns to prove himself a hero. The actor, said Huston, "may be on the lot at Metro or may be a guy in Iowa or South Missouri where they never see motion pictures."

Reinhardt wanted an actor on the lot, Montgomery Clift. Huston had another idea. Why not, he said, get the most decorated hero of World War II to play the role of the young man in the film? Huston then interviewed and liked the young war hero Audie Murphy, though Murphy remained relatively unresponsive throughout their interview.

With Mayer in the background ready to say, "I told you so," Reinhardt and Schary were uneasy about several aspects of the project. Huston's agent, Paul Kohner, was apparently getting uneasy too and sent Huston's script to a psychologist for assurance that the young soldier's actions as Huston had written them were plausible. Since Huston had been through a war and spent months in a mental hospital making *Let There Be Light,* one might have expected the studio to have a little more confidence in his decisions.

Huston went further. He did not cast a single "name" aside from comic character actor Andy Devine, who has one scene as the talkative soldier who helps Henry back to his lines. The second lead, Wilson, went to another war figure, Bill Mauldin. Mauldin, a cartoonist, had drawn the World War II cartoon "Willie and Joe" for the military newspaper *Stars and Stripes.* Huston liked the strip and sent for its creator. *Badge* was to be Mauldin's sole major acting credit.

Behind the scenes, Mayer was pulling for the film to fail and Schary was making changes out of fear the finished product would not be commercial enough.

Scenes were pulled after Huston fought to keep them. A gravedigging sequence that he felt particularly important was cut. Another scene deleted from the film featured Huston himself. He was to have been a seasoned veteran in a group of soldiers jeering at Henry and the new recruits.

Lillian Ross, who was present for the shooting of Huston's scene, described it:

> He had a three-day growth of beard on his face, and he put on the tattered costume of a veteran Union soldier and stood in the line of jeering veterans for a retake of the scene Schary had objected to. He delivered his line — "Hang your clothes on a hickory limb and don't go near the battle!" — in a callous manner, showing contempt for the Youth and the other raw recruits. Playing the bit galvanized him into tremendous activity. He went about his work still wearing his uniform.

In *The Treasure of the Sierra Madre,* Huston played the small role of an American who gives Dobbs several handouts at the beginning

Walter and John Huston about 1937.

A bespectacled John Huston shakes his father's hand on the set of *The Maltese Falcon* with Humphrey Bogart and cinematographer Arthur Edeson looking on. (National Film Archive)

On location in Mexico, Huston and Bogart clown with one of the actors playing a bandit in *The Treasure of the Sierra Madre*. (National Film Archive)

In a scene from *The Treasure of the Sierra Madre*, Tim Holt, Walter Huston, and Humphrey Bogart plan their quest for gold. (Warner Brothers)

At the Academy Award celebration in 1949, father and son congratulate each other on their awards.

Shooting of *The Asphalt Jungle* in New York City was held up by a Christmas party in honor of director Huston. Actor Sam Jaffe is in the background to the right. (National Film Archive)

Huston shows Louis Calhern what he wants for a shot in *The Asphalt Jungle*. (MGM)

Huston watches Audie Murphy and John Dierkes rehearse a scene for *The Red Badge of Courage*. (National Film Archive)

Richard Basehart, far left, listens to the promises of wealth from Gregory Peck's Ahab in a scene from *Moby Dick*. (Warner Brothers)

Marlon Brando as an agonized Major Penderton in *Reflections in a Golden Eye* turns away from his wife, Leonora, played by Elizabeth Taylor. (Warner Brothers—Seven Arts, Inc.)

Friends Ernest Hemingway and John Huston toured Biarritz in 1955.
(John Huston)

In *The Unforgiven*, Lillian Gish played the adopted mother of Audrey Hepburn.
(United Artists)

On the set of *The List of Adrian Messenger,* Anthony Huston and his father watch a rehearsal. (National Film Archive)

Huston demonstrates to Freud (Montgomery Clift) an expression he wants for a shot in *Freud.* (Universal International)

Huston directs daughter Anjelica in a scene for *A Walk with Love and Death*. (Twentieth Century-Fox)

A battle rages around Claudia (Anjelica Huston) and Heron (Assaf Dayan) in a scene from *A Walk with Love and Death*. (Twentieth Century-Fox)

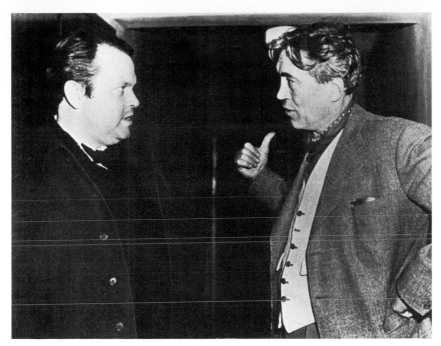

Director-actor John Huston makes a suggestion to actor-director Orson Welles for a scene in *The Kremlin Letter*. (Twentieth Century-Fox)

A group of spies played by Dean Jagger, Barbara Parkins, Patrick O'Neal, Nigel Green, Richard Boone, and George Sanders plans a trip to Russia in a scene from *The Kremlin Letter*. (Twentieth Century-Fox)

A bearded Huston tells an actor what he would like to see in a forthcoming shot in *The Mackintosh Man*. (National Film Archive)

Stacy Keach as a washed-up boxer gets ready to share a cup of coffee with a young boxer played by Jeff Bridges in *Fat City*. (Columbia Pictures)

As Judge Roy Bean, Paul Newman gazes enraptured at the poster of Lillie Langtry (Ava Gardner) in *The Life and Times of Judge Roy Bean*. (National Film Archive)

Actor Doghmi Larbi tries to strike a fearsome pose as Ootah, the doomed chieftain in *The Man Who Would Be King*. (Associated Artists)

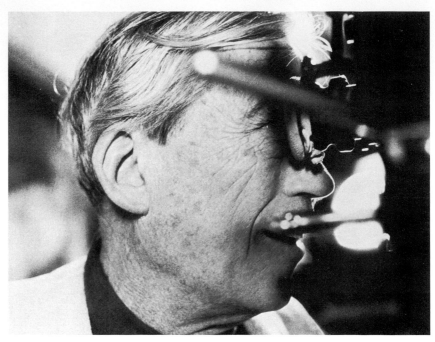

John Huston at work. (National Film Archive)

John Huston watching a fox hunt in Ireland. (National Film Archive)

of the story. After the third handout, he remarks, "From now on you are have to make it through life without my assistance." With some of the handout money, Dobbs buys part of a lottery ticket, which turns out to win him enough to become one of Howard's partners. From this point on, Dobbs proves that he cannot make it through life without the unnamed Huston character.

Huston's role in *The Red Badge of Courage* was that of Experience challenging Youth on the very point on which the young man is most vulnerable. The Huston character openly points out the Youth's fear and articulates Henry's internal problem.

The director's later appearances in his own films included *The Bible, Casino Royale, A Walk with Love and Death,* and *The Kremlin Letter.* In each, he was a character who questions the motivation of the protagonist, confronting him with a verbalization of the key moral problem and his shortcomings.

Sneak previews for the public of the much worked over *Red Badge of Courage* were a terrible disappointment, though Willy Wyler loved the film after seeing it at an early screening.

"The best scene in the film," Huston sighed to Ross, "was the one in which the Tall Soldier John Dierkes dies a kind of mystical death. 'Don't touch me,' he says, and then he falls dead. His death is witnessed by the hero Audie Murphy and by the Tattered Soldier Royal Dano, who begins to wander around in circles; then he too falls dead. This is particularly shocking because the viewer was not aware that the Tattered Soldier was even wounded until he drops dead. One third of the preview audience walked out at this point. The scene was too emotionally taxing, and so it was out."

Schary began to worry more after the previews, and it was decided that a narrator should be added to the film. The narrator would indicate that the story was based on a great classic and would, from time to time, read passages from the novel over the action. Huston acquiesced.

Reinhardt wanted Spencer Tracy to narrate but was unable to get him. Eventually James Whitmore, who had appeared as Gus in *The Asphalt Jungle,* was chosen.

During the shooting of the film, Huston's pregnant wife, Rica, had moved to a home they were renting at Malibu Beach. Pablo, now 14, stayed with Huston during much of the shooting and the director got to Malibu often.

Huston became a father on April 16, 1950. The child, a boy, was named Walter Anthony Huston.

During the prolonged making of *The Red Badge of Courage,* Huston celebrated his forty-fifth birthday with a party at Chasen's restaurant attended by, among others, Wyler, Edward G. Robinson, and John Garfield. Lillian Ross reported that Huston wore the ribbon of the Legion of Merit on his dinner jacket at the party. The award had been given to him for his Army Signal Corps films.

It was an unusually quiet Huston party, ending in a poker game and no battles, broken bones, or bloody noses. *The Red Badge of Courage* had become a very serious matter.

When the reshooting was completed, Huston absented himself from the continued squabbling about changes and left the fight to Reinhardt, but the producer kept asking Huston's support to salvage a scene or fight for a line or idea.

Huston, at work with Agee on the script for *The African Queen,* began to feel the pressure. At one point, he exploded: "I really hate the city. I've got to get out to the country and get on a horse. I get all mixed up in the city. You know where I'd like to be this very minute, Jim? I'd like to be in Mexico."

Huston decided to head for Africa. Reinhardt's long letters outlining changes and counterchanges, dubbing of voices, and addition of further narration followed Huston to London, then Africa. He responded with enthusiastic telegrams about elephant hunting. To one impassioned plea for help, the director replied:

DEAR GOTTFRIED STOP JUST GOT YOUR LETTER, KNOW YOU FOUGHT GOOD FIGHT STOP HOPE YOU NOT TOO BLOODY MY ACCOUNT STOP LET'S MAKE NEXT ONE REINHARDT NOT A HUSTON PICTURE STOP JOHN.

Reviews of the film were generally favorable. *Newsweek* said, "*The Red Badge of Courage* bids fair to become one of the classic American motion pictures," adding that the film "fills the screen with starkly remarkable images, like the Civil War photographs of Matthew Brady springing into motion." The magazine also noted "wrenching bits . . . as when a bespectacled trooper falls on the field, losing his glasses as he falls. Like almost any myopic man, he reaches immediately for his glasses and places them on again. Only then does he drop dead."

Even with the changes and cuts in the film, there is still much that reflects Huston's thematic and visual interests. Again, there is a group with a quest that may result in death. Members of the small group of soldiers argue, support each other, pretend they are not frightened, brag, and often die.

In the course of the action, both the Youth and the audience discover that the taking of an isolated field is not as important as the ability of the young men to face death without fear. The waterfall image of Huston's youth and his skirmishes with death during World War II may well have attracted him to the project in the first place.

As in so many Huston pictures, the characters involved in the quest discover that the object they have sought is not nearly as important as they have been led to believe. The quest in a sense has been futile. *The Red Badge of Courage,* for example, ends when passing soldiers tell the Youth that he has not even been involved in the major battle of the day.

Also, as in other Huston films, the two central figures, the Youth and Wilson, lie about their attitudes, putting on figurative masks. Their friendship solidifies only when both confess that they have been afraid during the battle and have run.

To emphasize Henry's confusion about the war, Huston set up many difficult shots involving camera movement through woods and trees. The camera runs with Henry and bobs in confusion when he is lost. At only a few points is the viewer allowed to see anything that Henry does not see. One of the few things Henry does not see and the audience does is an officer praying. As in *San Pietro,* religion is of no importance in the search for courage.

The relationship between Henry and his young friend is explored in typical Huston visual strips. The two youths take turns moving to the foreground and filling most of the frame in profile while the other man is in the background. Reactions of the man in the foreground dominate. For example, early in the film, Henry, Wilson, and some of the other soldiers are in a tent preparing for the battle. Henry remains in the foreground, taking as much as one third of the space, though he does little of the talking. Behind him, at different levels of the picture, Wilson, Conklin, and the Tattered Soldier talk of the coming battle. The conversation is on three levels verbally too, with each of the three soldiers expressing a different attitude. The Youth dominates the frame, listening, watching, unable to decide and accept. He is also isolated in space from the other three, thrust forward. Late in the film, during their mutual confessions around a tree, the Youth and Wilson change places several times to show the similarity of their attitudes.

Huston would rather not discuss the film as it now stands. "I couldn't bring myself to look at the present version," he told Phillips. "I have been given to understand that MGM is thinking of re-releasing the original version."

So far, MGM has made no announcement of such a re-release.

CHAPTER 10

The Rumpot and the Queen

The African Queen was almost made in 1938 at Warner Brothers. If it had not been for Bette Davis, Humphrey Bogart would not have won his acting Oscar and John Huston would have missed his biggest financial success.

According to David Niven in *Bring on the Empty Horses,* Warner Brothers had bought the 1935 C. S. Forester novel for Bette Davis, and "in 1938 their producer, Henry Blanke, borrowed me from Samuel Goldwyn to play the Cockney 'river rat' opposite her. The deal was signed, and bemused by my glorious opportunity, I had spent four weeks polishing up a Cockney accent. I even grew a beard which made me look like a diseased yak, but at the last minute, Bette Davis fell out with Blanke and told him she refused to be photographed out-of-doors (a likely story), so the picture was canceled and the property sold to Twentieth Century-Fox, where twelve years later John Huston unearthed it."

One day in the fall of 1950, while *The Red Badge of Courage* was still a point of conflict at MGM, Huston called Bogart on the telephone.

"I have a great story," Huston said, according to Joe Hyams in *Bogie.* "The hero is a lowlife. You are the biggest lowlife in town and therefore most suitable for the part." Huston had decided to tailor the part of Charlie Allnut, the skipper of *The African Queen* riverboat, for his friend by converting the Cockney to a Canadian so Bogart could be a British Commonwealth subject and not need an accent.

Bogart joined Huston for drinks at Romanoff's, where the actor was completely convinced, and with a few drinks under their belts, the two headed over to see Katharine Hepburn. Huston and Bogart quickly persuaded her to accept the other lead in this film about spinster missionary Rose Sayer and drunk Charlie Allnut who fall in love and blow up a German warship during World War I.

With two stars in the bag, John contacted his long-time admirer, critic James Agee. In a memorial introduction to *Agee on Film: Five Film Scripts,* Huston described his friend as "about six-two and heavy but neither muscular nor fat . . . His clothes were dark and shiny. I can't imagine him with a new suit . . . He held his body in very slight regard altogether, feeding it with whatever was at hand, allowing it to go to sleep when there was nothing else for it to do, begrudging it anything beneficial such as medicine when he was sick. On the other hand, he was a chain smoker and a bottle-a-night man."

When the script was in what Huston considered to be reasonably good shape, he packed up and headed for London, leaving Rica at the Malibu house just before the couple's daughter, Anjelica, was born.

In London, Huston called in Peter Viertel, his co-writer on *We Were Strangers,* for consultation on the script. As a result, Viertel was to briefly accompany Huston to Africa and, the following year, write a book about the experience. This novel, *White Hunter, Black Heart,* is an unflattering portrait of a Hollywood director named John Wilson who calls in a writer named Pete Verrill to consult on the script he plans to direct about a man and a woman in Africa. The parallel to Huston and the experience of *The African Queen* is so thinly disguised that the book can barely be called a novel. Huston had thus inspired two books about him within two years, *Picture* and Viertel's. Eventually another novel, *The Crazy Kill,* would deal with a character modeled on Huston during the making of *Moby Dick.* And a book would be written on the making of *The Misfits.*

Sam Spiegel raised a number of questions about the Agee-Huston script, particularly the ending, in which Charlie and Rosie die. Huston liked the idea and wanted to stick with it, even though in Forester's novel both characters live. In Viertel's novel, Wilson, the director, who calls everyone "Kid," argues that the man and the woman in his film should die, acknowledging that such an ending might well doom the project to box-office failure.

"I realized that you can't serve two masters very early in life," Wilson says. "Money or art, I said to myself. Money *and* art, I answered, just as you did. But I knew immediately that I couldn't keep the two separated. I had to make art and money at the same time, and I knew that could only work in Hollywood. And it did. I became a success. Artistically, that is. However, my pictures don't make money. In the years to come I will make five, or six, or ten critical triumphs that will fail at the box office and the banks will ultimately say, 'Throw the bastard out or we'll grow mushrooms in those sound stages.' And the bosses will oblige."

Wilson goes on to say that he will probably die in a flophouse and a special Academy Award will be named after him. "And all the wrong guys will get it, and I'll sit in hell, laughing my head off."

However, Wilson changed his mind about the unhappy ending of his film, as did Huston.

Script completed, Huston headed for Africa. "As far as I was concerned," Huston wrote in *Theatre Arts* in 1952 after the film was released, *"The African Queen* had to be made on location . . . The point about location filming is that if the actors are living in a certain way, it will come out in their performances. Their very hardships give character to the finished film . . . I had a foretaste of what was to come during the six months before we actually undertook the journey. For I spent much of that time in Africa, searching for the proper locations for the film, covering 25,000 air-miles looking for sites which had the settings we needed and which we could reach by truck, boat and plane." Most of the film was eventually shot in almost inaccessible spots in the Belgian Congo and Uganda.

Searching for locations, Huston took plenty of time to hunt. He wrote to Rica:

Last year there were some man-eating lions about and they seized the natives out of their huts and dined on them. Every morning and evening we go after elephant. I'd like to get one with really big tusks . . . Stalking elephant is most exciting. They don't see at all well and if one stays downwind of them one can get very close. Yesterday morning we were after them in some forest and we weren't more than six or eight yards away from them finally. Just a wall of vines between us and them. I tell you it gave me a very funny feeling.

Bogart made the trip to Africa with his wife, Lauren Bacall, who was not to appear in the picture. Instead, she willingly came along as cook.

Huston and Bogart were particularly concerned about how the prim Hepburn would respond to the ungodly conditions. According to Huston, it was so miserable at the locations that the actors didn't "have to imagine that it's hot, that it's so humid and wet that cigarettes turn green with mold as soon as the cellophane is ripped off; it really *is* hot and clothes do mildew overnight and when actors are supposed to be perspiring, they're sweating."

Hepburn arrived and immediately announced that she found Africa "divine." She was the only one of the thirty-four-person cast and crew to remain eternally cheerful throughout the filming, even during illness. Her acceptance of the miserable conditions almost drove Bogart mad.

Eventually everyone in the crew became ill with dysentery or malaria except Huston and Bogart. The actor, however, reported that the two people who didn't get sick were himself and Bacall. Both Bogart and Huston credited Scotch with protecting them. Supposedly Bogart and Bacall even brushed their teeth with it and never touched water. Bogart boasted that when the mosquitoes bit him, they would roll over dead or drunk. "His strength," commented Huston wryly, "was in Scotch."

Hepburn, however, threatened to destroy this protective layer of liquor. In the final version of the film, Rosie does dispose of Charlie's entire stock of liquor, filling the river with bottles. In real life, Hepburn's lectures on the evil of alcohol to Huston and Bogart had no effect.

According to Charles Higham, "Kate's feelings about Huston were ambiguous: looking at the tall, loping giraffelike figure, the long hangdog humorous face, she felt she detected a certain pretension, a posing as a Hemingwayish big-game hunter among men."

"He couldn't hit a tin can with a peashooter," she said, "but he liked to give the impression he could kill an elephant."

Bogart and Hepburn were, according to Huston, remarkably creative together on screen. Their chief contribution, the director said in *Theatre Arts,* was the comic element: Comedy, "absent from both the novel and the screenplay, grew out of the relationship between Hepburn and Bogart. This situation has never happened to me before, although I had worked with Bogie on four other films. Katie and he were just funny together, one calling forth that quality in the other, and the combination of their two characterizations brought out the humor of dramatic situations which, originally, none of us thought existed."

Bogart, in spite of his discomfort, was willing to go along with Huston's most extreme ideas. For example, there is a sequence in which Charlie must get out and pull *The African Queen* through thick, oozy water. When he emerges from the water, he is covered with leeches. He shudders violently, and he and a groaning Rosie hurry to pull the creatures from him. The shudder was real and so were the leeches. Such scenes would help bring Bogart his Academy Award.

In another scene, Huston wanted Hepburn to go into the river. "The river's full of crocodiles," she told him. "Don't worry," Huston responded. "I'll have the prop men fire a few rounds of ammunition into the water. The crocodiles will be scared by the noise." "Yes," replied Hepburn, "but what about the deaf ones?"

For the first part of the film, the crew shot near the relative comfort of a camp on the Ruiki River in the Belgian Congo. Art director Wilfred Shingelton had arranged for amenities exceedingly rare for that remote spot in Africa. "We even had shower baths — buckets with little spigots — so that we lived in what really was great comfort," Huston remembers.

But problems still abounded, as did dangers. The shooting crew worked on a large raft that accompanied *The African Queen*. Almost every member of the crew, including Huston, eventually fell into the crocodile-infested waters. But the crocodiles were not the worst of it. "The waters," says Huston, "are infested with parasitic worms that cause a disease worse than anything crocodiles can do to you."

Crew members frequently became so ill that they couldn't work. However, the only time that shooting actually had to stop for several weeks was when Hepburn became too ill to continue.

At one point the raft, with all its equipment, started to sink. Huston and the crew had to bail water furiously to keep it afloat. Another time, *The African Queen* sank, and it took five days to raise her.

Sam Spiegel began to worry about the budget. This was a Horizon picture, so, to a large degree, it was his and Huston's money on the table. Spiegel flew to Africa, but Huston says he hit on a scheme to avoid financial discussions. He paid a group of natives to follow the producer around from the moment he got off the plane. The natives chanted Spiegel's name as if in welcome and played drums. The noise was tremendous and Huston acted as if he had to get back to work quickly. Unable to carry on a sustained conversation, Spiegel departed.

On top of all the other problems, the campsite was besieged one night by millions of army ants, known to attack both animals and men. Huston's crew poured oil on them and, encouraged by Bogart, made noise, but there were too many ants. Huston and crew packed as quickly as possible and headed for Uganda.

"Actually," he recalls, "the film was not quite completed in Uganda. We had to finish a few scenes in London studios because people began to get sick and there was too much illness to risk remaining in Africa longer."

Back in London, Huston began to shoot the scenes that would appear early in the film. One scene involved Robert Morley as Hepburn's missionary brother who dies after being knocked down by Germans who destroy the village.

Morley, acting in the play *The Little Hut* in London at the time, had not learned his lines when he reported to the studio. "I judged wrongly," he remembered in his autobiography, "that there would be time as the film progressed. I was wrong and on the first day I fluffed and stammered my way through a scene with the two stars who were both supremely professional and word perfect." After the scene, Morley rushed back to the theater where he was appearing and later sat up all night memorizing his part.

"Huston never said anything to me about the incident," says Morley, "but I learned from a friend that night he had been to a party and someone asked him how he fared with me on that first day. 'Not well,' he replied. 'Not well at all. To tell the truth, Morley sent down his substitute!' "

After weeks of editing *The African Queen,* Huston was satisfied. The finished work was in many ways quite unlike his previous films and many of those that would follow. A primary difference stems from the affirmative ending, which, as Viertel points out, was so foreign to the director. To have a quest that succeeds and the adventurers survive happily may, indeed, have been a factor contributing to the film's box-office success.

Another important contrast with much of Huston's other work lies in the fact that neither Charlie nor Rosie is ever presented as wearing figurative masks, as pretending to be anything he or she is not. Briefly Charlie pretends to go along with Rosie's plan to destroy the German boat, but his pretense is feeble and he joins her reluctantly but openly. Charlie can't even lie when questioned by the Germans about what he is doing near their boat. He is far removed from Dobbs, Spade, and Rick in *Across the Pacific,* who were Bogart/Huston liars.

Other aspects of Huston's interests are also strongly present. The film opens with a scene in the mission's church, but, once again, religion proves to be ineffectual. The missionary shows himself to be an amiable but weak man. Ironically, there are moments of divine intervention in the film that Huston may well see as comic. For example, Charlie says that they must take their boat past a German fort. Rosie says naively, "Good. Then the sun will be in their eyes." When they do reach the fort, the sun is in the eyes of a German with a rifle for only a fraction of a second, the very fraction of a second when he has Charlie in his sights.

Later, *The African Queen* is mired in swamp and weeds, and Charlie says they will surely die without a miracle. We know, as Charlie and Rose do not, that they are only a few dozen yards from the lake they are seeking. God or Huston-as-God intervenes and sends a flood that lifts the small ship up and sends it onto the lake.

Huston's anti-German attitude is evident in this film, as the Germans prove to be heartless and unfeeling in the face of Charlie and Rosie's love. In the film, but not the novel, when the Germans are about to hang the couple, Charlie asks the German captain to marry them, which he does, concluding with: "I pronounce you man and wife. Proceed with the execution."

Visually, Huston continued to explore an important aspect of his style, the placement of characters in a frame so that their size and position reflect what they are saying and doing. He had explored this relationship with Bogart, Holt, and Walter Huston in *The Treasure of the Sierra Madre* and Audie Murphy and Bill Mauldin in *The Red Badge of Courage,* but much had been cut in *Badge.* In *The African Queen,* he had ample opportunity to work on his ideas.

For example, early in the film after Rosie's brother dies, there is a scene with Rosie seated on the front porch of the mission. Charlie, in the foreground, dominates the screen while Rosie, in the background, is small. As Charlie starts to take control of the situation and tell Rosie what must be done, he raises his hand to the rail and his arm covers our view of her. Charlie is in command.

Later, on the boat, Rosie begins to assert herself and pressure Charlie to join her in the quest to destroy the German ship. As she starts to dominate him, she fills the screen, while Charlie appears in the background, as she did earlier.

As they fall in love, the two begin to share screen space, either balanced from shot to shot or alternating foreground positions.

The African Queen, released in 1951, was both a critical and financial success. Huston was nominated for an Academy Award for best direction and for his screenplay, but the director's award went to George Stevens for *A Place in the Sun.* Bogart was nominated as best actor and won.

When his name was announced, Bogart kissed his wife, hurried to the stage to receive his Oscar, and then blew his memorized acceptance speech. Backstage after the awards, he announced that the Oscar was not a true award for ability. The real test, he said, was to have all the actors nominated play the same role. Nonetheless, he did not turn down the tribute.

Huston attributed much of the success of *The African Queen* to James Agee. When Agee died, Huston wrote in his introduction to a collection of the writer's screenplays that Agee "never attempted to win anyone to his way of thinking, far less to try to prove anyone mistaken or in the wrong. He would take a contrary opinion — regardless of how foolish it was — and hold it up to the light and turn it this way and that, examining its facets as though it were a gem of great worth, and if it turned out to be a piece of cracked glass, why then he himself must have misunderstood — the other fellow had meant something else, hadn't he . . . *this,* perhaps? And sure enough Jim would come up with some variation of the opinion that would make it flawless as a specimen jewel. And the other fellow would be very proud of having meant precisely that, and they would go on from there."

CHAPTER II

The Dwarf and the Devil

JOHN HUSTON owned several paintings by Henri de Toulouse-Lautrec. The director had known the French artist's work and life from the days when he had bummed about in Paris and London learning to paint.

The idea of doing something about the life of Lautrec had stayed in the back of Huston's mind waiting for the form and time. This process of slow evolution had produced *The Red Badge of Courage* and *The Treasure of the Sierra Madre* and later would give birth to *Moby Dick* and *The Man Who Would Be King,* a story he had read and loved as a boy. The model for the film on Lautrec was a 1950 novel, *Moulin Rouge,* by French writer Pierre La Mure which Huston had found while filming *The African Queen.*

Huston readily accepted La Mure's distortions of the artist's life and incorporated these liberties into his film. For example, the novel and film barely mention Lautrec's obsession with brothels, although according to Lautrec himself in M. G. Dortu and Philippe Huisman's *Lautrec by Lautrec,* he spent much of his time in them. The novel and film also deal with several love affairs that in fact never took place. The central created affair is between Lautrec and Marie, a streetwalker. The film also avoids Lautrec's stay in a madhouse and his mental problems.

But Huston clearly was more interested in Lautrec's art than his life. It was not a biography of Lautrec he wanted to make, but a tale in the style of the paintings he so admired. The myth of Lautrec and Huston's own artistic interests would thus be served the better, he reasoned.

As soon as he got to London and completed editing *The African*

Queen, Huston called actor José Ferrer in New York. Ferrer was his immediate choice to play Lautrec. Ferrer was also his own choice to play the role. In fact, Huston discovered that the actor owned the rights to the novel *Moulin Rouge.* Ferrer, it seems, had already planned to turn it into a play with himself as star. This was a happy coincidence.

Huston convinced Ferrer that he could do on film what would be impossible on stage, that he could deal with the film as if it were an Impressionist painting. Ferrer was convinced and a deal was made. Huston would not only write and direct the film but would also produce it.

To write the screenplay, Huston rented a chateau at Chantilly outside of Paris and hired screen-writer Anthony Veiller, whom he had worked with on the screenplay of *The Killers.* Between writing sessions with Veiller, Huston and a group of friends, including Art Buchwald, John Steinbeck, Gene Kelly, and Anatole Litvak, frequently went to the races. At one point Huston called his friend jockey Billy Pearson to Paris to do some racing. Pearson had been a frequent companion and friend of Huston's on such films as *The Red Badge of Courage,* in which he had been given a walk-on role.

Huston's love of horses prompted him to buy a horse and enter it and Pearson in French races, but the jockey lost regularly and so did Huston. Even before the shooting of *Moulin Rouge* began, the director was broke from having bet on his own horse. Pearson said he raised some money for Huston, who managed to remain relatively solvent until his next advance came.

The film was shot in the Paris of the 1950s, but each location was carefully designed by art directors Marcel Vertes and Paul Sheriff to resemble the Paris of the 1890s.

To portray the stunted artist, Ferrer had to wear a special rig devised by Huston that strapped the actor's calves backward painfully so that he could wear his shoes on his knees. Ferrer got to the point where he could walk naturally in the rig, but when he took it off, his legs had to be massaged for long periods to return enough circulation so that he could walk normally. Ferrer did not always have to wear the rig, as he also played Lautrec's father. For scenes in which both characters appeared, Huston used a real dwarf instead of Ferrer in long-distance shots.

Huston does clarify one point about Lautrec in his film. The artist was not born a dwarf. His deformity was caused because his legs failed to grow after he fell from a chair as a child. Huston used a more dramatic fall down a stairway to explain the deformity.

Huston respected Ferrer tremendously. "Never saw such an amazing guy," he marveled. "So many talents. I knew he spoke French fluently, and Spanish. Then one day Silvana Mangano visited the set; he spoke Italian fluently too. Anything he tries he does well and he tries everything. I don't think he'd ridden a horse since he was a kid, but he heard I was going to Ireland to do some riding and he came along and soon he was taking jumps as if he'd been riding all his life."

Huston's comment about Ferrer's Lautrec was, "One thing you'll notice is that in playing this grotesque, he never for one minute gives the character any self-pity. It's a proud and whole character, which is what Lautrec should be."

When the filming was over, Huston made the discovery that he had unknowingly been observed. "It wasn't until we'd finished shooting," says Huston, "that I found Picasso had been on the set every day we'd been on location. He'd had someone who tipped him off every day where we'd be shooting the next day and he'd rent a room in a house or a hotel there and peek out and watch what was going on."

Huston is not sure why Picasso, whom he dearly wanted to meet, did this, but he speculates that the artist may have thought that it would give him some insight into how he might some day be treated on film.

The second assistant director on the film was David A. Mage, who later wrote an account of his experiences entitled "The Way John Huston Works." The first time Mage saw the director he was wearing a burgundy waistcoat, a pink shirt, and an enormous green cap. He continued to wear this bizarre costume throughout the filming.

From what he had read about Huston and seen in his films, Mage expected to find a bitter and cynical man. "He proved," wrote Mage, "to be surrounded by an aura of such easy charm that one could not help but be attracted to him. He was polite and cordial at all times and quite genial to everybody, from the first assistant down to the last electrician. He had no tenseness whatsoever."

One of the most remarkable aspects of *Moulin Rouge* is its use of color. "We drove Technicolor crazy," the director told Al Hine of *Holiday* magazine in 1953.

Huston said he wanted to find some "way to get into color the feeling of Toulouse-Lautrec, and to get color that looked real, not just splashy and bright." To achieve that effect, Huston as producer hired *Life* magazine photographer Eliot Elisofon as special color consultant. Elisofon and cameraman Oswald Morris tackled the problem. "They worked it out with filters and with lighting and with other filters," explained Huston, "not just on the camera. These were big gelatin filters in front of the lights.

"Then the battle began with Technicolor. They couldn't understand what we were trying to do . . . All their thinking was to make everything equally bright and sharp and clear. Like a beer ad, where you can see every bubble in the foam."

What Huston wanted, and got, was color that was sometimes hazy and sometimes light or dark, depending on the mood he wanted to create. Sometimes he used color to show characters clearly in the foreground but let the background fade into a blur of color. The idea of not having everything sharp in a color film would gradually become accepted, but in 1952 it was a new concept and difficult for Technicolor to accept.

"They told us we were crazy," Huston said. "They wrote letters to us and to the money, trying to get pressure on us, or to stop us from doing this evil thing. We went ahead and did it."

With the question of color temporarily settled, Huston moved into the streets, houses, and nightclubs of Paris to shoot.

Initially, Huston was not totally satisfied with the supporting cast. In fact, there was a period of hostility toward Zsa Zsa Gabor, who played singer Jane Avril, a favorite Lautrec model. At first, Huston was unmerciful to Gabor, who had trouble with her lines. He had her repeat scenes over and over and sing the film's theme song dozens of times. He criticized her for dropping words at the ends of sentences, and she replied that this was her natural Hungarian inflection. His hostility toward Gabor stopped some time after he discovered that she was a horse lover. He became attentive and friendly, even driving her to the airport after her role was done.

Huston was also displeased at first by the performance of the French dancer Colette Marchand as the streetwalker who almost drives Lautrec to suicide. In one scene, Marchand was to display repressed anger. Something went wrong take after take. The French actors blew their English lines or someone was in the wrong position.

In addition, Huston didn't like Marchand's performance. She wasn't getting nervous and angry enough.

Mage recalled that "to obtain that nervousness, he purposely goaded her. After a few takes she was so nervous and angry that she asked for a rest. She went to her room."

Huston held the set ready and the camera crew at attention. He began to shoot the instant she came back and captured her real repressed anger and nervousness as she did the scene.

The most difficult scene in the picture was filmed in and near the Deux Magots, a popular café. Huston had to shoot Ferrer, Christopher Lee, and other actors while 45,000 square feet of a busy Paris street were kept clear of vehicles and Parisians. Cars were often backed up for miles during the shooting. To keep the street clear for two days, Huston needed thirty policemen and three of his own assistants. He further required three men to be in charge of 150 extras. And he had to have three one-horse carriages, a two-horse van, and a two-horse bus for the scene.

Adding to all these problems was Paris in the midst of one of its most severe heat waves. Lights often built the temperature on the actors in the café to well over 100 degrees.

Mage recalled that, all through the heat and din, Huston, who had returned from Africa not long before, remained perfectly cool. He concentrated on the actors and seemed impervious to the rest of the world.

Once, at ten o'clock at night, Huston stopped shooting for nearly two hours for the sake of a minor detail. He had decided that one woman's costume was not complete without a feather boa. Stores were closed, but someone finally persuaded a female impersonator in a nearby nightclub to lend his boa.

According to Mage, one irate Parisian woman who wanted to be in the film decided to disrupt shooting by making noises, banging garbage cans or doing anything she could. Huston finally got rid of her by hiring a fortuneteller to tell the woman that her doom was near if she continued the noise attack.

The finished film, for the first time, clearly relates Huston's interest in painting directly to film. Huston himself becomes an impressionistic filmmaker to capture the spirit of the subject's era. This interest in the relation of color to subject was to reemerge during the making of both *Moby Dick* and *Reflections in a Golden Eye*.

Thematically, *Moulin Rouge* is a return to Huston's pessimism and exploration of futility. The director's identification with Lautrec seems strong indeed. Lautrec is the only central figure in any Huston film who is an artist. Lautrec, like Huston, is separated from his parents as a young man and must come to terms with an ambivalence toward dependence and independence from them. Lautrec, like Huston, is given to late hours, ironic views of himself, performing for others, sardonic wit, and a frequent bitterness toward women. Lautrec, like Huston, trusts only his art and is jealous of it. Lautrec, like Huston, loved horses, and frequently painted pictures of them.

In this comic scene, one can see Huston behaving just as Lautrec does: A rich old woman objects to Lautrec's painting of a woman "undressing." The drunken Lautrec calmly explains that the woman is not undressing at all. She is, he says, dressing, and she and her husband are about to celebrate their twenty-seventh wedding anniversary, in which they will be joined by their oldest son, a taxidermist.

The vision of Lautrec alone with his memories as the film ends corresponds strongly to Peter Viertel's novelized recollection of Huston's forecast for himself.

It is interesting that Huston should identify with a character who so little resembled him physically but so strongly resembled him in artistic temperament.

Moulin Rouge was released in January of 1953 and was an immediate box-office success. It was nominated for an Academy Award for best picture; Huston was nominated for best director and Ferrer for best actor. The three lost out to Cecil B. De Mille's *The Greatest Show on Earth*, John Ford for *The Quiet Man*, and Gary Cooper in *High Noon*. *Moulin Rouge* did win Oscars for art direction and costume design.

Huston next announced that he and Ferrer were planning a film about bullfighting based on Barnaby Conrad's novel *Matador*. The film was never made.

Commenting on *Moulin Rouge* in 1965, Huston told *New York Times* reporter Robert F. Hawkins, "Everyone raved about that one at the time. Now no one asks me about it any more . . .

"*Moulin Rouge* got mixed reviews and was successful at the box office, but I didn't like it. It was kind of interesting physically. It just wasn't Toulouse-Lautrec, that's all. You could put him on the screen today; you couldn't then. He was sentimentalized. Actually, he was a clinically cold little realist, with the courage to look life in the teeth. He was sardonic, not bitter. There's never been another like him in life."

When Huston began to earn money from *Moulin Rouge,* he decided to move to Ireland, the home of his father's grandparents, and take up the life of a country gentleman, riding to hounds and occasionally directing a motion picture. Huston had purchased a house in County Kildare the previous year. Now he and his wife, Rica, decided to make Ireland their permanent home.

While making *The African Queen* Huston had asked Bogart to read *Beat the Devil,* a novel by an Irishman named James Helvick. Helvick, it seems, was a neighbor of Huston's in Ireland. Bogart read the book, liked it, and, when he got back to the United States, purchased the rights to it. He saw the possibility of another *Maltese Falcon* or *Across the Pacific* in the tale about a gang of criminals involved in a uranium swindle in Italy and Africa. He called Huston in Paris and told him that he had bought the rights, and Huston said he would get the author to work on the screenplay.

Weeks later, Bogart got a cable from Huston saying that Helvick was broke and needed money. Huston had none to give him. Bogart sent money. Eventually, Bogart, who became co-producer of the film with Huston, would sink over $400,000 into the venture, none of which he got back.

Huston gave some money to Helvick and then called Anthony Veiller. Veiller, who was living in Venice, worked on the Helvick script and shipped it to Huston in Ireland. Huston worked on it further and shipped it to Peter Viertel, who worked on it in Switzerland. The script was completed after three months and sent to Bogart, who thought it was awful.

Nonetheless, Huston convinced the actor to join him in Italy to shoot the picture with the promise that Truman Capote would be on hand to change it. Capote had been suggested by producer David O. Selznick, whose wife, Jennifer Jones, was scheduled to be in the film. Capote had just written dialogue for Jones on *Indiscretion of an American Wife.*

As usual, Huston had found an ideal spot in which to shoot the film. He remembered Ravello, an almost inaccessible, mountainous town south of Naples, from his Army Signal Corps days.

The cast, Huston told Bogart, would include Peter Lorre from *The Maltese Falcon* team; Robert Morley, who would play a Sydney Greenstreet role as leader of the gang; Gina Lollobrigida as Bogart's Italian wife; Jennifer Jones, who had been in Huston's *We Were Strangers,* as a tourist; and relative unknown Edward Underdown as Jones's husband.

Huston and Bogart met in Rome to further discuss the script before they commenced shooting. Afterward, they began the drive up to Naples to start filming. Their driver smashed into a stone wall, destroying the car. In the crash, Bogart hit his head and his teeth bit through his tongue. Huston and Bogart stopped the bleeding and hurried to Naples, fearing the accident would turn into a costly delay. In Naples, actor George Sanders found them a local German doctor, who stitched Bogart's tongue without anesthetic. "Bogie had guts," said Huston. The actor's teeth were permanently damaged and eventually had to be recapped.

With Capote working on the screenplay, converting it to a strange parody of adventure, Helvick's novel was almost completely lost.

Bogart still had doubts about the script and tried to convince Huston to shoot it in the then popular 3–D but failed. His doubts increased when he received a cable from Selznick, who had read the script and was urging Bogart and Huston to abandon the project and take one of his instead.

Huston pressed on, gathering his cast and crew and heading for the mountains. The Italian actors and crew could speak no English, so a translator had to give Huston's orders. The Italian actors had to learn their lines phonetically, not understanding a word of what they were saying.

Bogart was suspicious of Capote initially and took opportunities to poke fun at him from time to time. That changed one day, according to Capote, when Bogart jokingly challenged him to Indian wrestle. Much to Bogart's amazement, the little writer beat him handily each time they fought and won several hundred dollars betting on each challenge from the actor. Annoyed, Bogart began to really wrestle with Capote, an exercise he engaged in regularly with Huston. He threw his arms around Capote and began to squeeze. Capote put out his leg and gave Bogart a push, sending him flat on his back. At least this is the version of the incident quoted by Joe Hyams in *Bogie.* It was the scene between Bogart and the Japanese judo expert from *Across the Pacific* enacted in real life. Bogart was so impressed by Capote's display that the two became close friends.

In another incident, Morley was supposed to be filmed in a car, but, for various reasons, was not in the car when the camera rolled. During the shot, the empty car was accidentally destroyed. "If I had been in that car, I might have been killed," Morley said he told Huston. "Yes, but you weren't, were you, kid? So now you're fine, just fine," Huston replied. "Huston," continued Morley, "always told everyone he was fine. Once, while walking down Fifth Avenue with a party of friends, he came across a dead man on the pavement. Everyone else avoided the corpse, but not John. The story according to Lillian Ross goes that he knelt down beside the man and taking his limp lifeless hand held it for a few critical seconds before replacing it carefully on the pavement. 'He'll be just fine,' he told the waiting ambulancemen. 'He'll be just fine.' "

When location shooting was finished, Huston went back to Ireland to put final touches on the film. Disaster struck. Something got stuck in his foot while he was fox hunting and he had to be hospitalized. While waiting to recuperate, he called in his friends and held poker games in the hospital. Burl Ives came to visit and provided entertainment and song.

"God," exclaimed a beaming Huston. "Aren't those songs just wonderful. I think, Burl boy, you and I, we're going to make a film in Ireland." Huston planned a film in which Ives would portray a wandering minstrel in the early eighteenth century, but the film was never made.

Once out of the hospital, Huston finished *Beat the Devil,* a comic hodgepodge with a story clearly in the Huston tradition. A group of criminals pretending to be businessmen are on a quest for uranium. Bogart and Lollobrigida play con artists pretending to be tourists. Jones and Underdown, who appear to be the naive couple thrown into a nest of thieves, prove to be the biggest fakes of all when the husband walks off with the riches.

Once again, Huston pursued the familiar theme of the quest. Characters face the futility of their pursuit and failure prevails, though the failure this time is perceived as comic.

Released in March 1954, the film was an instant box-office disaster. It eventually became a favorite cult film frequently cited as an early example of black humor, but, as Huston was to remark, he has frequently either been too early or too late with a film idea. In this case, he was much too early.

In spite of the awful box office, *Beat the Devil* received several good reviews in New York City. But it was so disliked by the public that a theater owner in Michigan ran an ad stating: "If you don't see this picture you are not missing much. The picture at The Temple did not come up to our expectations. We would like to discontinue it, but are forced to play it until Wednesday. Please accept our apologies. After the first show tonight we will give passes to the first ten people who tell us they actually liked it."

"Funny thing about that film," Huston told reporter Hawkins, more than ten years later. "After I made it, it fell flat on its face. No one seemed to care for it. Now it's playing all over the place; people seem to be discovering it."

Huston now turned his mind from *Beat the Devil* to a new project, another novel he had read as a boy and loved, a novel he could convert to film and shoot near Ireland around his horses and hunting. His next project would be *Moby Dick*.

CHAPTER 12

The White Rubber Whale

THE YEAR 1953 opened with John Huston $20,673.10 in arrears in his property settlement with ex-wife Evelyn Keyes and filled with enthusiasm for a project that had been on his mind more than a dozen years.

In 1942 Huston had begun talking about making a film version of Herman Melville's *Moby Dick,* starring his father as Captain Ahab. After the success of *Moulin Rouge,* he formed Moulin Productions and went to work on the idea.

The film would take three years to shoot, making Huston's search for Moby Dick longer than Ahab's quest in the novel. More than $4,500,000 would be spent on the picture, and actor Gregory Peck, as Ahab, would come close to losing his life.

When Huston got in touch with Peck about the role, the actor was so enthusiastic that he signed a contract without seeing a script. Though contracted for twelve weeks, Peck never lost his enthusiasm over six months of shooting, much of it on the Atlantic Ocean in far from calm water.

Peck believes that Huston really wanted to play Ahab himself but needed a star for the film. "He had visualized the captain as a sort of cross between his father and himself," Peck told Renee Francine in 1960, "and the toughest thing about that role was keeping Ahab's wooden leg away from him."

Before Huston could get to his first shot, however, he needed a script. He had started writing one in 1942, but World War II had interrupted him. With the few pages he did have, Huston contacted science-fiction writer Ray Bradbury to ask if he were interested in working in Ireland on the *Moby Dick* script. Huston had recently read Bradbury's *The Martian Chronicles* and liked it immensely.

Bradbury met with Huston and asked for a day to consider the offer. Bradbury really needed the day because he had never read *Moby Dick*. "As a boy," he said, "I'd tried it and given up." Knowing that he couldn't work on a project he didn't feel strongly about, Bradbury sampled the book, liked it, and went back to read it through from cover to cover, staying up all night to do so. In the morning, he called Huston and accepted the job.

Bradbury and Huston worked in Dublin and in St. Clerans, the director's home in County Kildare, for over six months. Huston's plan was not only to write the script in Ireland, but to shoot most of it near there as well. He wanted to be near his home and family and be able to go fox hunting as well.

"When I was a kid I never had a home to come back to and lick my wounds when I needed help," Huston explained to Louella Parsons in a 1955 interview. "My parents were theatrical people and we lived in hotels. I want a home for Walter Anthony, age 5, and Anjelica, age 4, to come home to when life seems to defeat them. Too few children have real homes."

Throughout the writing of the script, Huston continued to hunt with a recklessness that worried Bradbury. The biggest accident, however, did not happen to Huston, but to his wife. When they married, Huston had hired an Irish teacher to give Rica riding lessons, but, as he put it, "she did have a bit of bad luck" while the *Moby Dick* script was in progress.

"I saw her flying out of the saddle on a jump," he explained to Parsons, "and I told myself, 'Holy Toledo, there goes the mother of my children.' But she was lucky. She only broke all her lower teeth. No broken bones. I had to send her back to the States to have her teeth repaired."

Huston paused in his reminiscence to savor the danger of the hunt. "People are off horses, coming off and lying in ditches. Gad, it can be funny sometimes."

All the while preshooting preparation was going on, Huston not only hunted four or five days a week, he also went to the horse races and played poker. The director explained his ability to do so much by pointing out that initially the time difference in Los Angeles and County Kildare had confused him, so he kept waking up at 4:00 A.M. Since he invariably went to bed early in the morning, this might have been a problem. "I have solved it," he said at the time to reporter Dick Williams, "by simply not sleeping much. A touch of Irish whiskey helps too, of course."

Meanwhile the writing went on, but with a great many difficulties. Huston's original idea had been to simply convert the Melville novel into a film.

"Our biggest problem," he told *Saturday Review* film critic Arthur Knight in 1964, "was to turn Melville's expositional passages into characteristic dialogue. We had decided at the outset that our picture was going to be as close to the original novel as we could possibly make it, barring, of course, certain scatological references to the whale itself. Also, while *Moby Dick* [the novel] has some tremendous action sequences, it has little actual plot. For dramatic purposes we had to make some changes in Melville's construction."

The most obvious change is the elimination of Fedallah, Ahab's servant, whose character is merged with that of Queequeg, the canni-bal.* Also, Starbuck's attempt to kill Ahab comes at a different point in the film than in the novel. And Ahab dies lashed to the whale instead of being pulled by a line attached to its tail.

Huston discussed the film's theme in 1965 with Gideon Bachmann: "I always thought *Moby Dick* was a great blasphemy. Here was a man who shook his fist at God. The thematic line in *Moby Dick* seemed to me always to have been, who's to judge when the judge himself is dragged before the bar? Who's to condemn, but he, Ahab."

The Huston-Bradbury friendship began to deteriorate during the filming and had broken down by the time shooting was over. Just before the film was released, Bradbury was informed that Huston would receive co-script credit. "There never was any collaboration," the writer told Arnold R. Kunert, "in spite of the fact that his name appears on the credits."

Bradbury appealed to the Screen Writers' Guild to have Huston's name removed from the script credit. However, Huston, who had been out of the country during the Guild's hearing, returned to the United States, contested the decision, and got the Guild to change its ruling.

Huston, said Bradbury, "has done this on more than one occasion and I don't know what all the motives are . . . in case after case he

---

*Queequeg was played by Friedrich Ledebur, an Austrian count, who had his head shaved and submitted to a daily two-hour make-up job for the duration of the film.

has shared screen credit, which makes me wonder how much he has contributed."

"Ray and I tried to be as faithful to the meaning of the book as our own understanding and the special demands of the movie medium would allow," Huston told Arthur Knight in an interview for *Saturday Review* just after the film was finished. "And by that I don't mean a love interest. There wasn't a woman in the book and there are none in our picture."

That is not quite true. The scene in which the *Pequod* sets sail in the film concentrates on the faces of women who must watch as their men go to sea. It is reminiscent of a similar scene in Robert Flaherty's *Man of Aran,* a film Huston particularly admires.

Moby Dick was to be a Huston-produced film released through Warner Brothers, and at one point, after months of script work, Huston received a telegram signed "Jack Warner" instructing the director and Bradbury to add a love interest to the picture and to somehow put a woman on board the *Pequod.* Huston solemnly handed the telegram to Bradbury, who became furious and began to curse the distant Warner until he noticed Huston in a corner rolling with laughter. The telegram had been a Huston special.

Huston came up with one of his most morbid jokes while the film was being shot. Spotting a ship approaching the *Pequod,* Huston yelled at the entire cast, clad in eighteenth-century whaling costumes, to lie around the deck and play dead. When the approaching ship passed by, a group of people on its deck gazed in horror at what must have looked to them like a ghost ship.

Huston continued to work on the script, this time with Irish neighbor John Kilbracken, who, though not an actor, struck the director as the perfect Ishmael. Huston had already cast another nonactor, his friend Seamus Kelly, a Dublin newspaperman, as the third mate, Flask.

Kilbracken waited in agony for the part but didn't hear from Huston. Eventually he was offered a small role in which he would carry a pig, but he was unavailable for some of the shooting. Then, surprisingly, Huston hired him to work on the script on location. He also got to stand in once for Richard Basehart in the role of Ishmael.

Kilbracken's final assessment of Huston after months of following the director about, being praised and humiliated, summoned at odd hours and forgotten for days, was noted in *Living like a Lord* and seems a summary of the attitudes many people held about the "Monster":

He is one of those men of fantastic personal magnetism and charm who can behave completely outrageously, and then, with a smile and a gesture, make one again instantly devoted to him. He is also a man of real genius; to an extent beyond anything I had realized, he is responsible for all that matters in every single department of every movie he directs. In his moments of inspiration, one stands aghast at his virtuosity. Yet, at times, he makes errors of judgment, of taste, of understanding, so gross that one feels it cannot be the same man. As I got to know him, I came to realize consciously that my feeling for him was of extreme, almost perfect ambivalence.

Huston began to shoot his film in the small Irish port town of Youghal (pronounced "yawl"). The town's entire waterfront was redesigned to make it look like 1840 in New Bedford, where the early scenes take place. Even telephone lines were removed. A British ship was found to serve as the *Pequod,* and it too was completely overhauled and redesigned.

To play the title character, Moby Dick, three elaborate, 100-foot, rubberized, steel-reinforced whales were built. Since the actual shooting was to be done at sea, there was always the risk that one of the whales might get lost and a double would be needed. In fact, two of the whales were lost. And at one point, a towline broke and the third whale disappeared in a dense fog with Gregory Peck on its back.

Peck recalled this extraordinary incident as one of the most remarkable in his life: "I remember thinking of how foolish it would be to die like that, in full costume on the back of a rubber whale in the Irish Sea. I was sure it would have amused John, but I called and called and finally the crew of the towing ship found me. One of those rubber whales is still out there in the Irish sea. I remember they sent out warnings to fishermen the day it was lost telling them to look out for a huge artificial whale."

From Youghal, Huston and his crew moved the *Pequod* to Fishguard, Wales, to shoot further offshore scenes. The rigors of shooting at sea caused delays when Basehart broke three bones in his foot jumping into a whaleboat, Peck hurt his kneecap on the rig built for his peg leg, and Leo Genn, who played Starbuck, slipped a disc in his back and got pneumonia from the cold days at sea.

Huston happily left Wales and took the *Pequod* to Madeira, where whaling was still being done with harpoons by the Portuguese. Here Huston had the *Pequod*'s crew actually hunt and kill whales at sea, both for sport, and to learn how it was done.

Huston remembers the excitement of the filming as well as the tribulations: "Three times we were sure we'd lost the *Pequod*. Sure, we could have done it in a studio, and some of the shots actually were made in a studio, but there's nothing that compares with the fury of a real storm at sea. We got as much of that on film as we possibly could."

When location shooting was completed, Huston moved his cast and crew to Elstree Studios in London. His primary set was the deck of the *Pequod,* which occupied half of an old warehouse. Facing the deck throughout the shooting was the set for a World War II film, *The Dam Busters,* complete with sections of British bombers.

For one of the key scenes shot on land, Huston got Orson Welles to play Father Mapple, who gives a sermon from the poop-deck pulpit of his church.

"It was," recalled Huston to Rosemary Lord in a 1974 interview, "a long, long speech that went on for five minutes. Orson got up into the pulpit and started turning pages and asked for a drink. We gave him a bottle of brandy. I asked him if he was ready to rehearse. We planned to take about three days for the scene.

"Orson took a drink and looked at the script with the whole congregation waiting. I finally called for a rehearsal and Orson said, 'Let's shoot the rehearsal.' Well, bang, he went right through, did five pages and I moved the cameras in closer and he did it again right through. A marvelous performance. We finished it in three hours and it was, as far as I'm concerned, the finest thing in the film."

Huston sees Father Mapple's sermon on submitting to the will of God as being in conflict with Melville's philosophical concepts. He believes it is religious while the rest of the novel is not. It also struck Huston "that the story of Noah is the story of Ahab in reverse." Interestingly, when Huston made his film version of *The Bible,* he himself played Noah — and God.

A particularly complex studio shot involved filming Ahab strapped to the back of the dying whale. An 80,000-gallon tank was prepared and a three-sectioned metal and rubber whale constructed.

A hand-operated mechanism made it rise and fall in the water. Twenty smaller versions were also built for various close shots. At one point, Peck was to be lashed to the big whale and pulled out of the water for the final shot of him dead. Huston didn't tell the actor that the mechanism had failed to lift the whale from the water the first time he had tried it. If it had failed to work when Peck was tied to the whale, he really could have been dead when they got it up. That, says Peck smiling, "would have provided John with the last touch of realism he was after."

For clearly allegorical reasons, Huston specified that the final clash with the whale and Ahab's death take place at Bikini, the atoll where the atomic bomb was tested. According to Kilbracken, Huston claimed that he deduced this location from the novel, but there is no such evidence in Melville's book.

Even when shooting was finished, Huston continued to be concerned with, as he put it, "finding fresh ways to deal with the substance of Melville's book."

One way involved a unique approach to color, but one quite different from that in *Moulin Rouge*. With Oswald Morris, who had been cameraman on *Moulin Rouge,* Huston "sought to discover the tones that would tell *Moby Dick* as a picture . . . So we devised a new color photography process . . . We shot *Moby Dick* in Technicolor. From the color film we made two sets of negatives, one in color, one in black and white. The two negatives were printed together on the final print, achieving a completely new tonality," according to the Arthur Knight interview.

The result of the color process was to give the image a hard edge, to remove the softness Huston had exaggerated in *Moulin Rouge*. The impressionistic amoral images of *Moulin Rouge* gave way to the hard, moral world of Captain Ahab.

The completed film is both like the Melville novel and unlike it, as Huston wished. Huston's Ahab is a demented, mysterious creature who has an hypnotic effect on his crew. Melville's Ahab is obsessed but able to manipulate his men gradually. Huston's Ahab is direct and open about his goals, and neither the film nor the captain sways from the single narrative of pursuit. Melville's novel is filled with digressions about whaling, coffin-making, and history, all of which help to build a picture of how small Ahab and the *Pequod* are in God's universe and how enormous is their blasphemy.

In both film and novel, it is explicit that to attack the whale is to defy God. The film, however, stays within Ahab's world. The novel expands out to the whole of history.

Certainly, the narrative as developed by Huston and Bradbury is in keeping with the director's preoccupation with failed quests. Only one man, Ishmael, survives the quest. All the other men of the *Pequod* go down in Ahab's futile attempt to destroy the whale. But Huston sees Ahab in his actions and his final gesture as a noble creature who has chosen to go down fighting.

Huston's attitude toward death is evident in a scene that contrasts with the novel. Strangely, it is a scene that people usually believe came from the novel. In it, Ishmael tries to persuade his friend Queequeg not to commit suicide by refusing to eat. In the film, the uncomprehending Ishmael tries to get Queequeg to drink water. He then tells him that he will be angry if he refuses to eat. Finally, the totally confused, emotional Ishmael forbids his friend to die. It is only when Ishmael reminds Queequeg of a promise he once made of lasting friendship that the cannibal is willing to remain alive. His word, once given, is the only thing that will deter him from his decision to face death directly and with dignity.

Huston and Peck toured the United States supposedly promoting the film but actually telling interviewers about a stable of horses they had just bought. Huston said he was thinking of filming Melville's first novel, *Typee,* with Peck and jockey Billy Pearson as leads. He also indicated that he was planning to film Aristophanes' *Lysistrata* with Marilyn Monroe and Ava Gardner. "For this one," he told Louella Parsons, "I'd love to collect all the delectable female flesh in Christendom, put it into one big pot, and stir it well."

He also talked of remaking *The Devil and Daniel Webster* and of obtaining rights to film *The Lark, The Sleeping Prince,* and the life story of photographer Robert Capa. As usual, Huston's mind was on his next film, not the one he had just spent three years of his life on. Not unusually, the projects he was discussing publicly never got made.

Moby Dick won the New York Film Critics award for best direction, and the Motion Picture National Board of Review named Huston the best director of the year.

"I hope," said Huston when *Moby Dick* was receiving its awards and favorable reviews, "the picture will be successful because production costs are in the millions and unfortunately you can't get funds for anything that is in the least way a departure from the established pattern."

Hoping for a big success with *Moby Dick,* Huston took off for India to scout locations for his long-desired version of *The Man Who Would Be King.* He and Peter Viertel had been working on the screenplay, and it looked as if the time might be right to shoot it. Huston wound up shooting a Bengal tiger but no film. *Moby Dick* had failed to be a big moneymaker, perhaps because of the seriousness of the subject matter or the period dialogue.

Huston always lived well and had recently spent a great deal of money renovating and furnishing St. Clerans with paintings by Monet, Utrillo, Juan Gris, and Lautrec, expensive antiques, and such diverse items as African sculpture, Aztec masks, and Napoleon's bed. He even had a moat put in around his yard, not as an affectation, but to keep all of his animals from trampling on the extensive formal gardens. He also had two children in school, alimony to pay, and a stable in Switzerland he owned with Peck.

Fifty years old and thousands of dollars in debt, John Huston next accepted a high-paying three-picture contract with Twentieth Century-Fox.

CHAPTER 13

The Nun and the Geisha

EARLY IN 1956, Twentieth Century-Fox handed John Huston *Heaven Knows, Mr. Allison,* a novel by Charles Shaw. The studio had bought the rights to the book five years earlier in the hope that William Wyler would forge a script from it and direct the film.

Providing a script from the novel was particularly difficult, as it deals with the love that develops between a U.S. Marine and a nun who are hiding on a Japanese-held island during World War II.

The studio had ample evidence that the Catholic Church would come down hard on a film that even suggested the development of such a love affair. Part of the evidence was in the Church's reaction to *Black Narcissus,* a 1947 film in which a group of nuns are vulnerable to worldly temptations, including men. Deborah Kerr, who was to be Sister Angela, the female lead, in *Heaven Knows, Mr. Allison,* had portrayed one of the nuns in *Black Narcissus.*

Wyler had worked with writers to prepare a script that would avoid church disapproval. He solved the problem by having the woman announce that she is not really a nun but has stolen the nun's habit to escape from the Japanese in disguise.* The Church approved the script, but Wyler never made the film.

Huston worked with John Lee Mahin, scriptwriter for such films as *Red Dust* and *Captains Courageous,* on a somewhat different approach. They made it clear that the nun has not taken her final vows, and, adds Huston, "We kept away from any implication of sex." In 1970, Mahin told Gene Phillips that of all the films he had written, *Heaven Knows, Mr. Allison* gave him the most satisfaction as script and film.

*Interestingly, the story outline bears a striking resemblance to Don Siegel's 1970 film, *Two Mules For Sister Sara.*

As reviewers were quick to note, the film bore resemblances to *The African Queen*. A rugged, profane, hard-drinking, uneducated man encounters a religious woman whose male religious companion has just died. The rugged individual and the woman must learn to exist together, and the man falls in love with her. In confrontations with the enemy, the man shows courage and resourcefulness. Just as it looks as if the couple will be killed, they are rescued and the enemy is destroyed.

There are, however, key differences between the two films. First, Allison (Robert Mitchum) is not an easily manipulated character on the fringe of society as was Charlie Allnut. He is a marine who defines the marines as his home and religion. His conviction matches Sister Angela's. "You got your cross. I got my globe and anchor," he announces proudly. In fact, she learns to depend on him more and more for food, shelter, and moral strength. In *The African Queen* there was the hint of divine, if comic, intervention. In *Heaven Knows, Mr. Allison,* salvation is entirely in Allison's hands.

The Marine must fight not only the Japanese but his own frustration with religion. The Catholic Church deprives him of the woman he has come to love, but he does not die in a fit of rage. He calls on his moral strength and, after one drunken protest, comes to terms with his desires. Actually, desire is only part of his feeling toward Sister Angela. He states quite clearly that he has, in this primitive setting, come to enjoy taking care of her and proposes that he continue to do so.

The contrasts between Allison's and Sister Angela's backgrounds are constantly brought out. They talk about their vocations in personal terms and they talk about the difficulties of their training. He tells of his drill instructor and she of a Mother Superior called "The Holy Terror." This scene contrasts with one in which it is clear that they both literally and figuratively speak different languages. She is Irish and educated. He is American and has had little schooling. She cannot understand his slang, and he cannot understand much of her vocabulary.

Heaven Knows, Mr. Allison was Huston's first film in Cinemascope, the wide-screen process that only a few directors, like Otto Preminger and Nicholas Ray, were comfortable with.

Cinematographer Oswald Morris and Huston experimented with format. The sides of the picture are frequently framed with natural objects that point to the center of the image like fingers. In a shot supposedly seen through Allison's eyes, trees point to a tower in which a Japanese guard is standing.

Huston also used natural objects to divide the frame into sections. In a darkened room, a door opens. The camera shows Japanese soldiers in the next room through the door. The Japanese are in the center with the black border of the door on each side. In another shot, Huston cuts off the left half of the Cinemascope frame with a building and shows Japanese lining up at the right of the frame. Throughout the film, Huston blocks off parts of the elongated frame, shifting the viewer's attention around the space of the screen, playing with the new shape.

Huston shot his film in Tobago, a British island about twenty miles from Trinidad. Tobago was, as a title at the start of the film indicates, supposed to represent an island "somewhere in the Pacific" in 1944.

The film was unusual in that only Mitchum and Kerr had English-speaking roles. The eight actors who play Japanese soldiers all speak Japanese exclusively. The marines who rescue the couple at the end of the picture (100 actors were brought in for several days for this) have no lines.

Such casting would appear to make the task of obtaining actors quite easy, but, thousands of miles from Japan, Huston had difficulty finding actors who could speak Japanese. He finally got a few from South America, but also had to use Chinese to bring the number of soldiers to eight. The search for them took almost two months, and the delays were costly.

As usual, Huston found time to play one of his morbid jokes. This time the victim was *Saturday Review* film critic Hollis Alpert, who had been receptive to Huston's films in the past and had come to the island to watch some shooting.

Huston told Alpert that after the actors playing the Japanese were removed from a tower, he would tell his crew to blow it up. Almost immediately after Huston said this, the tower exploded. Alpert turned pale. He was convinced that he had witnessed the accidental death of a handful of actors. Huston did not reveal his joke until he'd had a few minutes to enjoy the critic's reaction. It marked one of the few times in history when a director could prove that a scene had affected a reviewer.

As usual, there were accidents. Mitchum, who scurries over hills and rock, plunges into water, and is pulled through the sea by a real giant turtle, suffered several injuries, including a severe cut on one foot, a badly twisted ankle, and a number of bruises. He had heard about Huston before he accepted the role and was not surprised by the ensuing events.

Huston in an interview with Rosemary Lord for *Transatlantic Review* called Mitchum "a great favorite of mine. I only worked with him in that one complete picture. He is a great actor. He's never even scratched the surface. He should have played Shakespeare. Wonderful actor, and he's always so retiring; so modest in his self-estimation. Only sometimes do you get a glimpse of the center of this extraordinary man."

Heaven Knows, Mr. Allison took four months to shoot and cost about $3 million. For recreation, Huston played poker, enjoyed the sun, and went to boxing matches in Trinidad. He even purchased the contract of a heavyweight, whom he sent to England for training.

Reviews of the film were mixed, but Huston and Mahin received an Academy Award nomination for best screenplay. The Oscar went to Alan Jay Lerner for *Gigi.*

With *Heaven Knows, Mr. Allison* doing well at the box office, Huston received a temporary release from his three-picture deal with Twentieth Century-Fox. David O. Selznick wanted him to direct the second film version of Ernest Hemingway's *A Farewell To Arms,* and Hemingway had enthusiastically agreed with his choice.

Ben Hecht, perhaps the best-known writer in Hollywood, had already prepared a script that Selznick liked. When Huston came in at a flat $250,000 salary, he had major objections to this version and wanted to return to the Hemingway novel. The director worked with Hecht for two months, then went to Italy to begin shooting. While he was on his way, Selznick read the revised script and ordered a substantial number of the Huston-Hecht revisions deleted.

With only a few days to go until shooting began, Huston received a new script and a long memo from Selznick telling him to shoot what he had just received. Selznick wrote: "I don't want you to feel like a 'prostitute,' as you stated was your feeling when we talked the other night, by doing a picture you don't believe in. I most certainly don't want you to be depressed by any feeling that you are not honoring any pledges you may have made to Hemingway."

Huston quit. Charles Vidor took over, and Huston went back to Twentieth Century-Fox to complete the second of the three films he owed the studio.

The Townsend Harris Story, later changed by the studio to *The Barbarian and the Geisha,* was Huston's next film. It was 1958 and he was in good spirits on his way to Japan with his pal Sam Jaffe and the promise of a $300,000 salary.

Like *Heaven Knows, Mr. Allison, Barbarian* involves two people — again the only two major characters in the film who speak English — who must confront hostile Japanese. Scripted by Charles Grayson, the film tells the story of the first U.S. ambassador to Japan, Townsend Harris. The year is 1855, and the Japanese are highly suspicious of Harris (John Wayne) and his translator (Jaffe). Harris bullies his way onto the land and forces himself on the local governor, demanding to see the Shogun. The governor refuses and sends a spy, a geisha, to Harris' house. When a European ship brings cholera to the area, Harris and Huston fight the disease and finally burn down a village to control its spread. A grateful governor arranges a parade for Harris to see the Shogun, who turns out to be a young boy. The ambassador gives him presents, including a chair and a telescope. The Shogun's advisers discuss the signing of a treaty with the United States, and a group opposed to the idea attempts to kill Harris. But the geisha, who is supposed to help in the assassination, takes his place and dies. The governor cannot bring himself to kill Harris, though he has been ordered to do so by his clan. Instead, he commits suicide.

The original idea for the story had not been Huston's. In fact, he had not heard of Harris until a few months before he shot the picture, but he was intrigued. "After I saw *Rashomon* and *Gate of Hell,*" he told Los Angeles *Times* entertainment editor Cecil Smith in 1958, "I wanted to make a Japanese picture, using a complete Japanese crew, with the Japanese sense of color and design. It didn't quite work out that way. I used Americans in key technical spots, but still it's Japanese."

Huston was immediately fascinated by Japanese locations and artifacts. "I had one set," he recalls, "with not an object on it less than 300 years old, and each one was a work of art . . . In Kyoto I found treasures to use as props. I dressed an actress in clothes that an empress wore. I wanted to wind the time machine backward, to create this exotic world that was the old Japanese empire, that was so distant from our world as to be almost beyond belief."

Huston was pleased with the choice of Wayne as Harris because he liked the contrast between the big actor and the smaller Japanese. To get that contrast, Twentieth Century-Fox had to pay Wayne $700,000 for fourteen weeks of work.

"This huge figure in his innocence and naiveté, with his edges rough, moving among these minute people and all this exotic art work. I felt this would symbolize the huge and awkward United States of 100 years ago," Huston explained to Smith.

"At this point in history," he continued, "the Japanese were not only antiforeign but confused and frightened. In the beginning they would see this giant as a threat to their safety, and then gradually it would be revealed that he was simply flesh and blood."

The director readily admits that the geisha in the film probably never existed, though the Japanese have incorporated her into their stories about Harris. Huston thought this was fine. He auditioned dozens of actresses to play the role, but, in his frequently idiosyncratic way, he chose Eiko Ando, who had been a chorus girl in a Tokyo burlesque house.

Huston saw Japan as "a crowded little country" and, he said, he had to have "the feeling of crowds." To this end, he used as many as 800 extras in full costume in a single shot. In one such crowd scene, Huston spotted a small boy laughing at Wayne. "If a child laughs now at this foreigner, a child would have laughed a century ago," he reasoned. He had the laugh repeated for the camera, and added an amused reaction by Wayne to it.

In spite of Huston's enthusiasm and his usual ability to beguile actors, Wayne remained uncharmed.

In Wayne's biography *Shooting Star,* Maurice Zolotow said that the actor still writhes remembering how slowly Huston directed his scenes. According to Zolotow, Wayne believes that Huston was not only fascinated by the Japanese style of filming but by irrelevant details and shots. Wayne said he was convinced that Huston was overrated. When the actor said he could not think of one good picture Huston had directed, Zolotow cited *The Maltese Falcon* and *The Treasure of the Sierra Madre.* Then, Zolotow writes, "Duke insisted — with no basis except the fact that he disliked Huston and felt he had been artistically mistreated by him — that these pictures had succeeded because of Huston's father, because Walter Huston had been in both these films and had assisted his son. So I said what about *The Asphalt Jungle*? And Duke changed the subject."

In an article titled "On Location" in *Here's Hollywood,* Charles Grayson recalled one touchy situation between the director and the Duke. Huston was about to shoot the scene in which Harris and his translator burn down the village to keep the cholera from spreading, and Wayne couldn't understand why the Japanese wouldn't kill Harris:

"They'd chop the busybody bastard," he growled. "Why don't they?"

"Mostly because the picture's just starting," Huston replied, heading toward a corner to rewrite the sequence.

Huston then worked on the script and returned it to Wayne, who complained that a valuable line had been cut. Huston restored the line and called for the scene to be shot.

Wayne and Jaffe began by setting fire to the houses. Extras ran about and flames burst near the actors. The set was soon an inferno. When Wayne and Jaffe finished the shot, Huston shouted "Again," and the two actors ran back into the flames as the fire grew even bigger. When they came through the second time, Huston's voice shouted for yet another take. Wayne and Jaffe plunged back into the blaze. Extras and crew were moving away from the fire, and this time Huston shouted "Fine" when the shot ended. Fire engines hurried in to put out the set.

Grayson reported that at this point:

Charlie [Charles G. Clarke], the burly cameraman, walked to a stool and sank down to hold his face in his hands. A first-aid man came running — one of Duke's arms was scorched. Sam danced off slapping at the seat of his sizzling pants. The sun touched a distant mountaintop. John [Huston] casually descended from the platform. He glanced at the sun as if he would like to thumb his nose at it. But that would have revealed that he too had been worried about the risk he had taken . . . "Close, eh?" he asked taking off his cap. His hair seemed grayer than it had that morning. Pausing, he looked fondly back at the smoldering debris and the dispersing people. "I think we got some good stuff," he said and grinned. "Who says the excitement has gone out of making pictures?"

In a sense, *The Barbarian and the Geisha* experiments with visual art. Huston did indeed attempt to make a Japanese film, with long sequences of contemplation, attention to detail, and limited action.

The one major physical confrontation is the fight between Harris and the small judo expert. The conflict between director and star most certainly stemmed partly from each man's conception of what a movie should be.

Seen as an exercise in Cinemascope, an attempt to re-create not only the aura of Japanese film but the style of Japanese formal prints, *The Barbarian and the Geisha* is remarkable, but a film with John Wayne and little action was a disaster. Writing in *Films in Review,* Japanese critic I. Tanaka called the picture a "pointless falsification of history," adding that "the art direction and set decoration were far below the high standard of *Gate of Hell.*"

Publicity tours for the film were minimal, and Huston was unhappy with the studio's final editing.

"I have often been asked," Huston told Gene Phillips, "if I have had final cut on my films since becoming an established director. My answer is always the same. No director ever has final cut because ultimately the picture always belongs to someone else who may tamper with it after you think the film is finished and have it delivered for distribution . . . The studio altered the film [*Barbarian*] considerably. When I saw it a year later I wanted to take my name off it. Even the plot was unrecognizable."

At this point Huston gained a partner who has remained with him for more than twenty years. Gladys Hill had met Huston while working for Sam Spiegel, when Spiegel and Huston formed Horizon Films to make *The African Queen.* She married and left the industry briefly, but when she was divorced, Huston sent her a telegram: "I understand you're working temporarily and since you like to travel, why don't you come to Ireland and work for me forever and ever?"

Since that telegram, Gladys Hill has been Huston's writing partner, typist, assistant, and automobile driver. Jim Watters, writing for the *New York Times,* recently described Miss Hill as "a woman of indeterminate age but definite, plainspoken strength. She is all things — save one — to Huston."

CHAPTER 14

Return to Africa

JOHN HUSTON read *The Roots of Heaven,* by writer, soldier, and diplomat Romain Gary when it appeared in English in 1958. The novel had already sold 300,000 copies in France and had won the highest French literary honor, the Prix Goncourt. Huston was attracted by the African location, the subject matter — hunting — and the story of a one-man crusade to save African elephants that turns into an international folk tale.

He immediately informed Twentieth Century-Fox that he would be pleased if the studio obtained the rights to the novel for him. The reply was that the film rights had already been obtained for Fox's vice president in charge of production, Darryl Zanuck.

After his experience with David O. Selznick on *A Farewell to Arms,* Huston was reluctant to work for another of Hollywood's super-producers, but he wanted very much to do the film and arranged a meeting with Zanuck. The meeting went well and the fifty-one-year-old Huston was in, as he reported, at a salary slightly higher than the flat $300,000 he had received for *The Barbarian and the Geisha.*

Almost immediately, the logical question was put to him. Wasn't there something inconsistent in a big-game hunter, who often wore his jacket with the lucky bones of a tiger he had killed, making a film about a man trying to save Africa's elephants by attacking hunters?

"Contrary to prevailing opinion," Huston responded cryptically to *New York Times* reporter Richard W. Nason, "I never found an elephant big enough to justify the sin of killing one."

Nason then inquired about what philosophical points the director would make in the film. Waving a big cigar, Huston replied, "I don't consciously inject philosophy in my films. In France I learned that they've got me all figured out as an existentialist who preaches a philosophy of failure. I admit there's a lot of that in my films . . . but if I have any conscious view, it's simply that what fruits there are lie in the process of attaining the goal, in the getting there and not the attainment."

Huston and Patrick Leigh-Fermor immediately began to rewrite the script Zanuck had commissioned from novelist Gary. According to Gary, Zanuck had assured him the script wouldn't be changed, but when the writer saw the finished film he said only one line of his original was left. Meanwhile Zanuck gathered a cast. His first choice for Morel, the crusading hunter, was William Holden, but Holden was committed to another project and British actor Trevor Howard got the part. The female lead, Minna, went to French singer Juliette Greco, Zanuck's "protégée," who had had some supporting roles in French films and appeared in Henry King's *The Sun Also Rises.* The other important roles included Errol Flynn as Major Forsythe, a drunken ex-officer who joins Morel's band; Eddie Albert as Abe Fields, an American photographer; Orson Welles as Cy Sedgewick, a gross American television commentator who turns Morel into a folk hero; and Paul Lukas as Saint Denis, a government official. An important minor role, Peter Qvist, a Danish naturalist who joins Morel, went to Huston's friend Count Friedrich Ledebur, who had played Queequeg in *Moby Dick.*

As soon as he could, Huston headed for Africa with cinematographer Oswald Morris and a cast and crew of 164. The first location was French Equatorial Africa, where the director felt he had the greatest possibility for natural local color and finding elephants.

"The heat was terrific," he recalled. "One hundred and thirty or one hundred and forty degrees all the time; one hundred at night. You drank, drank, drank all the time, but you sweated it out before it reached your stomach."

One of those joining Huston in his drinking was Errol Flynn. The two had been friends since their near-legendary Hollywood encounter in which the actor had convincingly beaten the director in a garden brawl.

For Flynn, at forty-nine, the film was a godsend. His career had been dropping steadily and his drinking increasing. His looks were gone, but his pleasant disposition and smile remained. He had good reason for the smile, for when Holden dropped out of the cast, Flynn became the best-known actor in the film and was moved to top billing, even though he had a supporting role.

In *My Wicked, Wicked Ways,* Flynn said that the six months he spent working with Huston were fascinating, "in some ways the most astonishing period of my life." He remembered that almost everyone got sick from heat, malaria, or venereal disease. "One Italian," he recalled, "didn't take his anti-malaria pills and caught the most virulent type of African malaria, the mortality rate of which is tremendously high, and he died."

Zanuck did his best to make conditions comfortable for Greco and the rest of the group by flying 'n fresh water and providing lots of mosquito netting and plenty of liquor. Flynn was almost the only person who didn't get seriously ill, a fact he attributed to his diet of vodka and fruit juice. It may have been that very diet, however, that caused him to take a fall on a staircase later in the shooting and wind up in a Paris hospital.

One of the malaria victims was Bobby Jacks, Zanuck's son-in-law, who had to be flown to Europe. Greco also became ill several times, stopping production for days. At one point, Eddie Albert was stricken by the extreme heat, collapsed, and was delirious for a long while. According to Zanuck (in Mel Gussow's *Don't Say Yes Until I Finish Talking),* "Eddie Albert was out of his mind for three weeks, completely out of his mind. When he was in the worst stages, he was lying naked on the cement floor of his hut. I told him this later and he didn't believe me. He'd refuse to go to the toilet. We got two boys to tie him to a pole and carry him to the toilet." Trevor Howard's face was constantly turning beet red from the heat and had to be made up frequently to made his skin look normal. A regular plane run to civilization for the sick was established.

Huston, however, suffered only one minor brush with illness. Once while looking for a location, he and several others realized that it might be too dark to get back to their camp. They asked a local chief to put them up for the night and he had them taken to a shack in the jungle. The shack, which was used as the tribal jail, was furnished with only an old automobile seat.

With mosquitoes coming through the openings that served as windows, and swarming around them, Huston and his group began to finish off some of the Scotch they carried as a gift for the natives.

They stayed up all night playing cards and drinking, except one man who went to sleep on the auto seat. In the morning, Huston and the other card players were badly bitten and had to take a few days off work. The man who had gone to sleep was so severely stung that he had to be hospitalized for weeks.

During delays for others' illnesses, Huston and Flynn went hunting. Flynn did no shooting on the safari. "Frankly," he wrote, "I just don't like to kill." Huston, however, was delighted with a big water buffalo he shot. The director, recalled Flynn, "was obviously very good in the jungle, I thought I was pretty good on foot, but this fellow Huston, no youngster, leaped along like a big spider swinging through the trees."

Holiday reporter Alfred Bester, who met Huston when *The Roots of Heaven* was being filmed, described him as "tall and lean as a basketball player and co-ordinated like a cavalryman. He dresses like a horseman in narrow twills, hacking jackets and Tattersall waistcoats. His thin grooved face, brown as teakwood, looks Chinese; his iron-gray hair is cut in no discernible fashion."

Though he was in poor shape, Flynn volunteered to do his own stunts in the film when, as he said, "a double might have done just as well. I found myself singing a bawdy Australian song while pretending to be drunk, swimming in an African river and hanging onto a horse's tail, the horse kicking me in the crotch."

The workday had to be cut because no one could tolerate the sun past noon. By the time location shooting in Africa was finished, over 900 cases of illness had been reported among the cast and crew. One man developed an illness so obscure that he was sent to the Pasteur Institute in Paris for special study. Friedrich Ledebur got an eye infection and spent six months in the American Hospital in Paris. Greco contracted a rare blood disease. Her memories of the African experience were not as affirmative as Flynn's.

"We lived in little huts," she recalled for Alfred Bester for a 1959 article in *Holiday*. "I was the only woman. I had the feeling at night that I was in a military house. All those men snoring." She remembered that Trevor Howard always woke up smiling and happy but that Huston's mood varied.

She also recalled the director's style. "He never told us when we were good or bad. That drove me mad the first day. I was crying . . . but sometimes he would look at you like a snake and say, 'Fine,

fine' through his teeth. 'Fine, honey' is the most he can say. 'Fine, honey.' "

In a scene between her and Paul Lukas, Huston's approach, according to Greco, consisted of saying, "And now, kids, what do you feel? Tell me. Show me. Show me what you are feeling. Do what you want to do."

"And," said Greco, "we did. And he never said a word. He never told us it was good or bad."

Howard's description was somewhat similar. Huston, he told visiting reporter Cynthia Grencer, "leaves a lot up to the actor. Of course, I don't mind that. He lets you do what you want."

Huston readily admits that he never sets up any pattern for his work with actors, but in a 1958 interview with *Newsweek* he did list a visual rule he works by: "The essence, the genius of the screen, is motion. If you can compose with motion, which a painter can't do, setting one motion against another, you've hit it. But don't change your setup each time you shoot. Let the camera move as the subjects move.

"... If you want to ennoble somebody or make him powerful, you shoot up at him. This comes from childhood, looking up. You can never look up at somebody and make him funny ... the two most normal positions for the camera are sitting down or standing up. Variations from them must be thoughtful. They must have a purpose — otherwise the camera is hamming, substituting virtuosity for perception ... Often you see people moving the camera around indiscriminately. But I only move the camera up on you if you're fascinating me, if I want to see what you're thinking."

Cast and crew moved to France for studio interiors and a few exteriors, but shooting was held up by Flynn's fall on the stairs and Greco's blood ailment.

Zanuck explained to Cynthia Grencer, "Juliette's got low blood pressure, developed out there from all the heat. Doctors say she'll be all right in time, but it's a long process building up blood pressure. She's got to rest a lot."

The producer also pointed out the difficulty of building a town in the jungle. "This," he told Grencer not unsadly, "will be the year's most expensive production with the exception of *Ben Hur.*" The final cost of the film turned out to be slightly under $4,500,000.

As production drew to an end, Huston said, "I still don't want to work with a producer again, but if I had to, I'd certainly choose Darryl. He's been very good, co-operative and decent throughout."

In one of the final shots, Forsythe is shot and Minna shouts in anger, "You killed him" and attacks a native soldier. In the first take, Greco, recently up from a hospital bed, worked up such a rage in her attack that she knocked the actor playing the soldier out of camera range. Huston calmly called for another take, but one of the actors grinned this time and the director calmly informed Greco that the scene had to be done again. Zanuck asked Huston if all this might not be too tiring for her. Huston calmly called for another take.

This continued for four takes, with Greco as furiously attacking the actor each time as she had the first. Grencer said that she did so "with inexhaustible energy and enthusiasm, as if she were working off an enormous quantity of pent-up aggression." It is not unlikely that the object of the aggression was the ever-tranquil and healthy Huston.

With only a few more shots remaining, Huston said, "It's always a little odd, the last days of a film. The work's really all done: all behind you. There's just a few loose ends to be tied off. Every film is a kind of world. You're very close with people who, at the end of the film, you may never see again in your life. The end of a film is something like the end of the world."

The Roots of Heaven is yet another example of Huston's exploration of an apparently doomed quest by a group of vastly different people led by a man obsessed. In spite of the odds, the group persists in its mission and some of its members die. As in many Huston films, the quest is not a total failure; there is the likelihood of continuation, if not success, but the price that must be paid is high in human lives.

Morel's crusade is clearly seen as a religious obsession. His followers are disciples, elevated by the righteousness of his cause and ready to follow him to their deaths. The setting and the framework give Huston ample opportunity to make use of the colorful and the Biblical, which he had always found so attractive.

In answer to the question "What are the roots of heaven?" one of Morel's followers responds, "They're the oceans, the forests, the races of animals, mankind. Poison heaven at its roots and the tree will wither and die. The stars will go out and heaven will be destroyed." But the director does not seem to be as interested in the morality of the Old or New Testaments as in the stylized presentation of dialogue and the kind of mythic figures against the sky that such dialogue evokes.

Reviews varied. Some called the picture "excellent" and "artistically fine and spiritually exuberant"; others said it was "a disappointment" and "an interesting but curiously unconvincing picture."

Huston told reporter Brian St. Pierre in 1966: "I am completely responsible for the badness of *The Roots of Heaven*. I really wanted to make it, and Darryl Zanuck got me everything I wanted. But I had the screenplay done by someone who had never done one before, and it was bad. By then the cast, crew and me were in Africa; it was too late to turn back." There were "problems of foolish haste, rushing slap-dash into production before it was ready. There were depths to the story that were never, never touched," he told the Los Angeles *Times* in 1969.

When the film was released in September 1958, Huston's agent Paul Kohner announced in New York City that the director would make five pictures for Elliot Hyman's Seven Arts Production, a subsidiary of United Artists.

Huston outlined two of the projects. The first would be a film on Sigmund Freud. At this point, Huston believed that he would cover only the three-month period in Freud's life during which he met the man who most influenced him, Jean Martin Charcot, a specialist in hysteria. This project might be followed by a pet idea of Huston's, a film about Montezuma and Cortez. But, he pointed out, such a production "would cost so many millions that it would finish my credit."

"Montezuma," he explained, would deal with "the conquest by Cortez of Mexico and the passing of what was a superior culture. That will be the hard-ticket show to end all hard-ticket shows."

The film on Freud would eventually be made, but the Montezuma project is still in the director's head.

In a 1956 interview with Edouard Laurot in *Film Culture*, Huston had said that "Westerns have become a noble convention; they tell the same kind of story in the same way and there is no reason to change this approach. From time to time, people say to me, 'We'd like to see you make a Western.' If I ever made a Western, I'd make the same kind of Western. I don't want to put my brand on the Western; it has its adequate style already."

Late in 1958, Huston signed a contract to direct a Western for the production company of Hecht-Hill-Lancaster, whose first big hit had been the Academy Award–winning *Marty*. The film would star Burt Lancaster and be based on the novel *The Unforgiven* by Alan LeMay.

Huston and Ben Maddow, with whom he had written *The Asphalt Jungle*, began the adaptation. To save money, the film, set in the western United States in the late 1860s, would be shot near Durango, in Mexico, a country that Huston knew well and felt happy working in.

In an interview with the Hollywood *Citizen-News* in 1959, Huston announced, "In *The Unforgiven* . . . the gross salary of any of the stars — Audrey Hepburn, Tony Curtis, Burt Lancaster — is more than the entire cost of *The Maltese Falcon,* which was made for less than $300,000." Curtis would drop out of this cast and be replaced by Audie Murphy, but the cost of the film would not drop. It would eventually hit more than $5,000,000, making the project the most expensive Huston had done to that point in his career.

There were a number of reasons for the expense. One involved a long delay that occurred when Audrey Hepburn was injured falling from a horse — a recurrent danger in Huston films because of the director's insistence upon using horses — and had to be hospitalized with a bad back.

Another major expense was the house that had to be constructed. There are only two apparently simple houses in the film, one in which the Zachary family (Lancaster, Hepburn, Murphy, Lillian Gish, and Doug McClure) live and the other in which the Rawlins family (Charles Bickford, Albert Salmi, June Walker, Kipp Hamilton, and Arnold Merritt) live. The Zachary house, however, proved to be one of the most expensive sets Huston ever had made. Built against a fake mountain that itself had to be constructed, the house was made in specially fitted sections so it could be taken apart easily for shots at various positions. It was a marvel of engineering, supervised by art director Stephen Grimes.

"The house," said Huston, "was almost as ingenious as the whales built for *Moby Dick*. It served as a studio as well as our main set because we did our film cutting right there, in the back of the house under the artificial hill."

After each day of shooting, the color film would be flown to England for processing and then flown back to be viewed by Huston.

In the finished film, which runs over two and a half hours in its uncut form, the Zachary family, led by the eldest brother, Ben (Lancaster), is in partnership with the Rawlins family in cattle ranching. The Zachary father had been killed in a Kiowa attack and the Zacharys — particularly Cash (Murphy) — bear a deep hatred for the Indians.

A mysterious figure, Kelsey (Joseph Wiseman), dressed in a Union uniform arrives one day and tells the Indians and then the Rawlins family that Rachel Zachary (Hepburn) is really a full-blooded Kiowa. The Zacharys admit that she is a foundling but deny she is Indian.

When the oldest Rawlins boy, Charlie (Albert Salmi), is killed by the Kiowa after he courts Rachel, Kelsey is brought in to be hanged for helping the Indians. He again insists that Rachel is an Indian and that he had been with the dead Zachary father when the child was found. The Zacharys deny this and refuse to allow Rachel to be examined. Zeb Rawlins (Bickford) renounces his partnership and sends the Zachary family off alone to fight the Kiowas, who have vowed to take Rachel. The Zacharys find an Indian message indicating Kelsey's story is true. Mattilda (Gish) admits the truth, and Cash denounces Rachel and leaves.

The Zacharys then fight the Indians through the night. Mattilda is killed and Andy (McClure) wounded. Cash returns to help at the last minute, and Rachel kills her own brother, the Indian who has led the war party to get her. Ben announces his plan to marry Rachel and the film ends.

The similarity to Huston's other films can be seen in the search for a truth hidden in the past, a truth that reveals someone has been posing as something he or she is not. This recurrent Huston theme was to be developed even more explicitly in *Freud* and *The List of Adrian Messenger.*

Again, a small group must stand alone against great odds and risk their lives for a goal or principle, for the first time in a Huston film a principle that involves a group of people held together by racial prejudice.

The film is filled with Biblical dialogue and Old Testament references. "The Lord sayeth, be fruitful and multiply," says the patriarchal Zeb. This verselike Biblical prose was to be used even more in Huston's only other Western, *The Life and Times of Judge Roy Bean.*

There is a strange undercurrent of mysticism in the film. Cash, for example, has special powers and is able to sense the presence of Indians. During the siege of the family house, when he is ten miles away, he tells the Rawlins' daughter (Walker) exactly what is happening. Kelsey appears as a prophet out of the mist to forecast doom just as Elijah (Royal Dano) in *Moby Dick* did before the voyage, but still the characters move forward, committed to their path.

While the film does adhere to conventions of the Western in many ways, it also introduces some rather bizarre touches. The ghostly presentation of Kelsey throughout the film is one example, but the use of the piano may be even more striking.

Ben brings a piano back home from Wichita so that Mattilda can play Mozart. When the Indians play their war flutes — not drums — in the night during the seige, Ben moves the piano outdoors and his mother counters with light classics. The image is surreal and followed by an equally strange sequence in which six Indians are killed in a frenzied attack on the piano.

Unfortunately, while reviews were mostly good, *The Unforgiven* was not popular with audiences.

At this point, Huston had made three films away from his home in Ireland and had thoughts about heading back there to work on his Freud project, but he was to be delayed for almost two more years by a film that took him back to the United States.

CHAPTER 15

The Fit and the Misfit

IN 1958, when John Huston was in Paris shooting the last scenes of *The Roots of Heaven,* playwright Arthur Miller sent him a script to read. In 1957 Miller had written a novelette about contemporary cowboys who round up wild horses for dog food. The story, published in *Esquire,* had been written as a result of Miller's 1956 experiences in Nevada while waiting for a divorce from his first wife. He wrote the tale of three cowboys who capture the misfit horses after briefly staying with a trio of cowboys who did just that for a living.

Shortly after the story appeared, Miller married actress Marilyn Monroe. When she lost a baby at the beginning of the following summer, Miller took his short story and rewrote it as a screenplay, adding a female character, Roslyn, patterned after Monroe, whom he wished to play the role.

That same summer, 1958, Miller read the play to his friend Frank Taylor, editorial director of Dell books. Taylor knew John Huston, his love of horses, and his interest in the kind of group venture that involved the cowboys and the girl. It was then that Taylor and Miller sent the script to Huston in Paris. Huston responded with a one-word telegram: MAGNIFICENT. He followed this with a message stating that he was willing to work on the script and direct the film as soon as possible. Monroe was delighted, since she respected Huston and had always thought her small role in *The Asphalt Jungle* one of her best performances.

Almost immediately, Clark Gable, Montgomery Clift, and Eli Wallach agreed to play the cowboys, and it looked as if the project would soon be on with Taylor as producer.

Huston contacted Elliott Hyman, with whom he had recently

entered into an agreement to do a series of films. Hyman agreed that his company would finance the project.

The film was scheduled to start in the fall of 1959, but a problem arose over the availability of actors. Gable was on a film and Monroe was committed to Twentieth Century-Fox to do *Let's Make Love* with Yves Montand. Nevertheless, Huston, Taylor, and Miller went to Reno late in December 1959 for a day to select possible locations. At first Huston had worked to shoot the film in Mexico, not only because of his familiarity with and affection for the country but for tax purposes. Miller and Taylor, however, held out for Nevada, and Huston eventually agreed.

One of Huston's first acts was to get art director Stephen Grimes, who had worked on *The Unforgiven,* for the new film.

Miller and Huston went to St. Clerans in Ireland to work on the screenplay, expecting to start shooting early in the spring. When delays on *Let's Make Love* postponed *The Misfits'* starting date again, Huston accepted *The Unforgiven* and Gable accepted *It Happened in Naples* with Sophia Loren.

A year later, everyone was available and Huston for the first time in eight years was making a film in the United States. His filmmaking travels had taken him from Africa to Paris to Italy to Ireland to Wales to Madeira to London to Tobago to Japan to Africa and Paris again and to Mexico. His last stint in the United States had been on *The Red Badge of Courage.*

Shooting on *The Misfits* began in July of 1960. Huston, Miller, and Taylor agreed that the film would be shot sequentially and chronologically. This meant that the script would be followed through from page one to the last page. This was and continues to be the exception in filmmaking. For financial reasons, almost all films are shot out of order so that all scenes in a particular location or on a particular set will be shot on the same day or days to cut the costs of keeping sets standing or moving valuable equipment around. In addition, most actors are paid according to how many weeks or days they work on a film. Therefore, an expensive actor's scenes are usually shot as close together as possible to keep the cost of his time down.

In addition to shooting the film sequentially, Huston, Miller, and Taylor decided to shoot it in black and white. At a final cost of $4,000,000, it would prove to be one of the most expensive black and white films ever made.

The trio gathered in Reno with a crew of more than 200, including three airplane pilots, ten cowboys, and a rodeo clown.

One early sequence required a brief appearance by a drunk. An actor named Freddy Parker, who could play a drunk perfectly, was found, but as soon as shooting started, he froze. Huston solved the problem by actually getting Parker drunk and filming the scene.

For his first appearance in the film Gable arrived fit and ready. He had lost thirty-five pounds for his role of Gay Langland, the aging cowboy. The film was strenuous and there was some question about how the loss of weight and heavy activity would affect the fifty-nine-year-old actor. In the first scene, Gay was to say goodby to a woman boarding a train. Gable suggested that a New York socialite friend of Huston's, Marietta Tree, would be fine for the role. The director agreed and the scene went without a problem.

Huston's enthusiasm was high. He told James Goode, who would eventually write a book on the making of *The Misfits,* that he had agreed to do the film because "It is about people who sell their work but won't sell themselves. Anybody who holds out is a misfit. If he loses, he is a failure, and if he is successful, he is rare. This movie is about a world in change. There was meaning in our lives before World War II, but we have lost meaning now. Now the cowboys ride pickup trucks and a rodeo rider is an actor of sorts. Once they sold the wild horses for children's ponies. And now for dog food. This is a dog-eat-horse-society."

Huston also explained that he no longer used drawings for each setup as he had done before. Now, he said, he knew each scene automatically. "I court accident," he told Goode. "I try to keep actors spontaneous. I like very much going into a little room. It has its own requirements. Confronted with limitations, thinking is less prosaic."

On his first free Sunday in July, the fifty-three-year-old director played tennis for six hours after having spent the night without sleep, gambling at dice tables in the Mapes Casino in Reno and Harrah's in Lake Tahoe. Throughout shooting, Huston would spend his nights betting and go straight from the dice tables to the set in the morning. Eventually, the director would lose $50,000 gambling while making the film — one sixth of his salary.

Before the first month of shooting had ended, problems began to arise with Marilyn Monroe. She was frequently indisposed, refused to work more than a few hours a day, and would start only in the afternoon.

Eli Wallach enjoyed working with Huston. The director, he said, "elicits a performance, gives you clues, suggests, doesn't stomp on it, draws it out of you. He's very amenable to suggestions. I feel it. It's up to him to orchestrate it."

One time, as a joke, Wallach made himself up as Sigmund Freud for a photograph to be put on an album that would be given to Huston on his birthday. The film about Freud was definitely to be the director's next project.

On August 5, thirty-five days into shooting, a surprise birthday party was held for Huston at Reno's Mapes Hotel. Among those attending were Count Friedrich Ledebur, who had acted in both *Moby Dick* and *The Roots of Heaven;* jockey Billy Pearson, a constant Huston companion; Burl Ives, who had serenaded Huston in an Irish hospital when he was injured during *Moby Dick;* and the cast of the film. In addition, a bagpipe player was flown in and a ninety-five-year-old Paiute Indian chief went through a tongue-in-cheek ceremony to make Huston a member of the tribe. Comedian Mort Sahl came to perform without charge.

When shooting began the next day, Thelma Ritter immediately announced that she liked doing the picture chronologically. The veteran actress indicated that she found it difficult to come on a picture cold and not only play a scene with an actor whom she may never have met but establish her character and her relationship to the actor for the rest of the shooting under hot lights with a crew of forty looking on. "I think," she said, "that pictures require more concentration than anyone would think possible. More than a play."

With another week of shooting behind him, Huston spent one day off in Auburn, California, waiting for Ledebur to finish a 100-mile horse race that ended in the town. Ledebur finished last. Huston made the journey with Pearson and several others, including Gladys Hill.

By the middle of August, Miller and Huston had decided to use real wild horses and not tame ones for the film. The decision would result in some convincing footage and a number of injuries for the cast and cowboys.

For the rodeo sequence, Montgomery Clift actually had to mount a bucking horse. His shirt was torn and he took a few good bumps even though a cowboy double was used for the actual riding. The rodeo scenes were shot in Dayton, Nevada, where the crew had to construct an entire rodeo set, including grandstands and chutes.

Throughout the shooting it was clear that Miller admired Huston's ability as a director, though on a number of issues the two had strong disagreements. According to the writer, Huston "sees the geometry of the shot, which is important. He understands the magnification of the camera. I'm more interested in the interpretation of lines. I would tend to neglect the visual elements more. John relies on the actor. I'd rather have it this way."

By the end of August, delays began piling up, primarily because of the reported emotional illnesses of Marilyn Monroe. She entered Westside Hospital in Los Angeles and shooting was suspended. This was the second film in a row for Huston in which shooting was delayed significantly because of injury to or the illnesses of his leading lady.

At the same time, rumors were flying that Monroe's indisposition was a result of her supposed love for Yves Montand, and Miller was kept busy hiding from the press. By the time *The Misfits* was to finish shooting, the Miller-Monroe marriage had ended.

To amuse himself while waiting for shooting to resume, Huston entered a camel race with Billy Pearson. The Labor Day event was held in Virginia City, Nevada, and had only three riders, Huston, Pearson, and a local man. Huston's camel had never been ridden, but Pearson's ran off the road and Huston won the race. He announced afterward in a radio interview, "I owe my splendid victory to a deep understanding of the camel. You're really living when you're up there between those humps. It has its ups and downs, but so has life."

One of the downs continued to be the schedule of *The Misfits.* By the middle of September, when shooting was supposed to be over, more than one fourth of the film had not been completed.

Huston spent some of the delay time discussing the Freud script with his agent, Paul Kohner, and producer Wolfgang Reinhardt in California. He also checked with Monroe's physician to try to find out when she might be available, if at all. According to Fred Lawrence Guiles in *Norma Jean: The Life of Marilyn Monroe,* Huston was informed that Monroe had been taking an unusually large number of Nembutals. Huston assured Guiles that the company doctor had refused to give her such pills but that she had found a doctor who would.

While waiting for Monroe to recuperate, Huston spent much of his time reading a script a day in the hope of finding future projects. He also pursued Aaron Copland to write the music for *The Misfits,* but Frank Taylor was forced to veto the idea when Copland wanted $55,000 for about a half-hour of music. It was agreed, instead, that Alex North, who had composed the music for the film version of Miller's *Death of a Salesman,* would do *The Misfits.*

Late in September, after treatment by a psychiatrist, Monroe returned and was welcomed heartily by Huston and the crew. She said that she expected to finish *The Misfits* without further delay and added that the project was decidedly easier than her previous film, *Let's Make Love.* She nonetheless continued to show up late for shooting.

Expenses were growing. Gable's salary was $750,000 for the film, with overtime of $48,000 a week beyond the regular schedule. Monroe's salary for the picture was a straight $300,000, the same as Huston's.

By early October, Huston had bronchitis and was feuding with Miller over the script and the development of Guido, the character played by Wallach. Huston wanted a scene explaining Guido's motives, feeling that he was too mysterious in his actions.

Even the usually calm Gable began to grow impatient with the many delays. The pace of the film was taking a lot out of him, and he had the right by contract to veto any script changes from the version he had approved. Instead, he acted as a mediator between director and author. "If I hadn't liked this story," he told Goode, "I wouldn't have done it no matter how much money they offered me. I have to like the story or I won't do it. I'm doing what I like to do."

The most difficult physical scenes for Gable were near the end. In one sequence, he had to fight with the horses, and Huston called for him to be dragged 400 feet at about thirty-five miles an hour.

While Huston shot the final scene, an exhausted Arthur Miller fell asleep. He had been on the project for three years and on location on and off for three months.

Following a birthday party for Miller and Clift, Huston headed for Los Angeles to work on the sound and editing. Early in November, Gable called him to announce that he was about to become a father for the first time. The day after he called Huston, Gable suffered a heart attack. Eleven days later he was dead.

In *The Misfits,* Gay Langland utters one of the many prophetic lines of the film, considering the tragedies surrounding it. "We've all got to go sometime, dying's as natural as living. A man who's afraid to die is afraid to live."

It wasn't until January 1961 that Huston had a final print of the film ready.

"I think Clark is great in it," he told Bob Thomas. "Our first desire was to get the picture out in time for the Academy Awards because I felt sure he'd be nominated. It would have been nice to have it happen while his memory was still fresh. But the picture would have suffered if we had hurried that much. So next year he can be nominated." Gable never did receive the nomination.

Huston also said that just before he died, Gable had agreed to appear in *The Man Who Would Be King,* which was being planned again. "I had known Clark for a number of years but never very well," he told Bob Thomas. "I had the impression of him as having a kind of lethargy. I discovered in working with him that this was only a façade. Underneath he was very earnest, even eager to please. Whenever he had a call, he was always on the set a half-hour early, always ready with his lines. Only once did he ever blow up."

The blowup, Huston explained, was the result of Gable's being asked to remain for a rehearsal while his wife, believing she might be pregnant, went to see an obstetrician in California. When Gable discovered that there was to be no rehearsal and he could have been with his wife, he became furious.

Huston announced that in spite of the publicity about Marilyn Monroe, he would be willing to work with her again. "When people talk about her," he said, "they are generally talking about themselves. They don't really know her."

Not only did Gable die, but within months Clift was in an automobile accident and suffered injuries that would eventually take his life. In a few years, both Monroe and Thelma Ritter would also be dead.

Monroe died in 1962. Thirteen years later, Huston said to Rosemary Lord, "It disturbs me a little, seeing all the birds lighting on the body and just exploiting a tragic memory. She was a good-hearted girl."

It is ironic that of all Huston's films to this point, *The Misfits* is the only one in which no one is killed.

During the filming, Arthur Miller told a reporter that his cowboys were not Hemingway heroes. Huston had clearly made the film his own as much as Miller's in this respect. It is ultimately more like Hemingway than Miller might admit and more like Huston than Miller may have realized.

Again there is the group on a sad and fruitless quest. This time they are searching for horses. But they find far fewer than they had expected. The expedition becomes a bust and the trio of friends are at odds over a woman, Roslyn, who opposes their quest and the killing and capturing of the horses.

With the exception of Guido, the characters represent the least masked or disguised group in Huston's films. Perhaps it is this very element of never-penetrated disguise in Guido that upset Huston about the character and drove him to push for a motivation scene, an emotional unmasking.

Certainly all three men face death without fear, as Huston heroes usually do. It is specifically a point of honor in the case of Perce (Clift) that he risk his life in rodeos. It is also explicit that he is very frustrated over his alienation from his mother. In one scene early in the film, Perce calls his mother while the others wait outside the phone booth. He is clearly upset over the presence at the other end of his stepfather, over his belief that his mother has somehow betrayed him, and the memory of his natural father. After talking to her, the injured Perce immediately sets out to join the rodeo.

The introduction of Roslyn presents the interesting confrontation of a Miller character — emotional, vulnerable, full of feeling and sympathy that she is willing to show — with a Huston character, Gay, who is fiercely independent and overtly self-sufficient.

The scene in the film that shows this tension between author and director was one that drew applause from the veteran crew when it was shot: Gay is drunk and misses a meeting in a bar with his two children. He runs out into the street crying and calling their names while Roslyn tries to comfort him and cowboys watch. He stumbles against a car and weeps. The Huston hero breaks. His self-sufficiency and independence break down when weakened by alcohol and, for the moment, he proves to be as vulnerable as the highly unstable Roslyn. But Gay pulls himself together, accepts what he has done, and makes it clear that he is not ashamed and does not wish to live with sadness and guilt.

The end is a compromise. In a truck alone, Gay states that he is not going to change but acknowledges that he wants Roslyn and is willing to respect her attitude toward life and death if she will try to respect his. It is a strange pair that heads for home following a star in the sky, for compromise is not within either.

Critical response varied and though the film was relatively popular, it did not approach the box-office success Huston had hoped for.

CHAPTER 16

Freud and the Foxes

HUSTON AND CHARLES KAUFMAN, who had written the director's postwar documentary about mental rehabilitation, *Let There Be Light,* had for a long time had the idea of some day doing a film about Sigmund Freud. Kaufman had tried for years to get studios to move ahead on a biography, but Freud's children had strongly opposed any film about their father.

Gradually, however, Huston and Kaufman came to the conclusion that the psychiatrist was a public figure and, as such, his heirs could not prevent a depiction of him unless it proved libelous. Freud had already appeared as a key character in plays and a number of fantasized histories. Fictionalization of Freud would go to an extreme, perhaps, when in 1975 Nicholas Meyer wrote *The Seven Per-Cent Solution* in which Freud undertakes a cure of the drug-addicted Sherlock Holmes.

By 1959 Kaufman and Wolfgang Reinhardt had written a screenplay about Freud, but Huston contacted Jean Paul Sartre to prepare a new one. "He wrote a 450-page script," recalls Huston. "Then he revised the first version into another script twice as long as the first. It would have been a ten-hour movie."

Huston finally settled on the Kaufman and Reinhardt version but told Gene Phillips that the final script still contained "the strongest of his [Sartre's] ideas and is still very much his script."

Because of his good working relationship with Montgomery Clift on *The Misfits,* Huston selected him to play the role of Freud. For the second lead, Dr. Joseph Breuer, Huston chose Larry Parks. Parks had gained sudden and great fame a dozen years earlier as the star of *The Jolson Story* and *Jolson Sings Again,* but his troubles with the House Un-American Activities Committee had nearly ruined his career. Huston, as always, remembered those whom he had helped to defend.

For the role of Cecily, the patient with whom Freud makes his major breakthrough discoveries, Huston selected a relative newcomer, Susannah York.

Almost immediately, the bad luck that had plagued the director on *The Misfits* continued with *Freud*. "The picture," he told Phillips, "was difficult to make. Montgomery Clift was quite ill during shooting. Halfway through he could hardly see because he had developed cataracts on his eyes as a result of damage sustained in an automobile accident. The film was a real ordeal for him."

This is evident in the film. Clift looks pale and in agony, which perfectly suited the role, since Freud, during the period covered in the film — the few years before his thirty-third birthday — was developing his theories and facing the agony of his painful self-analysis.

The film, released by Universal as *Freud: The Secret Passion,* is not an attempt to duplicate scenes from Freud's life exactly. Encounters are presented out of the order in which they took place. Cecily is a composite of several patients Freud treated over a number of years. Events are presented as having happened more closely together than was the case. Huston was less concerned with being true to the details of Freud's life than with presenting an aspect of the life of the first psychiatrist dramatically as a kind of detective story in which the detective discovers not a killer but the source of the guilt that cripples millions of victims.

After having made six films experimenting in color, Huston had turned to black and white for *The Misfits* and stuck with the absence of color for *Freud*. "I would never have made *Moulin Rouge* in black-and-white," he said. "And I would never have made *Freud* in color. There was a certain projection of a unilateral thought, the development of logic. Color would only have distracted."

In avoiding distraction, Huston created one of his most unusual films. The percentage of close-ups is greater than in any other Huston film and almost any commercial narrative. The viewer is assaulted by huge faces: Freud's, Breuer's, their patients'. Backgrounds, when they are seen, are clearly symbolic, in keeping, surely, with the subject matter. For example, when two characters are shown, one inevitably Freud, there is frequently in view some object of the buried past that neither person refers to. When Freud lectures to disbelieving colleagues at the medical school, behind him there is a skeleton in view, the only other object in the frame. When Freud meets Von Schlosser (David McCallum), a patient, there is a dummy in his room with the tunic of Von Schlosser's father on it. It is Von Schlosser's hatred for his father that has caused him to be considered mad. Freud's inability to accept the sexuality of Von Schlosser's relationship to his parents results in the psychiatrist denouncing his patient and leaving him to die.

When Cecily is recovering, Freud sits with her mother. The camera is low, revealing between them a huge painting of Cecily's father. It has been the sexuality between the girl and her father that has been the primary cause of her mental condition.

Freud was shot on location in Munich and in Vienna at the Bavaria Studios. It took six months to make and cost $3,000,000.

A scene at the Hôpital de la Salpêtrière in Paris in 1885 proved to be one of the most unusual Huston had ever shot. It was here that Freud had the first revelation that he would later develop into psychoanalysis. In the film, a woman is brought into a hospital room in a wheelchair. Both of her legs are paralyzed. Another patient, a man, is brought in trembling uncontrollably.

To prove that the paralysis and trembling are psychological, Professor Jean Martin Charcot (played by French actor Fernand Ledoux) has the two patients hypnotized. He tells the paralytic to walk and the trembling man to stop trembling. They do. He then transfers their symptoms so that the man cannot walk and the woman trembles. "The hypnotist is not a magician," Charcot announces. "He can understand but he cannot cure."

It is this incident that led to Freud's belief in the unconscious.

The originality of the scene, however, is in the fact that the two patients in the film actually were mental patients with the hysterical symptoms depicted and that they actually were hypnotized for the scene and performed under hypnosis with physicians from their psychiatric hospital on the set.

The scene was so important to Huston that he found a painting of the Charcot experiment by a French painter, Brouillet, that included Freud. Huston duplicated the costumes and look of the people in the painting by choice of actors, make-up, composition, and costumes. He did this not so much to re-create the way the scene had actually looked but to re-create the image of the scene as it had been reported by a fellow artist.

When Huston had finished editing the film, it ran two hours and forty-five minutes. "This," he told Gene Phillips, "was the length needed to explain Freud's discovery of infantile sexuality to a movie audience."

Universal cut almost half an hour from the final version. "The audience had no time to relax during the whole running time of the film," said Huston. "It was too much to ask filmgoers to give such close attention to a film for that length of time. All of the cuts made in the film were at the film's expense since vital steps in the continuity and progression of the story were eliminated."

Some of the problems that resulted from the cuts are evident. For example, early in the film Freud's father gives his son a watch when he boards the train to see Charcot. Freud breaks the watch. Clearly, we can expect him to recall the incident later as part of the development of his ideas of the unconscious. In fact, the real Freud made much of the incident in his writing. In the film, it stands as a bizarre and unexplained moment without meaning or significance.

When the film was released, it did poorly at the box office. "In dealing with psychosexual matters so frankly, *Freud* was ahead of its time," Huston told Phillips in partial explanation. "I seem to have a knack for making films that are either a few years ahead of or behind the times, and one is as bad as the other."

As a Huston film, *Freud* has some particular interests: Huston serves as narrator, displaying an omnipotence and almost Biblical detachment that establishes Freud as a kind of savior and messiah.

The film opens with Huston's description of Freud as a kind of hero or God on a quest for mankind. "This is the story of Freud's descent," he says in his narration, "into a region as black as hell, man's unconscious, and how he let in the light." The bearded, thin look of the Freud who stands alone denounced before the tribunal of his own people also suggests the Christ parallel; also like Christ, Freud brings a message of possible salvation which is rejected and for which he is reluctantly denounced by his chief defender, Breuer.

Huston continued to be concerned with probing through masks and disguises to the truth that his characters must face with dignity even if it means defeat. Thus does he present Sigmund Freud, who not only has to penetrate the lies and disguises of his patients

— Cecily literally puts on paint to hide the truth — but also go through the same agonizing process in himself. Freud cannot break through to his understanding of the unconscious and infantile sexuality until he faces his own hatred of his father. The act of facing it is physically painful for him, and he literally falls down in a faint when he approaches the cemetery where his father is buried.

Biographical comparisons with Huston are also possibly evident in Freud, who fears that his mother will abandon him. Freud has a father whom he loves and who gives him things he finds difficult to accept. When the father dies, Freud feels guilt and a need to understand.

Reviews of the film were very good, but the public did not respond to the film.

Almost immediately, Huston agreed to do another project for Universal, a film version of *The List of Adrian Messenger,* a mystery dealing with the adventures of Anthony Gethryn, a character the author, Phillip MacDonald, had used in his previous work. One critic has commented that "after the intellectual rigors of *Freud,* John Huston must have enjoyed relaxing with this genial thriller."

He may, indeed, have relaxed while making it, but what may be the least critically regarded of Huston's films can be seen as one of two or three he has made that are the most personal and meaningful in his career. *Freud* had been an important project for Huston, and surely the disappointment of its financial failure may have led him to what appears to be the "fun" of *The List of Adrian Messenger.*

Huston's first act was to get frequent collaborator Anthony Veiller to work with him on the screenplay. After finishing the script in Ireland, Huston chose locations nearby and in London.

"I felt that it was absolutely necessary to shoot some parts of *The List of Adrian Messenger* in London and Ireland," he wrote in a 1963 article in *The Screen Producer's Guild Journal,* "but the major part of the picture was filmed on the stages at Universal. It was the first time in six years that I found myself shooting in a Hollywood studio and, I was, quite frankly, very glad to get back."

There were two stars in the film. Kirk Douglas, whose company, Joel, was producing the film for Universal, played the mass murderer George Brougham, and George C. Scott played the aristocratic detective Gethryn. Clive Brook played the Marquis of Gleneyre and, in his screen debut, thirteen-year-old Walter Anthony Huston played

Derek, grandson of the Marquis and the intended victim in the murder scheme.

In addition to the regular cast and a cameo by John Huston, Tony Curtis, Burt Lancaster, Robert Mitchum, and Frank Sinatra appear in disguise. Part of the film's publicity campaign involved trying to identify the guest stars and Douglas, who also dons numerous disguises. Each disguise was created using a new process involving an artificial skin and took Bud Westmore and his crew more than four hours of make-up time per actor each day of shooting.

In the film George takes years to kill off the men he had betrayed in a Burmese prison camp during World War II. Having worked out a plan to inherit the estate of his uncle, the Marquis, George wears various masks while systematically killing all of these men, including Adrian Messenger, who could call him traitor and thus jeopardize his inheritance. In the process, he also kills more than 130 others. Messenger dies in a plane George bombs, but he manages to leave a clue with a survivor, LeBorg (Jacques Roux). Gethryn and LeBorg begin to put pieces of the puzzle together, though they remain a step behind George, who, in disguise, finishes off the remaining member of the Burma campaign.

LeBorg, meanwhile, falls in love with Lady Jocelyn (Dana Wynter), Derek's mother and Adrian Messenger's cousin. The Marquis and Derek are ardent fox hunters, as is Gethryn to a lesser degree. With all his victims behind him, George appears at a family fox hunt undisguised. He proves to be an excellent horseman and charms the Marquis, Derek, and Jocelyn.

Gethryn, however, knows that George must kill Derek and then wait for the Marquis to die, so he tells George that he has a clue indicating that Messenger was murdered, knowing that George will have to make an attempt on his life. George makes an excuse not to join the next fox hunt and sets a trap to kill the detective. Gethryn anticipates the trap and in an open field lets his trained bloodhound point out his would-be killer, who is disguised as a farmer. To escape, George jumps on the gypsy horse Adrian Messenger had given Derek, but the boy calls out the Gypsy word that stops the horse, and the murderer tumbles into the machine on which Gethryn was supposed to die. With his last breath, George rips off his final disguise. The film ends with the foxes barking and the Marquis reminding us that the Brougham foxes always bark when a member of the family dies.

When "The End" title appears, Kirk Douglas' voice says, "Hold it. That's the end of our picture, but not the end of our mystery." The guest stars then appear and remove their disguises, revealing themselves with a characteristic gesture and a smile. Douglas appears in all of the disguises he has worn throughout the film and faces the audience to remove the first disguise he had worn. This marks the third time in the film Douglas is shown removing the complex make-up.

There are several major changes from book to film. Gethryn is a composite of two characters from the novel. In the book, he is married and never has been in love with Jocelyn. In the film, Gethryn quite clearly says he has been in love with her. In the book, Jocelyn is a big blonde who is compared to an Amazon. In the film, she is small, delicate, and dark, typical of Huston's women, who tend to be fragile and to need male protection. In the book, George Brougham has a giveaway tic that always makes his presence known to the observer regardless of his disguise. Huston characteristically keeps the disguise total until the final revelation. In the novel, the Marquis is killed and his widow, a strong-willed creature who does not exist in the film, appears. The novel ends in the United States and not on a fox hunt. In fact, the metaphor of the chase illustrated by the fox hunt is almost nonexistent in the novel.

In the film, two elements are constantly intertwined and related: first, the Victorian detective story, and second, the metaphor of the fox hunt, Huston's passion. The film constantly draws the parallel between the hunt for the fox and the hunt for the man. In the opening, Derek says, "Damn good hunt," which is exactly what we see on both levels of the film.

The Marquis then complains about fox hunting in America, saying, "They follow a drag." "What," says Derek "is a drag?" "An abomination," replies the grandfather.

A drag is the practice of putting the fox in a bag and dragging it so the dogs will follow the scent wherever the dragster wishes. It is unsporting. It is also what George, the Canadian, does symbolically, by creating a false trail as a murderer, and what he does literally in the climax of the film to kill Gethryn. He does not play according to the rules of the hunt. "Sham," announces the Marquis in the first scene. And that is exactly what George is.

Gethryn picks up the metaphor in his pursuit of George, whom he sees as a fox. "Can't have our fox going to ground," he tells one subordinate even before he knows whom he is pursuing.

When the Marquis first meets George, he uses the metaphor to greet him, though he doesn't know about any of the killing. "Are you," says the old man, "my brother's whelp?"

When a woman protesting the inhumanity of the hunt stops the Marquis, he coolly explains, "Madame, it is man's nature to hunt foxes, foxes' nature to be hunted." It is a natural state, a superior state, this facing and playing with death.

Of all Huston's films, *The List of Adrian Messenger* is the one that deals most literally with people in disguise. George, who describes himself as unexcused evil, hides behind a romantic or heroic mask that falls away when he is forced to face the detective, who functions very much like Freud. The detective penetrates the masks, revealing the evil, and the evil is destroyed.

The entire film is constructed as an elaborate play of false fronts and masks, games played with identity: Robert Mitchum plays a man disguised as his own crippled brother. Tony Curtis plays a policeman disguised as an organ grinder.

It is both ironic and fitting that Scott as Gethryn should trap George with his own trick of disguise, pretending to be a simple-minded fellow who has stumbled on a clue.

The film includes further puzzles within puzzles, each reflecting Huston's view of a world of disguise to be penetrated.

Gethryn recognizes LeBorg as a French resistance fighter he had known during the war. The code names, indicated casually in the film, were Ajax (LeBorg) and Polidor (Gethryn). Ajax was a hero of the Trojan War who drowned at sea. LeBorg had been rescued from the sea and, we are told, is a powerful, direct man, though ironically, the plane crash keeps him incapacitated throughout the film. Polidor was the patron divinity of sailors. In another mythic reference, we are told that the horse Messenger has left for Derek is named Avatar, the Hindu mythic name for a diety who descends to earth in the form of a man or animal to right wrongs. It is the horse Avatar who kills George.

LeBorg, the character who wins Jocelyn, is shown without disguise, direct in his proposals and revelations as George is not.

It is tempting to see biographical elements in the film. George, the villain, is, like Walter Huston, a Canadian and an actor who left home to tour on the stage. He is, also, like Walter, charming and presented as a consummate actor, but, unlike Walter, he is evil.

The Marquis' family bears a possible fantasy resemblance to Huston's family. The grandfather is an aristocratic fox hunter, surely an ideal ancestral parent for Huston. The grandson, Huston's own son, respects the memory of his father, who we are told was a World War II hero.

In one sense, the conflict is between the wild American side of the family and the sophisticated Old World side. For Huston, clearly the Old World side of the past survives and triumphs.

Huston's own appearance on horseback in the film is a kind of disguise that supports this idea. As Lord Ashton, he rides up after the attempt on Gethryn's life and says, "We've been following a drag, at Gleneyre. Unheard of . . ."

The appearance is both comic and possibly unconsciously meaningful, considering Huston's move to Ireland and aristocratic interests. As an aristocrat on horseback, he denounces the drag, the American tradition, and asks the reigning aristocrat for an explanation.

In a 1969 article in *Sight and Sound,* critic John Russell Taylor indicated that Huston's film may well have been unappreciated critically when it appeared. "In *The List of Adrian Messenger, "* he wrote, "now that we come to look at it again on television, it is evident that the digressions are the essential; the whole thing is a series of enigma variations on the theme of disguise, both within the film's proper context and beyond."

When the black and white film was released in 1963, it did well financially. However, the reviews were mixed.

Before the reviews were in, however, Huston took a plunge that altered his future professional course. At the age of fifty-seven, he accepted his first major acting role in a film. The result was to lead the director into a career that has come close to equaling his identity as a director.

CHAPTER 17

Actor

IN 1962, while John Huston was well into shooting *The List of Adrian Messenger,* director Otto Preminger began selecting his cast for *The Cardinal.*

During a casting discussion, Preminger's brother Ingo, the producer, suggested that Huston might be a good choice to play Cardinal Glennon, Bishop of Boston. Otto, who had known Huston in the theater and had produced the Huston-Koch play *In Time to Come* on Broadway in 1941, did not seriously consider the suggestion at first. Huston had never had a major film role and had not acted on stage for twenty years. Gradually, however, Preminger, who had frequently acted in movies by other directors, began to think of Huston in the part and decided to call him. Huston's fee was not cash but a painting by de Stael that he admired and wanted to add to his growing art collection in Ireland.

"It is very good for the soul of a director, once in a while, to be on the other side of the camera," said Huston when the deal was confirmed. "I've got to be a model actor. I've got to be obedient, or actors will always be throwing up to me how I behaved for Preminger."

Huston was indeed a model actor. At one point, for example, he suggested that he offer another character a cigar. "Never," shouted Preminger. "These are your private cigars. He's too young to smoke anyway." Huston quietly accepted this and other directions from Preminger, even when he had different ideas of how he should move or behave.

Occasionally, he suggested an action or bit of business Preminger liked. For example, he told his director, "If he's lighting a cigar, and he's a real cigar smoker, he'd make a thing out of it. I can do it with great elegance. I need wooden matches and a cutter, a small pen-knife." Preminger agreed and the cigar-lighting bit remained in the film.

Once into the role, Huston enjoyed himself so much that he was reluctant to remove his clerical robes when each day's shooting was finished.

Huston said of his work with Preminger, "Otto is very self-confident. I don't think he has any doubts about himself — that aren't legitimate."

When his role was finished, Huston, Preminger recalled, asked "that his costume [red cardinal's vestments, purchased at a New York ecclesiastical haberdashery] be sent to him, so we sent it. I asked him it he was going to wear it around the house, and he said no, but near his home in Ireland is a small town with a seminary. He wanted to dress up in his robes and walk through the town with everybody wondering who the new cardinal is."

Huston got the robes and announced that he was through with acting. He would, he said, stick to directing. "There was one great actor in my family, my dad, and that's enough," he announced. "I could never top him and I don't want to try."

But he had not anticipated the public and critical reaction to his performance. His acting was singled out in review after review as the highlight of the film.

Huston says, "Otto is the one who is entirely responsible for my acting career. It's all his fault; any complaints about my acting should be referred to him."

Variety wrote that Huston and Raf Vallone stole the picture. "Academy members would be hard put to decide between them for supporting performance honors . . . Seldom has any film been blessed with two such towering giants."

Judith Crist in the New York *Herald Tribune* wrote that "the film's outstanding performer is that outstanding director, John Huston, who brings throbbing vitality and sophistication to the role of Cardinal Glennon."

Bosley Crowther in the *New York Times* wrote: "It is this old boy, played by John Huston, who arrests and fascinates me. He's the one who reveals in just a few scenes toughness, authority, political acumen, compassion, and a fine philosophical turn of mind. In everything he does so adroitly in the brief time he is on the screen, I sense the presence and the essence of a strong administrator of the church."

Time wrote simply, "John Huston, with a ripsnorting vitality, all but steals the show. Huston is superb."

Huston was nominated for an Academy Award as best supporting actor but lost to Melvyn Douglas for *Hud*. Huston's first reaction was that the award nomination was nonsense, but when offers came in to act, he accepted them. He would also, from this point on, frequently make substantial appearances in his own films.

His choice of roles over the years has varied. He seems to like parts that allow him to put on broad disguises. Often the reviewers have been less than kind about his choices. His major roles have included:

— Dr. Dunlap in the 1968 Christian Marquand–directed version of Terry Southern's *Candy*. The film was broad sexual comedy which the reviewers thought in bad taste. Renata Adler wrote in the *Times* that "John Huston and Ringo Starr look as though they had been drawn in by a regrettable, humorless beautiful people syndrome."

— The evil abbé, uncle of the Marquis de Sade, in Cy Endfield's 1969 film, *De Sade*. When he received unfavorable reviews Huston responded, "Delighted to be accused of underplaying. I thought the performance got kind of baroque."

— The lusty ex-cowboy star Buck Loner in the 1970 Michael Sarne version of Gore Vidal's *Myra Breckinridge,* which was considered to be in even worse taste than *Candy*. He was offered the role partly as the result of a telegram he sent to Sarne praising his film *Joanna*.

— General Miles in Burt Kennedy's 1970 film *The Deserter*. Huston's Miles is a soldier who doesn't care for regulations, kicks dogs who get in his way, and turns his back on potential enemies.

— Sleigh, in the first film in which he received top billing, *The Bridge in the Jungle,* directed by Pancho Kohner. This rarely seen 1971 film was based on the novel by B. Traven, author of *The Treasure of the Sierra Madre*. (Huston's other top billing was in the 1977 horror film *Tentacles*.)

— Captain Henry in Richard Sarafian's 1971 release, *Man in the Wilderness*. In perhaps the strangest of his roles, Huston plays a demented trapper who rides around the American wilderness commanding a boat on wheels — clearly the part of Ahab he had missed in his own film. Pauline Kael in *The New Yorker* said it marked Huston "at his most idiosyncratic."

— The Lawgiver, in ape make-up, for Twentieth Century-Fox's *Battle for the Planet of the Apes,* directed by J. Lee Thompson. Huston was the ape who passes on the history of the ape civilization and serves as narrator for the film.

— Noah Cross, the evil manipulator in the cowboy hat in Roman Polanski's 1974 film, *Chinatown.* This is probably Huston's most widely known role. Polanski's version of Noah is the reverse of Huston's presentation of himself as the Biblical Noah in *The Bible.* In the Huston film, Noah is a gentle savior of life during a flood. In *Chinatown,* Noah is a bringer of death during a drought.

— President Teddy Roosevelt's advisor John Hay in the 1975 film, *The Wind and the Lion,* directed by John Milius. This was perhaps Huston's least flamboyant role.

— Robert Duvall's grandfather in the 1975 Tom Gries–directed film, *Breakout.*

— An old Hollywood director whose career is falling apart in Orson Welles's as-yet-to-be-released 1975 film, *The Other Side of the Wind.* After having directed Welles in three films, *Moby Dick, The Roots of Heaven,* and *The Kremlin Letter,* it was a strange experience to be on the other side of the camera. "Orson," he told Charles Champlin, "has all the dialogue on boards where the actors can read it. That's not my way, of course. When I'm directing I expect the actors to be on the set letter-perfect. When *I'm* acting, that's entirely different, naturally. I was having a bit of trouble getting a line and Orson said, 'John, stop torturing yourself; use the boards.' It's against my way of thinking but I learned something from the experience and I'll benefit from it. If I have an actor in trouble, I'll go to the boards."

Huston's other roles have included arch-villain Professor Moriarty in the 1976 made-for-television film *Sherlock Holmes in New York,* in which Roger Moore played Holmes.

Despite their variety, all of Huston's roles have resemblances: The Huston character is usually loud, self-confident, and a fraud or liar. His motives are frequently sinister and selfish. His forte is understated menace as he stands tall and lowers his serious, steady voice. He is invariably a leader, a man accustomed to giving orders and being obeyed, and he enjoys acting his social role as general, doctor, clergyman, or political manipulator.

Huston can also present the potential ridiculousness of this self-confident character, as evidenced not only by *Candy* and *Myra Breckinridge* but also strikingly by Huston's direction of himself as James Bond's boss, M, in *Casino Royale.*

Huston's face is a Mount Rushmore of crags. His smile or frown in close-up implies a vastness of experience. Some faces photograph as if they have depth and levels of meaning, but some of the finest actors are limited by faces that have no such implication. Christopher Plummer, whom Huston was to use in *The Man Who Would Be King,* is a perfect example of an actor whose youthful face showed little experience. Conversely, a face like Clint Eastwood's or Charles Bronson's shows experience.

Huston's roles in the films of other directors, with the exception of *The Cardinal,* are quite different from the way he usually uses himself as an actor in his own films. As we will see, in his own films Huston is most often the voice of reason or truth. In one film, in fact, *The Bible,* he is not only the gentle Noah, but the voice of God as well.

Huston's advice to actors is simple. "Enjoy acting," he says, "Don't take it seriously. It's a cinch, and they pay you damned near as much as you make directing."

CHAPTER 18

Defrocked

TENNESSEE WILLIAMS' play *The Night of the Iguana* opened on Broadway at the Royale Theater in December 1961. The stars were Bette Davis as Maxine, Margaret Leighton as Hannah, and Patrick O'Neal as Reverend Shannon. The play was a somber, bitter drama of a man who has lost his church and ideals and is trapped between two women at an isolated resort in the depths of Mexico. The Reverend's life is further complicated by the appearance of Nazi tourists. Under pressure from the vindictive Maxine, Shannon is driven to his death. The play won the New York Drama Critics Circle award as best play of the 1961–1962 season.

Huston read the play and arranged for Ray Stark and his Seven Arts Company to purchase the film rights using Williams as consultant.

Huston's film turned out to be radically different from the play. He called in Anthony Veiller and together they fashioned a script eliminating the Nazi, turning Shannon into a comic character without eliminating his loneliness and doubt, and altering the character of Maxine so that she became not the source of evil but of salvation. In the Huston-Veiller story, Shannon not only survives but apparently lives happily ever after with the generous Maxine.

Huston and Veiller worked on the script in Puerto Vallarta, a relatively inaccessible town on the west coast of Mexico where part of the film was set. The actual location for shooting was a mountainside near a cove in the Bay of Banderas, about twenty-five minutes by boat from Puerto Vallarta, and the fishing village of Mismaloya. At the mountain location, nicknamed "The Rock," Huston had twenty-five houses constructed for the cast and crew of 106. He also had Stephen Grimes construct a hotel that would serve as the principal set.

Huston so enjoyed working in Puerto Vallarta that he purchased a home there and began dividing his time between Mexico and Ireland.

The project got off to a good start when the bearded Tennessee Williams, from whom Huston expected trouble over script changes, agreed to the revisions after two conferences.

Huston's next task was to assemble a cast. His choices were Richard Burton for the role of Shannon, Ava Gardner for Maxine, and Deborah Kerr for Hannah. Sue Lyon, who had appeared in the title role in Stanley Kubrick's *Lolita,* was added as Charlotte, the fourth lead.

In August 1963, Huston called Ava Gardner in Spain. They had met in the forties when Huston was writing *The Killers* and had gotten along well. Their friendship had continued in Europe. The director flew to Madrid to talk to Gardner about playing Maxine. He had, he said, changed the part and even though Bette Davis was interested, he wanted Ava.

Huston told Charles Higham in 1973, "There was nobody in the world who could play Maxine but Ava. She was and is a fine actress though she thinks she's lousy. I knew she had the random, gallant, wild openness of Maxine along with the other side of Ava, the side which is very close and almost secretive."

When she came to Puerto Vallarta a few days before shooting was to begin, Huston went to see her. Her fears were evident and she talked of backing out. "We had a difficult session," he says.

Richard Burton showed up after finishing *Cleopatra.* With him were Elizabeth Taylor and three children from her previous marriages. Magazine and newspaper reporters created problems by swarming around them throughout the filming.

When Burton and Taylor's plane landed at the Mexico City airport, thousands of people greeted it. Taylor refused to leave the plane and became especially frightened when a stern-looking Mexican in a big sombrero climbed aboard, took her hand, and shouted, "Follow El Indio. You will be safe with me." El Indio held a pistol in one hand and another was clearly visible in his belt.

"Get this bloody maniac off the plane before I kill him," Burton screamed. Crew members jumped the intruder, managed to disarm him, and threw him from the plane.

It turned out, however, that El Indio had been sent by Huston. His real name was Emilio Fernandez, and he was a well-known Mexican film director and actor who was serving as Huston's assistant. Fernandez, best known as the Mexican general in Sam Peckinpah's *The Wild Bunch,* was to appear as a bartender in *The Night of the Iguana.* Fernandez had actually shot several men in moments of passion, including a producer with whom he had quarreled. He and Huston, however, got along just fine.

One of Burton's initial requests was that a bar be built at The Rock. Huston granted his wish and Burton was well supplied with alcohol throughout the shooting, as Taylor was supplied with hamburgers and Gardner with Mexican beer. At one point, Burton was so well supplied that he fell during a scene and cut his thigh, but he insisted on continuing. No matter what the actor did off the set, he was always ready for shooting each day. Since he was playing an alcoholic defrocked priest, Huston had no objection to his drinking and thought it went well with the character.

The third principal, Deborah Kerr, with whom Huston had worked on *Heaven Knows, Mr. Allison,* arrived with her husband, Huston's former collaborator Peter Viertel. Since Viertel's novel *White Hunter, Black Heart* had come out with its slightly veiled and less than flattering portrayal of Huston, the director probably had harbored few loving feelings for the writer, with whom he would now be living in close contact.

Sue Lyon also presented a problem. Her boyfriend, Hampton Francher III, had followed her to Mexico and become a particular irritant. For one thing, he began to give Huston suggestions about directing the picture. For another, he kept dragging Lyon off when she was not in a shot and necking with her furiously within eyeshot of the cast and crew. Finally, Deborah Kerr complained that she found it difficult to do her scenes when she and everyone else could see the couple. Huston agreed and barred Francher from the set.

Despite the location so remote from civilization, Huston was plagued by the outside world. Gardner, for example, brought with her her brother-in-law, two maids, a secretary, and a hairdresser. Francher's wife, from whom he was awaiting a divorce, arrived and caused further pandemonium. Taylor's children were constantly present and Huston occasionally found himself serving as momentary baby sitter, but he didn't mind this in the least. His ability to get along well with animals and children was very much accepted among his friends.

At one point, Huston called Burton, Gardner, Kerr, and Taylor together in the bar and presented each with a gold-plated derringer and five gold bullets, just enough to shoot the five of them.

As was usual in the remote locations and with the difficult shooting that Huston liked, there were accidents. In addition to the injury to Burton's thigh, Taylor required a minor surgical procedure to remove an insect that had entered her foot, cast and crew members suffered from dysentery and food poisoning, Sue Lyon was bitten by a scorpion, a balcony of one of the cottages collapsed with two members of the crew on it. One man was seriously injured and had to be flown to a Los Angeles hospital.

In spite of the agony that the location apparently caused the cast and crew, Huston loved it and began making plans to convert the fishing village to a resort. He even invited architect-designer Buckminster Fuller to visit the site with some ideas for the project.

A near-disaster occurred during one shot when a bus carrying Burton and a group of actors playing tourists nearly went off a narrow road and over a cliff. With the bus balanced on the edge, the actors got out carefully.

Burton was getting a flat $500,000 for the film. Gardner's salary was $400,000, Kerr's $250,000, and Lyon's $75,000. The film's budget was somewhere over $4,000,000. The entire amount, plus the lives of Burton and others, came within a wheel's turn of being lost.

However, Huston, when interviewed by Paul Kennedy of the New York *Times,* said "Offhand I would say it is the easiest picture I have done in years, maybe in all the years. It's almost too easy." Shooting was completed five days ahead of schedule and the director said, "To me it smells good. You get a sense about these things and this one looks really good."

As soon as filming was over, Huston went to Los Angeles to work out business problems and grant an interview to Hedda Hopper. The columnist went to the director's hotel room in the Beverly Hills Hotel and noted that he had a 200-year-old carved mastodon tusk and a pre-Columbian sculpture that he placed on top of the television set so he could watch both set and sculpture at the same time.

"Easiest picture I ever made," he told Hopper. "Everybody adored themselves and one another. A most serene experience."

As for Ava Gardner, Huston declared to Hopper, "She was a revelation. I'd never worked with her before. She couldn't have cared less about her appearance, wore no makeup, her hair was a-tangle. She was completely unself-conscious. I'm lost in admiration for her. At the end of the picture she told me it was the first time she'd ever liked working."

Gardner's biographer Charles Higham had a slightly different view of her participation and reported that she had been upset by the clothes she had to wear and embarrassed about doing one sequence in which she had to swim with two beach boys who were her lovers in the picture. Before the scene, Huston gave her several stiff drinks. Then the gangly director stripped to his shorts and plunged into the water, where he acted out Gardner's role with the two young men. After the drinks had taken effect, Gardner then took Huston's place and did the scene.

Huston's touch was evident in the film in a variety of ways. First, he again took a group of losers and put them together in an isolated location. The protagonist, Shannon, goes on a journey from American pulpit to tourist guide in the heart of Mexico. At the furthest reaches of despair and far from civilization, the quest for meaning ends and the protagonist is forced to face himself.

Huston again uses an animal symbolically, only this time it is not a horse or a whale, but a reptile. The iguana is initially presented as free and repulsive, but gradually he is trapped in the same way that Shannon is. Both must be let free.

Religion is an important theme. The film opens with Burton preaching a sermon to his congregation. It is a startling contrast to Father Mapple's sermon in *Moby Dick*. Shannon is lost, confused. His speech is gibberish, a seminonsense confession about being unable to control his appetites and emotions. It is a confession by a priest whose congregation turns away from him.

Then, as a tour guide, Shannon is pursued by Charlotte. Like other good Huston heroes, including Gay Langland and Sergeant Allison, Shannon wants to demonstrate his strength and independence from the sexuality and emotion a woman represents. Maxine is an earthy, uncomplicated woman. Hannah, on the other hand, lives in a kind of fantasy world. Shannon must choose between the two, both of whom Huston presents as attractive.

This choice between the practical and the fantastic is a constant theme in Huston's life and films. There is also a choice between illusion and reality, a choice Huston finds difficult to make. Religion, when it exists, is seen as part of the fantasy world, a dangerous fantasy that his characters must overcome if they are not to be destroyed or absorbed by it.

Characters throughout Huston films represent the conflict, and resolution is generally in favor of the practical and real. Illusion is viewed as ultimately destructive. This, incidentally, is not a universal truth for all filmmakers. For example, when faced with the same choice, Vincent Minnelli always chooses art and illusion.

Huston's instinct about the film proved to be correct. *The Night of the Iguana* was an instant box-office success. Before its first American run was completed and before there had been any foreign distribution, the film had returned its original investment.

Arthur Knight in *Saturday Review* wrote, "When all performances are so uniformly excellent, however, so uniformly right, the ultimate credit belongs properly to John Huston as the director."

Variety wrote, "This production is rich in talents . . . Direction by John Huston is resourceful and dynamic as he sympathetically weaves together the often-vague and philosophical threads that mark Williams' writing."

What had promised to be the most difficult film of Huston's career in terms of dealing with actors proved to be his easiest. A questionable box-office property based on a highly serious and flowery tragic play had been converted to a romance.

Huston was on top of the world again.

CHAPTER 19

The Bible

IN 1964, after completing *The Night of the Iguana,* John Huston became an Irish citizen. "I shall always feel very close to the United States and I shall always admire it, but," he told AP staff writer Eddy Gilmore in a 1969 interview, "the America I know best and loved best doesn't seem to exist anymore. This, the life over here [Ireland] and the people are more like the America I knew and loved."

"An artist," said Huston, "has the right to live and work anywhere in the world. It is what he creates that counts — not where. I like living in Ireland, for instance, because it offers the kind of recreation and relaxation I've always wanted. For one thing, the hunting there is ideal."

Apparently after a decade of living in Ireland, Huston had no trouble becoming an Irishman. He simply called the office of the Minister of Justice in Ireland and was told to come down and pick up a passport. "An Irish passport," said Huston, "is one of the most valuable. It has no restrictions. With it I can go anywhere, even to Red China if I want to."

Where he wanted to go for his next film turned out to be Italy. While working on *The Night of the Iguana,* Huston received a visit from Dino De Laurentiis. The short, bespectacled producer was a forty-four-year-old brilliant success who had just built the De Laurentiis Studios outside Rome. The studio had four sound stages, including two of the biggest in the world, one of them large enough to house an exact duplicate of the Sistine Chapel for the making of *The Agony and the Ecstasy.* De Laurentiis, son of a Naples spaghetti manufacturer, had produced more than sixty films since he was twenty-one, including *La Strada* and *Barabbas.*

It was while making *Barabbas* that De Laurentiis read the Old Testament for the first time. "In Italy," he explained to Lillian Ross for a 1965 *New Yorker* article, "we learn everything about religion from our priests."

De Laurentiis contacted poet-playright Christopher Fry, who had worked for William Wyler on the script of *Ben Hur* in Italy, to write a screenplay. Fry began work on a project that would turn out to take him several years to complete. Each of the stories of Genesis that he was supposed to convert to a script provided major problems. "What sort of creature, for instance," Fry later wrote in the preface to the 1966 Cardinal edition of *The Bible,* "is the Serpent before he tempted Eve? It was only afterwards, the Bible tells us, that he crawled upon his belly. Should it be played by a real snake, or by an actor-snake?"

Huston would solve the problem by alternating shots of snake and man.

Fry also worried about Cain's wife. "Who was she?" he asked. "Are we to suppose that the years went by until Cain married one of his nieces, or a great-niece, perhaps, who had somehow strayed into the land of Nod on the east of Eden?" The writer decided that such literal questions were unnecessary. "We should," he decided, "think of the characters as poetic figures, or types of the dawn of life, and not be concerned with pseudo-historical biography." Huston clearly agreed. Such questions are not raised in *The Bible.*

Fry further had to wrestle with the problem of which episodes and incidents in the first five books of the Bible to exclude from his script. He decided to omit the incident of Noah's drunkenness and the episode of the daughters of Lot lying with their father after they escaped from the city of Sodom, "at the risk of appearing to be dodging difficulties."

Fry decided to add scenes to the Old Testament. For example, in the journey of Abraham and Isaac to Moriah for the sacrifice, the writer has them pass through the destroyed city of Sodom — an incident that does not occur in the Bible. Fry argued that "it dramatizes the agony of the journey in Abraham's mind."

One of Fry's major problems was in deciding not only what words the characters would speak, since the Bible provides little dialogue, but what language to use. He settled on the dialogue in the King James English version plus his own additional lines in keeping with its spirit. "To those who know it well there must always be a feeling of lack when other words are used," he explained.

De Laurentiis' original idea had been to use separate directors for different stories in the Book of Genesis. French director Robert Bresson would direct the Creation and the Garden of Eden. American Orson Welles would do a section on Abraham and one on Jacob and Esau. Italian Luchino Visconti would do the story of Joseph and his brothers, while Italian Federico Fellini and Huston were to select other sections of Genesis to direct.

"Dino first came to see me in Mexico about my doing only one of the sequences and about the possibility of putting me in artistic charge of the whole picture," Huston told Lillian Ross. At the meeting, the director suggested that all of Genesis was too much to cover. "The picture," he said, "should describe man's emergence from the mists of mythology and legend into the first light of history. To me, that meant starting with the Creation and going on as far as Abraham, the first figure in the Bible of whose existence we have historical proof."

According to De Laurentiis, he talked to Huston "for an hour and it was as though we had been talking about this picture for a year." The producer returned to Italy and within a week offered Huston the job of directing the entire film. Huston accepted.

One of De Laurentiis' first moves was to rent a giant billboard in Times Square in New York City for $100,000 a year. For a while the message on the 265-by-60-foot sign read: "Dino De Laurentiis has reserved this space to announce the most important movie of all time." This was eventually replaced by a sign reading: "*The Bible* will cover these inspiring events — The Creation, Adam and Eve, Cain and Abel, Noah's Ark, Tower of Babel, Abraham." The gigantic sign remained up for almost two years before the film actually opened.

The Bible, originally budgeted at $13,000,000, was by far the most expensive film Huston was to direct. As time passed, the cost rose to $15,000,000 and, finally, to approximately $18,000,000.

De Laurentiis remained unperturbed. He said of Huston, "I do not ask him in advance what he is going to do. He has his ideas in his mind. It is like giving an artist paints and brushes. You do not say to the artist, 'What are you going to do with them?' "

Huston, in turn, commented, "I can't begin to describe the exquisite deference that Dino shows me."

After working with Fry on script revisions, Huston gathered leading Italian painters, sculptors, and designers to work on the film.

These artists included Manzu, who had fashioned the new central doors of St. Peter's. Manzu created the earth forms that become Adam and Eve in the Garden of Eden sequence, since, in the film, Eve does not come from Adam's rib. Artist Corrado Cagli designed the tree for the Garden of Eden and the three towers for the short Tower of Babel scene. One tower was constructed in the Sahara, south of Cairo, Egypt, for long shots and cost $375,000. Another was built in the De Laurentiis studio for close-ups at a cost of $500,000, and a miniature one was constructed for special effects shooting and cost several thousand dollars. The set and costumes for the Sodom sequence were designed by the Italian artist Mirko.

Since *The Bible* took two years to shoot, the longest schedule in the director's career, Huston took periodic trips to his home in Ireland and brought various groups of Italian artists with him to work on the film. He even gave them lessons in fox hunting.

Back in Italy Huston supervised construction of Noah's ark, which turned out to be 200 feet long and 50 feet high. It had three wooden decks and was steel-reinforced to hold the more than 300 animals and 1000 birds used in the sequence. A second, partially built ark was also constructed for the scenes that showed the boat being built.

Three other arks were eventually erected for various close-up shots. Artist Marco Chiari based his drawings on boats depicted on Middle Eastern tombs that were probably close in design to what was built in Noah's time.

In the ark sequence, Huston himself played Noah. His original choice for the role had been either Alec Guinness or Charlie Chaplain. "Alec Guinness couldn't make it during the dates in which we needed him," Huston recalled to Robert F. Hawkins in a 1965 *New York Times* interview. "Charlie Chaplin was tempted. Others had conflicts. So Dino talked me into it."

Huston's conception of Noah is that of a simple peasant puzzled at being chosen for the task of saving human and animal life. Huston's Noah is an innocent protected by his belief and lack of guile. "Noah," he says, "is the child figure in the Bible. He's always a little bit absurd and delightful."

Because Noah would have needed a forest to build the ark, Huston had more than a thousand trees transplanted on the lot.

The entry of the animals into the ark required almost five months of shooting at a cost of $3,000,000. A worldwide search was required to gather the hundreds of animals that were brought to Rome, fed, and trained by fifty full-time trainers and thirty laborers.

One of the animals' owners insisted that the animals be blindfolded for the trip up the ramp, claiming that if they could see they would panic and fall. Huston told them that was nonsense, and he was almost totally right.

One water buffalo charged up the gangplank, crashed through the ark, and was on his way out of Rome at a gallop when trainers caught up with him. During a rehearsal, Huston was knocked down by an elephant. Another tore off the director's robe searching for peanuts, and a camel fell off the ramp into a tank full of water placed there for just such an accident.

Finally, Huston decided to shoot the entry of the animals even though the head trainer objected that they weren't trained sufficiently. The director put on his Noah costume and walked down the line of animals, talking softly to each. As he came to the head of the line, he signaled the three cameras to roll and grabbed the ram's horn trumpet Noah uses to soothe the animals. To the astonishment of the trainers, the animals immediately began to march calmly into the ark with Huston gently urging them forward.

"Our hippo was the greatest actor in the picture," says Huston. "Every time that hippo heard me coming, he broke into the damnedest grin you ever saw." The director's affection for the hippo is evident in the shot in which he talks to the creature, gives it a bucket of milk, and then pats its snout. Another moment of remarkable rapport with an animal is captured when Huston and an ostrich mug with each other.

Huston enjoyed directing himself. He told Hawkins: "I find him [John Huston] wonderfully responsive and easy to work with. We have a wonderful rapport."

The Tower of Babel was only a slightly less difficult task for artist Chiari than the ark. He decided to base his design on the Ziggurat, a towerlike structure built by ancient Babylonians with an outside staircase leading to a shrine on top. Since thousands of extras had to climb the structure, it was constructed as solidly as a skyscraper. The finished ark and tower became major tourist attractions in Rome during the shooting and after it.

Huston combed the world for locations. The city of Sodom was constructed on the slopes of the still-active volcano, Mount Etna, in Sicily. The crater of Vesuvius, which destroyed Pompeii 2000 years ago, was selected as the backdrop for Cain's murder of Abel. The rough terrain resulted in the usual number of bruises for the scarcely clad actors, particularly Richard Harris, who played Cain.

After moving to the Sahara for the Tower of Babel long-shot scenes, Huston remained in the desert for the Abraham and Sarah sequence.

Many artists contributed to the film. Dancer Katherine Dunham choreographed dances showing the fall of Sodom. Toshiro Mayuzumi, a leading Japanese composer, was brought in to do the music. Giuseppe Rotunno, who had been working with Visconti, was cinematographer. Still photographer Ernst Haas was called in to shoot the scenes of creation. Haas had been considering a book of photographs of natural phenomena illustrating his theory that the world is in a state of continuing creation. Huston liked Haas's work and his idea and gave him a relatively free hand. With a ten-man crew, Haas toured the world for a year and a half shooting God's first six days of the earth's creation. He filmed erupting volcanoes in Iceland, rare animals on the Galapagos Islands, and mountains in Ecuador.

To create the Garden of Eden and keep it as lush as Huston wanted, twenty men worked round-the-clock shifts for months on the location near Rome. Each day, thousands of fresh flowers were brought in by truck. When Huston planned the sequence, he also decided that there should be a stream winding through the garden. A riverbed was dug twenty feet wide and several feet deep.

Visual questions kept cropping up unexpectedly. What did the mark of Cain look like? Huston decided that it should look like a tree that had been hit by lightning. What should an angel look like? Huston decided that all three angels who enter Sodom should be played by Peter O'Toole. What color was Eve's hair? Or Eve for that matter? Huston settled on a blonde after his choice of a brunette was protested. Ulla Bergryd, a Swedish anthropology student, was chosen for the role when one of Huston's Italian assistants spotted her at an art exhibit in Götenborg, Sweden.

Well into the film, Huston said to Hawkins, "I admit that there were films I made which I lost interest in when I saw they weren't turning out right. But this isn't one of them. Sure, we've had problems. Plenty of them. Every scene, every sequence had its obstacles, conceptual and otherwise. I think we've managed to lick most of them."

While filming, Huston was constantly searching for someone to narrate, to be the voice of the Bible and the voice of God. Huston himself had been doing the narration for the work prints, and De Laurentiis finally decided to let him serve as narrator for the final film.

"I didn't want to narrate it," Huston said, going on to explain that the actors he had tested had been "too recognizable. The narration should have an anonymous quality. I think my voice has that."

There are probably few people who would agree with the director. Certainly his voice is recognizable when Huston as Noah talks to Huston as God in the film. It was not, however, the first time such a confrontation with self had taken place in a Biblical epic. In Cecil B. De Mille's *The Ten Commandments,* Charlton Heston played both Moses and the voice of God.

De Laurentiis had begun the film without the promise of distribution. Before shooting was completed, however, Twentieth Century-Fox had for $15,000,000 acquired the rights to distribute it in the United States and all over the world with a few exceptions, notably Italy. The remarkable De Laurentiis had just about guaranteed his profit before the film was released.

The pleased producer was quick to announce that he was preparing his next project with Federico Fellini. De Laurentiis compared the two directors: "There are two ways in which John and Federico are identical. The first way is in their charm. It is a pleasure to talk to them. They can get you to do anything at all. The other thing they have in common is that they understand audiences . . . John and Federico know how to create art that gets across to humble people as well as to intellectuals."

De Laurentiis was also quick to point out differences between the two: "Federico's pictures have an autobiographical aspect; in all of them there is the quality of something he has deeply felt. What John does, on the other hand, is to make the characters his, and then present them to the audience."

The reviews of the film that Huston had worked on twice as long as any other in his career were mixed. *Variety* said that "the world's oldest story has been put upon the screen with consummate skill, taste, and reverence," but Bosley Crowther in the *New York Times* called the film "mechanically inventive" but "lacking a sense of conviction of God in magnitude or a galvanizing feeling of connection in the stories of Genesis."

Since the film is based on the fundamental religious work of the Western world, Huston has frequently been asked about his own religious beliefs. This question also crops up in relation to the religious subject matter of several of his other films, particularly *Moby Dick* and *The Night of the Iguana.*

Huston describes himself as a "philosophical atheist" with existential ideas. "I don't conjecture about the existence of a divinity," he told *Cahiers du Cinema* in 1966. "I think all churches, Catholic, Protestant, Jewish, all except perhaps some rattlesnake-eaters in the South, agree today that *The Bible* is a mixture of myth, legend, and history. I consider the book as such with its plots, its people, and poetry. It's the first adventure story, the first love story, the first murder story, the first suspense, the first story of faith."

Of all Huston's work, *The Bible* stands as the best opportunity to see the director's various religious ideas. The story of Adam and Eve's expulsion from the Garden of Eden is presented as a choice between mortality and pain, or comfort, a choice Huston characters frequently make. Adam and Eve fail to succeed in Eden, thus choosing pain. Cain's agony and rejection by God are the result of his asserting his individuality by attacking his brother. The story of Nimrod and the Tower of Babel is similar. Nimrod challenges God, builds his tower, shoots an arrow into the sky, and asserts his power and stature as a human being. For this, he is punished.

In the Noah and the ark and Abraham sections, man has become docile. Unlike Nimrod and Cain, who are Ahab-like figures, Noah is submissive; he and his group are saved by God, given privileged status. Abraham, whose section ends the film, is a man torn between the wish to assert himself as an individual and the fear of God. In a sense, Cain and Nimrod are Huston existential heroes, while Noah and Abraham, presented as simpler souls, are more traditional religious figures. These different attitudes are evident in much of Huston's work.

The sequence of Noah and the ark is, for example, as Huston himself has observed, a reversal of *Moby Dick.* In that film, Ahab takes his ship out to defy God and destroy one of His creatures, the white whale, not for sport, profit, or food but out of vengeance. Noah, on the other hand, goes to his ship solely to save the animals. He accepts God's will as Ahab denies it. Ahab is tense, secretive, compelling, and obsessed. Noah is at ease, open, with no natural leadership and no ambitions. He does not even take pride in being chosen by God. He simply accepts the decision.

As in other Huston films set in the past, the director makes a contemporary social allusion. *Moby Dick* concludes with an allegorical confrontation at Bikini, and the Sodom episode in *The Bible* climaxes with the destruction of the city in what is clearly an atom bomb blast. Lot's wife is turned to salt by looking at the blast as she would be burned in an atomic explosion.

Visually, the Bible offered Huston an opportunity to work with a number of artists he admired. Furthermore, he had not only an opportunity to explore his existential beliefs against a Biblical background but also an unusual opportunity for visual creation. For example, the outline of Adam in the dust is seen across the screen, then the wind blows it from dust to man. Another of Huston's many visual contributions was to shoot hundreds of feet of film on a gold-painted board. He then rewound the film in the camera and shot the Garden of Eden sequence on it, giving it a strange golden glow.

There are clearly constants not only in *The Bible* but in many of Huston's other works — man's ability to find solace in animals, the sensation of the physical world through contact with nature, challenges to oneself — but the world is unpredictable, governed by a whimsical God or no God at all. Each of Huston's characters seeks a way of coming to terms with that unpredictability, establishing rules of behavior by which he can live. But the Huston character, like Cain or Adam, is often weak. He is but a man, and frequently his best intentions will not carry him through to success or even survival. The more a man thinks in a Huston film, the more dangerous it is for his survival. The less a man thinks and the more he responds instinctively, like an animal, the more likely he will be to earn Huston's respect. Carried away by emotion or too much introspection, a man is doomed. Since the line between loss of control and rigid morality is difficult to walk, many Huston protagonists do not survive. It takes a Sam Spade, Sergeant Allison, or Abraham, very rare men indeed, to remain alive in this director's world.

De Laurentiis' faith in *The Bible* proved to be well founded.

Variety recently listed it among the seventy-five highest-grossing films of all time. It also made more money than any other Huston film.

At the age of sixty, the director spoke of finally making *The Man Who Would Be King* with Richard Burton and Peter O'Toole. He also talked about a De Laurentiis film with the same two actors, adding, "Liz is welcome to play a cameo bit, if she wants." The main problem in doing such a film was to find a country with cavalry who could serve as soldiers in the battle scenes. "Turkey has cavalry," he said. "So does Russia. Both are possibilities for a locale." Neither materialized.

Instead, Huston accepted the task of directing and acting in one quarter of a James Bond film, *Casino Royale,* next to *The Bible* his greatest financial success.

CHAPTER 20

Spies and Voyeurs

THE AESTHETIC DISTANCE between *The Bible* and *Casino Royale* is great. Huston had spent two years on one of the most somber and serious films ever made, and within weeks of completing it, he was at work on *Casino Royale,* one of the most irreverent films of all time. He was supposed to work only a few months on the James Bond parody and to be one of several directors for different segments.

The film was to be based on *Casino Royale,* Ian Fleming's first James Bond novel, in which Bond, with the assistance of a lady friend, Vesper, destroys the Smersh leader Le Chiffre by defeating him at baccarat. When Le Chiffre loses his and some of Smersh's money, he is executed. Bond then discovers that Vesper is really a double agent.

The novel was, to a great degree, based on Fleming's fantasy about winning a game he had never had any success with. At one point in his life, the writer had faced an adversary across the baccarat table and lost miserably. Re-creating himself as a victorious winner in the guise of James Bond in *Casino Royale,* Fleming started the series that made him a multimillionaire.

Casino Royale was budgeted at $6,000,000, but time and expenses went very quickly and it took more than $10,000,000 to finish the picture. First, the script for the whole film went through twelve rewrites; one a collaboration between Huston, novelist Terry Southern, screenwriter Wolf Mankowitz, Woody Allen, and Peter Sellers. Then the other four directors had to be chosen. They were Val Guest, Ken Hughes, Robert Parrish, and British television director Joe McGrath.

In the segment he directed, which opens the film, Huston plays M,

James Bond's boss. After a precredit gag involving Peter Sellers, Huston has the first lines in the film.

"Yes," he recalled to *Cahiers du Cinema* in 1966, "I played M, James Bond's boss, bald with a Guards mustache. I wanted Bob Morley, but he was busy. I tried a few others, all busy. Then Charlie Feldman said, 'I'll give you a painting if you play M.' So I did, not for a painting, but for a Greek bronze head I'd fallen for. It turned out to be not worth a damn, but I liked playing M. It was great fun."

Huston's section of the film was shot at Pinewood Studio in London and on location in Ireland. His co-stars were David Niven, who played Bond; Deborah Kerr, who played a spy; William Holden, who played a CIA official; and Charles Boyer, who played the head of French Intelligence.

The finished film contains dozens of "in" jokes, many directed at, but not by Huston. In a segment Huston did not direct, Peter Sellers, dressed up as Toulouse-Lautrec, looks remarkably like José Ferrer. In another scene, Deborah Kerr walks into Bond's office in her nun's costume from *Heaven Knows, Mr. Allison* to collect for charity.

In Huston's section, McTarry (Huston) and representatives from the Intelligence units of three other countries (Holden, Boyer, and Kurt Kasznar) come to the home of the retired James Bond to try to convince him to return to service for a special mission. Bond, the very picture of an English gentleman, not unlike Huston, replies that he is quite content away from it all. In the garden, Bond changes his decision when a mysterious bomb destroys his home, killing M, who is last seen with his red toupee flying off to reveal his bald head.

Bond then brings the toupee to M's home, an isolated country estate in Scotland, where he finds dozens of red-headed women, including Lady Fiona (Kerr), who make sexual advances toward him, but the agent is shy and a bit frightened. He is then challenged to a contest of round-rock catching by the huge male guards in the house and easily defeats them because of their inability to handle the balls and with his own strength. Lady Fiona falls in love with him, and the next morning, when he is out duck shooting, she rushes to warn him that the artificial ducks are bombs. With her help and accidental hindrance, he manages to shoot down some of the ducks and send the homing device planted on him back to the truck from which the ducks are being launched. A duck destroys the truck in a huge blast.

As in *The African Queen, Heaven Knows, Mr. Allison,* and *Key Largo,* the protagonist and heroine combine forces to defeat a strong enemy. Also, as in so many Huston films, the woman turns out to be evil, but in this comedy she has an extreme change of heart.

The stone-throwing sequence is a comic comment on Huston's own displays of masculinity including the ability to box, fight Indians, or battle gangsters.

When the film was released, the reviewers were a bit perplexed by the chaos, and their negative reviews reflected their confusion. Nonetheless, *Casino Royale* was a financial success, and Huston enjoyed making it.

Huston, now sixty-one, was ready to turn again to a serious subject, one that proved to be so serious, in fact, that it became one of the director's biggest disasters.

The project was *Reflections in a Golden Eye.* Based on a novel by Southern writer Carson McCullers, *Reflections* dealt with repressed sexuality and homosexuality in an American army post in the South in 1948. It starred Marlon Brando as Captain Penderton; Elizabeth Taylor as his wife, Leonora; Brian Keith as Major Langdon, her lover; Julie Harris as Alison, his wife; and newcomer Robert Forster as Private Williams, the unsuspecting object of Penderton's affection who lusts after Leonora.

Although set in the United States, none of the film was shot there. The entire army post was constructed in Rome under the supervision of Huston's long-time art director Stephen Grimes.

It was, says Huston, "one of the first American films to broach the subject of homosexuality."

Some of Huston's ideas for the adaptation had to be scrapped. He had hoped, for example, that McCullers could work on the film for a long time, but she had been extremely ill. Huston brought her to his home in Ireland to rest and recuperate. "She was bedridden," he remembered for *Réalités* in 1973, "and the only person we allowed to interview her was a leading Irish journalist. One of his questions was 'What is the purpose of the artist or writer?' In all sincerity, Carson answered, 'To search for God.' There was a very solemn moment, and the old Sicilian crucifix over her bed turned upside down . . . She began to laugh and so did we. She was a marvelous person." Carson McCullers was to die before *Reflections* was completed.

Huston had wanted Montgomery Clift to play Penderton, but the actor died in 1966. The director then chose Patrick O'Neal, who had played Shannon in the original Broadway production of *The Night of the Iguana*. He also considered Richard Burton and Lee Marvin, but Elizabeth Taylor wanted Brando, and she prevailed.

According to Gary Carey in his book *Brando!*, Brando said the main reason he was doing the film was "$750,000 plus 7½ percent of the gross receipts if we break even."

Working with Chapman Mortimer, a little-known English author he admired, and Gladys Hill, Huston reworked the McCullers novel. He promoted Penderton to major, made his homosexuality much more explicit than it was in the book, and chose not to make Alison as obviously demented as she was in the novel.

Although Huston himself does not appear in *Reflections*, his voice opens the film. We see Private Ellgee Williams and hear Huston's voice call out, "Private Williams, report to Major Penderton's house for a work detail." Huston gives the stage direction that starts the action and will lead eventually to Williams' death.

The director also plays with a line from McCullers' novel that appears on the screen at the start and finish of the movie: "There is a fort in the South where a few years ago a murder was committed." As Andrew Sarris observed in the *Village Voice,* the audience is set up for a Hitchcock-like situation. Throughout the film, Huston plays a game as to who will be murdered. At least once, every principal character is given the motivation and opportunity for murder, but the murder does not take place until the last three minutes of the film.

Reflections raises questions of the sexuality inherent in many of the themes that have most attracted Huston: riding horses, hunting, boxing, militarism. The honesty with which the director handles homosexuality is characteristic of his willingness to face what he finds antithetical to his own nature.

In the film, the equation of Leonora and her horse is presented as definitely sexual, and at one point Penderton actually beats the horse in a fury because he himself is impotent.

Huston also includes a boxing match in the film which is not in the novel. The immorally provocative Leonora watches the match, but Penderton watches another spectator, Williams.

Reflections becomes an almost comic labyrinth of voyeurism, with characters spying on other characters. Penderton spies on Williams,

spies on Leonora. Alison spies on her husband and Leonora.
ton constantly shows the audience eyes and then the unsuspect-
person being spied upon. In one striking series of shots, Anacleto
(ro David), Alison's Filipino companion, shows her a painting of
d with a golden eye. There is then a cut to Williams' eye in which
flected the image he is watching, Leonora walking upstairs nude
r taunting Penderton.

Villiams is frequently seen alone in the frame even when others
at the same location. Each principal character, in fact, is pre-
ed as being alone, as well as being ultimately shallow and stupid.
enderton suffers great agony with his emerging homosexuality
, busy searching for Williams, doesn't even listen when he is told
Alison's suicide. Leonora faces each person in the film without
itivity, often hurting feelings or offending without knowing it. In
scene, she describes a fox hunt in which a woman was badly
red. Alison, who has heard the story frequently, is on the point
ausea, but Leonora, taken with remembering the incident, is
ware of her feelings. This theme of human insensitivity is rare in
ton's works.

uston devised a series of visual shots he felt would be equivalent
McCullers' style. The major innovation was his use of desaturated
r, of removing much of the color on the film and concentrating
drained, golden caste. This desaturization is constant until the
der at the end of the film when full Technicolor comes on with
t while the camera pans rapidly back and forth between Pender-
Leonora in bed screaming, and the dead Williams.

eflections in a Golden Eye played only ten days in New York in
desaturated process. With box-office receipts down after luke-
m-to-poor reviews, Warner Brothers moved to replace Huston's
ion with prints already prepared in full color.

uston talked to Gene Phillips about the color experiment: "It is
result of considerable experimentation, and was perfectly suited
his study of a group of neurotic people. This color process basi-
y had a golden amber quality to it; other colors, toned, impinged
he screen, as it were, from behind this golden hue. This served
eparate the audience somewhat from the characters, who were in
ous ways withdrawn from reality, and to make their story a bit
e remote and exotic." The decision to use normal Technicolor,
rding to Huston, came from a Warner Brothers executive. "I

think," the director mused, "he had seen a beer ad at age eleven
that was the extent of his aesthetic growth."

As was usually the case, Huston had little trouble with his c
"I had no directorial problems with Elizabeth Taylor and Mar
Brando during shooting," he told Phillips. "I don't cast an actor
his technique but for his personality and because of my vision of w
he will do with his personality in a given part. My faith in the ac
in *Reflections in a Golden Eye,* I think, was justified. Taylor
Brando, Brian Keith and Julie Harris all had different acting sty
but people are different too."

Huston was disappointed with the response to *Reflections,* but
success of *The Bible* and *Casino Royale* and his earlier performan
still made him a highly marketable director.

However, instead of choosing a commercial property next, Hus
went home to Ireland to shoot *Sinful Davey,* a film about a rogu
1821, for producer Walter Mirisch.

At first, Huston tested his teen-age daughter, Anjelica, for a l
but decided against her. The principal actors in this film about a
who devotes his life to attempting to recommit and outdo all
crimes for which his father was hanged are John Hurt, Pam
Franklin, Nigel Davenport, and Robert Morley.

Sinful Davey proved to be another box-office disaster, prima
because most critics and audiences failed to see the humor in w
Huston considered high black comedy involving the dissection
corpses, hanging, and attempted murder. For Huston, one of
high points of the film is a fox hunt in which Davey steals a ho
to escape from the pursuing constables. The film's romantic nat
is affirmed at the conclusion, in which Davey is scheduled to
hanged but is rescued by an old friend and his girl, who walks
with him into the hills. Huston's interest in disguises is seen as Da
takes three names to elude the police and keeps shifting from
normal voice and social position to his guise of nobleman.

Although most reviewers mentioned that the 1969 release
minded them of Tony Richardson's *Tom Jones,* released six ye
earlier, they had little else favorable to say about it. The film
shown for one week in New York City and removed from circu
tion. Huston blamed producer Mirisch's editing for the problem
a 1972 interview in *Interview* with Curtice Taylor and Glenn O'Bri
"I can't imagine how that one lasted three days, after the fuck
that Walter Mirisch made of it."

Back at St. Clerans, Huston, at the age of sixty-two, decided to turn to serious painting forty years after he had begun his original study in Paris. He set up a studio and began to spend more time painting than fox hunting. His method of working, according to one actor, was to spend hours at the canvas and then clean up the studio completely so that it would be spotless for his next session. Two of Huston's principal projects were a painting of a nude woman from a pre-Columbian figurine and a portrait of his daughter, Anjelica.

Huston once paused in his painting to make a few observations about life. "Life," he told Associated Press reporter Hal Boyle, "fascinates me, each moment as it comes along. I don't know that I have a philosophy, but I never do anything that doesn't entertain me. That way a man can't be bored. . . . What defeats most men in life? Probably the fact that they make false gods for themselves and strive to attain things that don't have an enduring value for them."

He told Boyle that what he liked best were "highly seasoned things, both foods and people, the long twilights of Ireland, which are a small eternity, any music by Bach, the sounds of hounds in full cry, the sound of crows, primitive sculpture, good vodka, rogues, and quality of mind in people because that means they have fresh outlooks."

His dislikes, he said, were "any dish containing chicken, mawkish popular songs, the sound of automobile metals in collision, drunken women, any writing that tries too hard for effect, and people with too much propriety, people who strain after social correctness but achieve only pomposity and self-complacency."

ove and Death in Europe

BELIEVE," says John Huston, "I'm the only one in film history o has directed himself, his father, and his daughter."

Daughter Anjelica was an inexperienced teen-ager of sixteen when ston selected her to star in *A Walk with Love and Death* based New Yorker* writer Hans Koningsberger's 1961 novel of the same ne set in northern France during the Peasants' Revolt of 1358. When questioned about his choice of a star, Huston happily admit- that he was engaged in favoritism. "Can she act?" a UPI reporter ed in September 1968. "Oh yes," replied Huston, "she does it all time." When shooting started, Anjelica said, "There are some s when I am scared, others when I'm not. I feel best when I can eam or cry. I find it hardest to be still and jolly."

According to Huston, he was unaware when he cast nineteen-year- Assaf Dayan as his other star in the film that the young man was son of Israeli war hero Moshe Dayan.

Having chosen two unknowns as his leads, Huston proceeded to t a real princess, Antoinette Reuss of Austria, as a charcoal- ing peasant. "I couldn't find anyone else who looked like a peas- ," he explained to the Los Angeles *Herald-Examiner*.

Huston also gave himself an important role in the film as Robert Elder, a nobleman who joins the peasants in their revolt and is ed by the nobles.

Koningsberger, who consulted on the screenplay for the film and rked with Huston and writer Dale Wasserman, recalled an exam- of Huston's technique of screen adaptation in an article for *Film arterly* in 1969. In the novel, the two young lovers flee across ance after the girl's nobleman father is killed. They find refuge in abandoned manor house.

"During this time, in the novel," according to Koningsberg "the girl brings the young man a text of Scripture she has bou from a gypsy woman and which supposedly bears on their futu Huston wanted to use this, but he neither wanted the girl to sim say where the text came from, nor did he want to show the gy woman. Another person on the screen would disrupt the sense isolation and insulation of the episode. I rewrote the scene with the gypsy, but with the student and the girl reading each othe futures out of the palms of their hands. They say in essence the sa thing the gypsy woman's text said. That's how it went into shooting script, but when Huston filmed it, he ended up by or showing the girl reading the boy's palm, in pantomime, smiling him, putting a kiss in his hand, and closing his hand around it, a fi visual simplification of what had begun as a word idea."

A Walk with Love and Death was set to start shooting France, and Huston was dealing with preproduction proble when the massive 1968 student riots began in Paris. In the mid of the tumult, Huston got a call from a Twentieth Century-F executive telling him to come immediately to London for a ca ing meeting. Huston explained that riots were in progress rig outside his hotel room and that it was impossible to do so. T executive was insistent and Huston, according to the *Hera Examiner,* shouted, "My God, France is in a catastrophe a you're mewling about a damn movie."

But the situation in France made it too difficult to continue pr duction, so the crew moved to a location in Austria, just outsi Vienna. Huston planned to begin shooting across the border ir village in Czechoslovakia. It was August 1968. When Huston's cr was set, the Czech revolt began and Russian troops moved in.

"We can't wait for the Russians to leave," he announced. "We move to Italy and finish shooting there." Filming was completed the Fossanova, the oldest Cistercian abbey in Italy.

Because of the political encounters in France and Czechosloval during the filming, Huston changed his original concept of the p ture. When *Walk* was completed, critics immediately saw parall to Vietnam, the French student riots, and civil rights unrest in t United States. They pointed out that the Dayan character had ju been expelled from the Sorbonne for writing a poem in praise orgasm and that at one point Claudia (Anjelica Huston) remarks, hate anybody who is twenty or older."

Koningsberger said that references to modern times were intended
h in the novel and script.
'It is an abstract of our time with a Middle Age frame around it,"
ston commented to the *Herald-Examiner.* "You see what you
nt to see in it. It's modern to some. To others, it's historical or
ional."
In the film, Heron of Foix (Dayan) is on his way from Paris to the
after being expelled from the university. Since France is in the
ddle of a bloody revolution, his way is dangerous. He gains refuge
the castle of a nobleman and falls in love with his daughter,
audia. When the nobleman is killed by peasants, the two young
ers flee. The girl wants revenge against the peasants and urges
ron to take part in a battle against a group of them. When he kills
outhful peasant, he is appalled by his deed.
His compassion is further raised by another nobleman, Robert the
der, a genial, understanding person who says he is joining the
asants, because their way is right and their victory inevitable. The
bles turn on Robert, Heron, and Claudia. When both Robert and
son die fighting, Heron and Claudia, completely without friends
long the peasants or noblemen, take refuge in an abbey. There they
separated by the monks and nuns and told to leave when they
k to be married.
Given one more night of sanctuary before they are expelled, the
o wake up in the morning to find that the nuns and priests have
d. Heron and Claudia perform their own marriage ceremony and
cide to remain in the abbey because there is no place to run. As
ght falls, they hear horses approaching. Their death is near regard-
s of which side arrives at the castle, and the film ends with the two
aiting their fate from the unseen enemy.
Huston again shows his love for horses in this film and for the sixth
ne gives a white horse a leading part. Heron must ride a white
orse bareback through fields and woods as fast as he can to get back
Claudia. In *Moulin Rouge,* the young Toulouse-Lautrec rides a
hite horse before the accident that cripples him. Later the horse
ands in the foreground before the deformed child. A naked Private
illiams rides a white horse in *Reflections in a Golden Eye,* and in
comic sequence in *Sinful Davey* the hero races from the constables
a white horse. Avatar, the horse that kills Adrian Messenger's
urderer, is also white, as is the horse Audrey Hepburn rides in *The
nforgiven.*

The only reliable creatures are horses in Huston's world. "But greatest defect," he once said, "is misplaced faith in certain hors

Huston's negative religious attitude is strong in *A Walk with L and Death,* in which there are three encounters with the clergy. the first, Heron is almost killed by a group of ascetic monks demand that he renounce the memory of Claudia and "repent knowledge of women." The young man barely escapes with his These religious zealots counsel a move away from the pleasure of world and human love, a world that Huston believes in.

In the second encounter, Heron finds Claudia in a church in wh an angry clergyman promises punishment of the wicked peasants announces that the "world is God's cathedral" in a sermon bef the frightened survivors of the peasant raid. His concern is with C and not humans. Claudia steals the priest's candlesticks to sell so two lovers can eat. Their life is more important to Huston than C is.

In the third episode, which ends the movie, the priests at the ab will give sanctuary to the lovers only if they remain separate deny their feelings, which they refuse to do. Huston glorifies decision in the sequence of the self-performed marriage.

Existentialist Jean Paul Sartre was a frequent guest of Huston' Ireland, and his influence on the director is apparent.

Huston told a writer for *Réalités* this story about Sartre: "O when Sartre was visiting me, I had a very eminent Catholic intel tual there at the same time, Monsignor Paddy Brown. Well, know Sartre, suspicious of the clergy. He probably thought Pa Brown came to proselytize him. I reassured him, but I think he didn't believe me. In any case, Paddy Brown told a really good di joke and that did it. Sartre was *sure* he was to be converted."

Many of Huston's films can be divided between those involv group quests that fail (*Moby Dick, The Red Badge of Courage, Were Strangers, The Asphalt Jungle, Beat the Devil,* the Treasure the Sierrra Madre, The Misfits, The Roots of Heaven*) and th involving a pair of potential lovers who must face a hostile wo (*Heaven Knows, Mr. Allison, The African Queen, Sinful Dave Generally, Huston's films about such lovers end in the union of couple or, at least, their survival. In that sense, *A Walk with L and Death,* starring his own daughter, proved to be the most pe mistic of his love stories.

n 1969, Huston's wife was killed in an automobile accident. Al-
ugh the two had spent much of their married life separated, they
nited constantly at St. Clerans and had two children together,
ıy and Anjelica. The tragedy was a terrible loss for the director
l the effect is shown in the ending of the film.

inful Davey had been a comedy about death, and *A Walk with
ıe and Death* was a romance about death. Both films were finan-
and critical failures. *Time* wrote, "John Huston, one formerly
whom much honor was due, filmed this woeful tale and even
jected his daughter to it." *Time* then listed the director, writer,
l producer as having "conspired together to produce this thing,
l all must share equally in the blame. There is, truly, more than
icient for each." Pauline Kael wrote, "One feels that Huston is
longer doing what's close to him."

Iuston was next hired by Ely Landau to direct *The Madwoman
Chaillot* to be based on the play by Jean Giradoux. Katharine
pburn was guaranteed for the film and she wanted Huston to
ect. Landau visited the director at St. Clerans to discuss the
ject, but the two had basic differences about the script and Huston
ised to change his position. Landau immediately hired Bryan
bes to replace him, which upset Hepburn.

With a string of three box-office failures behind him, Huston
ced of organizing an Irish film indusry and making a film based
Brian Moore's novel *The Lonely Passion of Judith Hearne.* In-
d he made *The Kremlin Letter,* based on Noel Behn's best-selling
el about a group of spies hired by the United States to perform
angerous mission in Moscow that proves to be a cover-up for the
l, more diabolical mission. Like so many spy films, *The Kremlin
tter* had a remarkably convoluted plot of treachery and deceit.
As *A Walk with Love and Death* had been Huston's most down-
t film about lovers, *The Kremlin Letter* would be his most nega-
 examination of the group quest.

'In this film," Huston told *Cue* in 1969, "nobody has a single
ral, ethical principle," which, he added, was why he wanted to
ke the film. "The movie is just a reduction mirror. I think this is
 way the world is. It's not the espionage that concerns me here.
 that espionage is not so different from anything else. When I read
 book, I thought that here was a reflection of the moral climate
our times."

Huston explained that he was shying away from nothing in his f
exploration of the depravity of contemporary civilizati
"*The Kremlin Letter* has a bit of everything," he told Los Ange
Times reporter Marika Aba, "from homosexuality to violence, r
sex and even a Lesbian scene, but the point is that we are
presenting sex, we are presenting a bunch of amoral people w
happen to be spies."

Huston wanted to shoot part of his film in Moscow, but
Russians were strongly opposed. In fact, when he decided to film
Helsinki, Finland, Russia protested and began denying visas to F
nish citizens. Finland responded by allowing Huston to redecor:
a section of the city, complete with a statue of Lenin, to look l
Moscow.

The reason for Russia's display "is beyond me," Huston told A
"because this is certainly not going to be a political or anti-Russi
film. No James Bond techniques, no good guys or bad guys,
lily-white Americans and evil Russians. It's not going to be the st
of the 'glorified spy' but the 'amoral, corrupt one.' Russians
Americans, they are all identical. They are all the commissars
depravity."

To play his depraved spies, Huston gathered a distinguished ca
including:

    — Academy Award winner George Sanders, who plays a female i
personator gathering information from unsuspecting Russians
    — Dean Jagger, another Academy Award winner, playing an old s
who has been deceived and is dying of cancer
    — Nigel Green, as a character called "The Whore," who trades
drugs and prostitutes to gather information
    — Academy Award winner Lila Kedrova, playing a depraved R
sian madame
    — Richard Boone, as the paternal Ward, who betrays everyone on
mission he is supposed to lead so he can revenge himself against an
enemy
    — Max Von Sydow, as a Russian intelligence officer who tortures
get information and takes the wife of one of his victims
    — Orson Welles, as Bresnavitch, a highly intelligent Russian, w
enjoys embarrassing others with their weaknesses and, like Huston, c
lects art objects
    — Barbara Parkins, playing B.A., who has been trained by her fath
to be a safecracker and to gain information by sleeping with men

[nto this totally corrupt crew is cast Rone (Patrick O'Neal), who
villing to be used as long as the mission is clear and exciting and
: money is good. O'Neal said of the film, "It's a very cynical
ture, but it shows a side that exists in everybody's nature."
[n his review in *Sight and Sound,* John Russell Taylor singled out
m Huston's own acting role. "There is little doubt," he wrote,
aat the film John Huston set out to make may be read in the light
the little scene he gives himself near the beginning." Huston plays
 admiral who angrily dismisses Rone, accusing him of putting
ne sort of whim or personal loyalty in front of his loyalty to the
up.
Huston wanted to film as quickly as possible and when there was
lelay with the New York locations, he moved the cast and crew
Rome and the De Laurentiis studios, where New York sets could
quickly constructed. After shooting New York interiors there, he
ved back to the real New York and the Museum and Library of
 Hispanic Society of America, which was converted to the Tillin-
 Institute, the spy headquarters, and to Central Park zoo for a
ne in which the spies observe the daughter of a Russian diplomat
y wish to blackmail.
Huston met his daughter, Anjelica, in New York, where she was
derstudying the role of Ophelia in a stage production of *Hamlet.*
is was the director's first trip to the city for filming since 1949,
en he did exteriors for *The Asphalt Jungle.*
Huston also managed to get back to Mexico to shoot a sequence
which Rone goes there to bring back "The Whore," who is living
th a group of prostitutes in a small town where he goads them to
ht for his pleasure.
The completed film is a tangle of people spying on other people.
is on the international level what *Reflections in a Golden Eye* was
 the private level. The primary difference is that while the charac-
s in *Reflections* were all ashamed of their secrets, those in *The
remlin Letter* are ready to profit from them.
The film concludes with Rone in a terrible dilemma. To save the
rl he loves, he must kill the family of a Russian diplomat. If he
ally loves the girl, can he coldly murder a family to save her, thus
turning him to the immoral state of his now dead group? Huston
aves the audience without an answer.
Of all Huston's groups, the one in *The Kremlin Letter* is the most
-fated. The only members who survive physically intact are Rone

and the evil Ward. It is as if the totally evil murderer in *The Lis*
Adrian Messenger had succeeded in his mission.

The pessimism of *The Kremlin Letter* is underlined by its loc
and climate. Most of the film takes place in Russia in the win

Reviews were, for the most part, unfavorable, but there were a f
exceptions and the film didn't fare badly at the box office.

In succession, Huston had directed a series of films that question
his past attitudes. In *Reflections in a Golden Eye,* he question
masculinity and militarism. In *Sinful Davey,* he ridiculed the idea
a young man trying to surpass his dead father's reputation a
image, seeing such an attempt as a journey leading to fame a
possible death. In *A Walk with Love and Death,* he questioned
possibility of lovers surviving in a world of chaos. In *The Krem*
Letter, he questioned the old values of group loyalty in an amo
world.

Huston was immediately plunged into what proved to be anoth
setback. At the end of 1970, Carter De Haven, who had produc
A Walk with Love and Death and *The Kremlin Letter,* asked Hust
to direct George C. Scott in *The Last Run.* Huston, who had work
with Scott on *The List of Adrian Messenger* and *The Bible,* agre

Filming began in Spain in January 1971. Almost immediately, Sc
and Huston began arguing over the director's rewrites of the A
Sharpe script. Scott also objected to Huston's choice of leading la
Tina Aumont, daughter of Jean-Pierre Aumont and the late Ma
Montez. Arguments turned to shouting matches and Huston left t
film. He was replaced by Richard Fleischer, and Aumont was
placed by Trish Van Devere, who would later marry Scott.

CHAPTER 22

Pug, a Legend, and a Spy

IS UNDERSTANDABLE, considering his recent reexaminations of
st values, that Huston would choose to make a film about boxing.
s boxing memories were of direct confrontations between two
n, of a simple world of simple people compared to the world of
e devious, cosmopolitan, and complex characters in *The Kremlin
tter.*

"I've been a boxer, and I've never actually served as a spy,"
iston told *Interview,* "so let's say I'm a little closer to the material.
s a very personal story."

For two years, the director's luck and temper had been running
ainst him. *Reflections in a Golden Eye* was ahead of its time. *Sinful
avey* received little critical attention and almost no commercial
lease. He was replaced on *The Madwoman of Chaillot* after one of
s frequent battles with producers. *A Walk With Love and Death*
ent the way of *Sinful Davey,* and he was replaced as director of
he Last Run.* His one partial critical and financial success in the
riod had been *The Kremlin Letter.*

At the age of sixty-four, Huston was on the ropes, so he turned
a project reflecting his own frustrations, one that dealt with defeat
the boxing ring. Although boxing had been an important part of
s youth and a continuing point of reference in his films, until 1970
had never turned to the sport for subject matter. The result was
e of his most personal films, as he himself has pointed out, and
obably his most successful film critically in twenty years.

For *Fat City,* based on the novel of the same name by Leonard
ardner, who was also to write the screenplay with Huston, the
rector returned to California, where his brief career as a boxer, or

"pug," and his long career as a writer-director-actor had begun. T
story was both set and shot in Stockton.

Huston's original choice for the broken-down boxer Tully v
Marlon Brando, but, he explained to *Interview*,: "Brando was un
cided about playing it and time was wasting. I saw Stacy Keach
The Traveling Executioner and here obviously was a wonderful t
ent that could lend itself to *Fat City*. I met Stacy and in the meanti
we were waiting to hear from Brando and didn't so we closed
Stacy."

For the other lead, a younger boxer named Ernie Munger, Hust
selected Jeff Bridges, noting later, "This was really his first big pa
It was just before *The Last Picture Show*. Except for them [Kea
and Bridges] the others were mostly boxing chums of mine a
people we discovered in Stockton."

Huston's friends included former boxer Art Aragon, who play
trainer, and Curtis Cokes, who plays the substantial role of Earl. E
and Tully are rivals for the constantly drunken Oma, played
Susan Tyrell.

"Curtis," said Huston, "is an ex-welterweight champion. He h
never done a bit of acting in his life. There is also a black boy w
does an Ali-type talk in the dressing room. He was a high school k
in Stockton."

Huston chose Tyrell for the role when he happened to see a scre
test she did with Keach for another part. "There was no doubt fro
the moment I saw that test," said Huston, "that she was the girl f
it . . . She is extraordinary in the film. A flower maiden if there ev
was one."

The scenes between Tully and Oma seem totally spontaneous an
unrehearsed. When the film was released, many reviewers assume
that these sequences had been ad-libbed.

"No," Huston told *Interview*, "they were rehearsed. They ha
rehearsed with each other privately and in my presence and the
were just wonderful. There was scarcely anything at all for me to d
There was no improvisation, though they tried to look spontaneous

Critics also singled out cinematographer Conrad Hall, who ha
just won an Academy Award for *Butch Cassidy and the Sundan
Kid*. His camera work for the scenes in Tully's room, the gym, an
the bar was cited as contributing to the aura of authenticity.

One of Hall's favorite scenes in *Fat City*, however, was remove

m the American version of the film. "They took out the dream
quences," said Hall, in the October 1973 edition of the American
lm Institute's *Dialogue on Film.* "I liked the dream stuff myself.
 shows Tully at an earlier time with his wife. That's one of the
ces I think is missing in this film, his life when he was on top. It's
e key to making his dilemma felt. It was a terrific sequence. It was
 different. He was in a suit and he looked young and handsome,
d he went into the ring the way they introduce big-time boxers,
u know, like Joe Louis. Tully gets up there and the crowd goes
ld. That's what's missing, what his life was like. In order to appre-
ate what happens when life goes down the drain, you have to know
e good times."

According to Huston, one bar scene was done without any artifi-
al lights to re-create the feeling of stepping from sunlight into dark.
When you go into a bar it's like stumbling into a theater," he said.
You can't find your way until your eyes adjust themselves. There
u reach around and try and find a barstool the same way you try
 find a seat in a theater. That is what led Conrad and me to do the
tsides with explosive skies and background and the interiors,
hich were all on the spot, almost in silhouettes."

Many boxing movies, from *Golden Boy* in 1939 to *The Great White
ope* in 1970, had explored the agony of defeat rather than the glory
 victory. In most of these films, however, the loser was given his
oment of glory, a shot at the title or a chance to redeem himself
rough sacrifice for friends, family, or society. *Fat City* would offer
s characters nothing.

The movie is about people without hope, people who have no
mbitions or even the ability to conceive of any but the most immedi-
te goals. Making it through the day with a minimum of pain is what
ey seek. "Help Me Make It through the Night," the soundtrack
ong, is the plea of all the primary characters.

In *Fat City,* the two protagonists, Tully and Ernie, exist on so little
ope that there are no expectations to be thwarted. As in most of
uston's films, the protagonists' plans do not work out as they
xpect or hope they will. But Huston's boxers are not disappointed,
ecause they never expect to escape from defeat.

This "lower depths" vision is played out on the social fringe of
rban Stockton, with the threat of a derelict life always inches away
rom the nose of Tully, whose only potential dignity and distance

from the other bums is the fact that he still might be able to box.
his ability is too little to earn him even temporary escape. When
engages in his only fight of the film and wins, we see his defea
Mexican opponent as the more dignified, independent man.

Tully speaks for Huston in the final scene when, watching a put
faced old man serve coffee in a skid-row hangout, he wonders alo
if we are all potentially like that. His preoccupation throughout
film has been with food, but he loses his best job, as a short-or
cook, and leaves the woman he is living with after ruining a biza
meal he cooks for her.

Huston has always had a desire to make it clear that no mat
what the genre — detective (*The Maltese Falcon*), gangster *(K
Largo)*, epic *(Moby Dick)*, melodrama *(The Misfits)*, spy *(The Ma
intosh Man)* — his films have a direct correlation with life. In
City, his metaphor is unmistakable and bleak.

"Fat City" — slang for "having it made" — is used ironically
the film about a world of bars and hangouts filled with bums.
escape this claustrophobic existence, Tully turns to the open spa
of the gymnasium, where, instead of facing lost souls, he must fa
other men physically. He has three such confrontations in the ri
or near it. The first is with Ernie, the second is with his form
manager, and the third is with the Mexican fighter. Tully appears
come out ahead in all three encounters, but he turns each one in
a disaster and heads back to the safety of the bars. In the few scen
in which Tully is seen outdoors, he gets nothing from his conta
with nature. He thinks only about his past and is fascinated by oth
peoples' stories of theirs. His world is indoors.

Tully cannot, at the age of twenty-nine, exist as anything but
bum. He tries to live in a sexual-familial relationship with an alc
holic, but he has neither the intelligence nor the courage to face suc
a situation.

Huston's protagonists often represent extremes. They are eith
ignorant, pathetic, and doomed by their lack of self-understandin
(Tully and Hobbs in *The Treasure of the Sierra Madre)* or intelligen
arrogant, and equally doomed by their lack of self-understandin
(Penderton in *Reflections in a Golden Eye* and Ahab in *Moby Dick*
Between these extremes is the cool, intelligent protagonist who wi
sacrifice everything for self-understanding and independence (Sar
Spade in *The Maltese Falcon,* Freud in *Freud*). Huston always find

the first group pathetic, the second tragic, and the third heroic. He reserves his greatest respect for the man who retains his dignity in spite of pain and disaster. In *Fat City,* this is the Mexican fighter, who never speaks and departs the stadium alone, well dressed and erect even after defeat.

Huston's use of the masks people wear or are forced to wear is consistent in this film. All the boxers are gradually shown to wear the same mask, the battered face of the derelict boxer, the face of universal defeat. Ernie, who is only eighteen, takes on this mask and is indistinguishable from the real former boxers who appear in the film and actually do have this face/mask. Tully, played by Keach in heavy make-up, looks in close-up like the other mush-faced veterans.

The few negative reviews of *Fat City* were overwhelmed by the affirmative ones. John Russell Taylor in *Sight and Sound* called the film "one of those late films by old masters that look effortless because they are effortless, come out right because the filmmaker has forgotten more about his craft than most of his juniors have ever learnt."

Taylor was also one of the few critics to recognize Huston's interest in the use of color:

From the Toulouse-Lautrec colors of *Moulin Rouge* and the nineteenth-century whaling-print effect of *Moby Dick* through the medieval tapestry textures of *A Walk with Love and Death,* this extreme and close concern with the overall visual effect of a film has been a Huston trademark. And so it is with *Fat City*: the color is deliberately faded, almost like a Fifties B-feature in some such process as Trucolor, and the interiors are shot by Conrad Hall in a bluish haze, as though through the atmosphere of a smoke-filled pool-hall.

"The success of *Fat City* was a pleasant surprise," says Huston. "I didn't expect a commercial success. I believed very much in the film but would have been happy if it were well received by a selective audience. I admire the down-and-outers depicted in the film, people who have the heroism to go taking it on the chin in life as well as in the ring."

Huston immediately moved on to his next project, another film to be shot in the United States and his only Western besides *The Unforgiven.*

When *Interview* asked him about the finished film, Huston replied that *The Life and Times of Judge Roy Bean* "is a Western but I've never seen a Western like it. It's outrageous. It doesn't go along with any set of rules or have any particular form. It violates all the conventions and I hope it's as amusing to see as it was to make. It doesn't take itself too seriously. There are sentimental moments but it is scarcely ever solemn and never pompous."

"It's wild," the director added. "Stacy Keach is in it in a wonderful brief sequence where he plays an albino gunman." In this scene, Keach eats raw onions, shoots a horse, and orders that it be cooked for his dinner. He then shoots the big toes off the railroad-station clerk.

Also in the cast was Ava Gardner, as Lillie Langtry, the actress who never ages and with whom Judge Roy Bean is in love from afar. Box-office insurance came in the form of Paul Newman as the judge. Newman was in partnership with John Foreman in the company that was to produce the film.

Part of Huston's interest in the story was that his old friend William Wyler had made *The Westerner,* a film revolving around Bean, in 1940. Walter Brennan played Bean and Gary Cooper was the cowboy who had to use his wits to stay alive around the strange judge. Brennan got an Academy Award as best supporting actor for his performance.

Huston's film, as scripted by John Milius, is not a remake of *The Westerner.* * It is a combination of folklore and fantasy and includes a sequence in which the legendary Bean apparently comes back from the dead to gather his cronies and rid the town he founded of the mercenary oil men who have taken over. Milius, who went on to direct such films as *Dillinger* and *The Wind and the Lion,* in which Huston played American statesman John Hay, credited the director with being a prime influence on his own directing career.

Huston's film is intended as a presentation of legend and not an exploration of the judge's history, but it does stick to a few basic facts. Bean was a justice of the peace in Pecos County, Texas, and he did use his saloon, The Jersey Lilly, named for Lillie Langtry, as a courthouse, and he did have a pet bear that drank beer. That is

*In fact, a new version of the earlier film was being discussed at a different studio, with Don Siegel as director, Academy Award winner Peter Stone as writer, Jack Lemmon as Bean, and Bill Cosby in the Gary Cooper role. However, plans were dropped when it was learned that Huston's film dealt with the same subject.

about the extent of fact that Huston retains. An interesting addition is the director's own appearance as Grizzly Adams, who arrives from the prairie to give Bean a bear he claims is his own son.

The movie was shot on location in Tucson, Arizona, and from the start Huston was enthusiastic about it.

"*Judge Roy Bean* couldn't be more different from *Fat City,*" he told Los Angeles *Times* reporter Dan Ford on location in 1972. "*Fat City* took place in one concentrated area, a big city slum. Judge Roy Bean is all over the map. We departed from the historical facts and made Bean more of a scalawag than he really was, but the film is, after all, more of a romance than a historical document. I think we have a hell of a picture here, a complete departure from reality, a pure fantasy."

Ford described Huston as having "a face that belongs in a mine or on the road somewhere. It's a thin face deeply grooved. Under bright black eyes that glow like sapphires are enormous puffy bags. The gaze is steady. Right to the soul. Wispy grey hair and beard frame it. Clearly it is a face weathered by life."

"Huston is," continued Ford, "always at ease, always composed, he doesn't look as if he could sweat or worry. It's a delivery that doesn't fit the rugged face. It is the contrast of virility and vanity, sweat and silk, steel and fat."

While working on *The Life and Times of Judge Roy Bean,* Huston married for the fifth time. His wife was thirty-one-year-old Californian Celeste Shane.

Huston's rapport with Paul Newman was instant. One visitor remembered seeing the two playing catch between takes with a ball improvised from aluminum foil from the dinner-plate covers brought to the location site.

"My god," Huston said to Ford, "Paul Newman is a good actor. He's just marvelous in this picture. He's never done anything quite like this and yet he's caught something unique and original. The picture definitely says something about a spirit of the past. There's something uniquely American about the judge."

There is also much of Huston in the feisty Bean. Both see themselves as legendary, virile, hard-drinking men with a strange sense of humor and a great confidence. Both have a commitment to what they see as the violent individualism of the Old West, and both have a strong antagonism toward civilization.

Huston's usual theme of group failure is reversed in the final confrontation of the film, in which Bean gathers his old friends to fight and defeat the uniformed militia of Frank Gass (Roddy McDowell). The judge gathers the town drunk, a cuspidor cleaner, and a bum to join him in a triumphant battle in which he rides his horse like a ghost through the flames of the burning town to destroy Gass and his men.

Huston said of the last battle, "There's a mysterious quality to that sequence. You don't know if it's the judge or his ghost that has returned to wreak vengenace on the violence that has occurred. The judge leads an insane attack on the forces of evil. It's as if the 19th century rose from its grave to destroy its prodigy, the 20th century."

One of Huston's favorite performers in the film was the bear, whom he introduced to Ford and other visitors on the set. "A fine actor," Huston would say solemnly of the bear. "Give Uncle John a kiss." And the foul-breathed creature would lick the smiling director's face. "A thorough professional," commented Huston. "He'd sell his soul for a Tootsie Roll."

One afternoon Huston took time to answer questions about Bean put to him by actor Billy Pearson's small daughter. The answers show the director's identification with the screen character.

"Judge Roy Bean just faced each day as it came," the director explained. "He thanked God each time he saw the sun rise and lived that day as fully as he could. And because he did it with a flair, that makes him very special."

Bean in the film, Huston continued, is not a mean man, "but he had to act mean . . . He just acted a certain way for people, just like Paul is doing in the movie. Roy Bean played the part of his own legend."

The film, which cost $4,000,000 to make, was released in December of 1972 to mixed reviews. It nonetheless began to pick up a following almost immediately, possibly from a combination of Newman fans and Western aficionados. This success was enough for Huston and Newman to decide to team up again, this time on a spy film.

The Mackintosh Man was based on a novel by Desmond Bagley called *The Freedom Trap*. One reason that Huston found the project appealing was that he could shoot most of the film in and around his own home in Ireland. In fact, location may have been equally as important as theme in choosing the film, which includes a chase through the Irish countryside and a scene in an Irish pub.

Multi-time Academy Award winner Edith Head, who had designed costumes for *The Life and Times of Judge Roy Bean,* and who had designed a great deal for Newman, was chosen for *The Mackintosh Man* as well.

"Working with John," she says, "is a very exciting experience. He is a charming, sophisticated, and completely fascinating human being, but besides all that he is extraordinarily involved in every facet of his films. Huston has long discussions before sketches are started, is interested in fabrics, colors, and above all things, either tests or looks at every costume before it goes on the film."

The film, starring Newman, Dominique Sanda, and James Mason, was Huston's second film about spies in three years. Unlike *The Kremlin Letter, The Mackintosh Man* is peopled with characters who operate from principle. Reardon (Newman) is a counterintelligence agent sentenced to prison for a diamond robbery. He is sprung along with Russian agent Sir George Wheeler (Mason) and passed along an underground route until forced to flee when his identity is discovered. He then starts the chase of the group that freed him. Reardon is an essentially moral man who wants to do the proper thing in an extremely complex situation. As in *The Kremlin Letter,* Huston's protagonist must make a moral decision at the end of the film.

When Reardon has Wheeler at gunpoint, he is persuaded that the humane, civilized thing to do is to let him live, that there is no reason for further bloodshed. The decision, however, is taken out of his hands by Mrs. Smith (Sanda), whose father's death has led her to a desire for personal vengeance. As in *The Kremlin Letter,* an act of revenge is at the heart of the violence. In the earlier film, the revenge is on behalf of a group of spies murdered by the villain. In *The Mackintosh Man,* it is on behalf of a murdered individual. The killing in the earlier film is cold and calculated; in the second film it is emotional.

The ending of *The Mackintosh Man* asks whether it is possible for men to live without violence in an endless stream of political and personal one-upmanship.

Huston's mask motif is most explicit in his mystery and spy films (*The Maltese Falcon, Across the Pacific, The List of Adrian Messen-*

ger, The Kremlin Letter), and *The Mackintosh Man* is no exception. There are particular similarities between this film and *The Kremlin Letter*. Each involves a protagonist surrounded by people with false fronts, people in figurative masks pretending to be other than what they are. All the spies in *The Kremlin Letter* must pretend to be Russians — Ward turns out to be a spy pretending to be a spy pretending to be a Russian. In *The Mackintosh Man*, Reardon must pretend to be someone other than he is as part of his assignment to trap the Russian agent in the guise of Sir George Wheeler.

Most of the reviews were unfavorable and the box office was poor.

Partly because of his new wife's preference for California, Huston sold his estate at St. Clerans. Although he owns a cottage by the sea in Lettermullen, Connemara, Ireland, he now spends most of his time when not on location at his home in Puerto Vallarta, Mexico.

CHAPTER 23

The King

FOR MORE THAN twenty years, John Huston had planned to make a film of "The Man Who Would Be King," a longish short story written by Rudyard Kipling at the age of twenty-one. Huston had first read the tale when he was a supposedly sickly boy of fourteen in a sanitarium. The fantastic adventures of Peachy Carnehan and Daniel Dravot, two soldiers of fortune who undertake a dangerous quest for wealth, have it in their grasp, and face death nobly when it comes in the unmapped land beyond Afghanistan in the late 1800s, was a strong influence on the imagination of the bedridden boy. Huston began devouring Kipling stories, novels, and poems and memorized long passages from many of them.

"I read so much Kipling," he told Jim Watters in a 1976 Chicago *Daily News* interview, "it's in my unconscious. You start a verse. I'll finish it. 'The Man Who Would Be King' appeals to the child in me, to the child in a lot of us."

Huston elaborated on his attraction to Kipling's story to Gideon Bachmann for *Film Comment:* "Kipling himself identified not only with people, but with animals and even things, living in a kind of pantheistic world when trees and rocks had identities. It's this universality in Kipling that I feel close to, although it goes much deeper than that."

In many ways, the film is a presentation of a long-cherished fantasy by a director facing old age.

Huston's original idea of casting Humphrey Bogart and Clark Gable in the leads was put aside when Bogart died. When Gable died it again was shelved, even though locations had been chosen, a script prepared, and sketches made. Five years later, Huston reworked the screenplay with the idea of Peter O'Toole and Richard Burton in the leads, and then Michael Caine and Burton, but he failed to get financial backing.

A decade later, producer John Foreman, who had recently had great success with *Butch Cassidy and the Sundance Kid* and who had produced *Judge Roy Bean* and *The Mackintosh Man,* visited Huston at his home in Ireland and noticed some of the director's sketches for the Kipling story. He asked Huston about them and was delighted to find that not only did a script exist but also the director's diaries of his visits to India and Afghanistan to select locations for the film.

Foreman set to work to obtain the backing of Allied Artists, and Huston began to rework the script with Gladys Hill. By the time it was completed, Foreman had raised over $8,000,000 to shoot the film.

One of Huston's first acts was to hire three-time Academy Award winner Oswald Morris, who had worked with him more than any other cinematographer. Their credits together included *Moulin Rouge, Beat the Devil, Moby Dick, Heaven Knows, Mr. Allison, The Roots of Heaven,* and *The Mackintosh Man.*

Because of financial and political problems, Huston was unable to shoot his film in Afghanistan. Instead he chose Morocco and the Atlas Mountains south of Marrakesh.

According to Michael Caine, who played Peachy, "Some people who've never read the Kipling story think it's a great vast tome about something or other, but he wrote about rascals and scoundrels and had a great old time. Well over half the lines in the movie are straight from Kipling."

In the film two former British soldiers decide to travel to a land beyond India where they will become kings. Because of their military skill, determination, courage, and luck, they succeed, but when Peachy decides that it is time to flee with the wealth of the kingdom, Daniel chooses to remain as king. Just as Peachy is set to leave, the natives discover Daniel has no supernatural powers. Since they had believed him a God, they kill him. Peachy is almost killed, but manages to get away and tell the tale to Rudyard Kipling.

While Huston does retain the outline of Kipling's tale, the original is only twenty-five pages long, so Huston and Hill had to create most of the film's dialogue. The dialogue in a key scene, the one in which

Peachy and Daniel (Sean Connery) come to the newspaperman's office, light their cigars, and sign their contract against drink and women, is taken word for word from the story.

In story and film, Daniel is disguised as a mad priest and Peachy as his servant. Also, in both versions, Daniel becomes a god, the two men are Masons, and the girl bites Daniel to prove that he bleeds and is therefore not a god. Peachy's line about Daniel's death is the same in story and film: . . . "and old Dan fell, turning round and round and round, twenty thousand miles, for he took half an hour to fall till he struck the water."

In the story, Daniel is described as a large man with a flowing red beard, a physical appearance that Kipling was fond of giving his heroes. The bandit hero of *Kim,* for example, is so described. Daniel, in the film, looks like both John Huston and a Kipling hero.

"I am sure," Huston told Bachmann, "that at some moment every man alive, no matter how lowly, has dreamed for a split second, at least, that he himself was a god. This goes for a painter as well as for a film director or a dice player." All three vocations, as we have seen, are Huston's.

Some significant differences between film and story are:

— The newspaperman who tells the tale in the first person is never identified in the story as Kipling. Huston chooses to make this explicit, to have his image of Kipling, as played by Christopher Plummer, appear on the screen. Kipling thus becomes not only a source but a character to explore.

— In the story, it is the newspaperman who turns Daniel and Peachy in to the authorities to stop them from blackmailing a rajah and to protect them, but in the film Kipling is a loyal Huston comrade and does not turn them in.

— Although Daniel and Peachy are Masons in the story, no big point is made of it. The importance of the Masonic order in the film is entirely Huston's. Huston explained to Bachmann: "I used a Masonic emblem to symbolize a universal connection between men, and my protagonists' lives are saved in a remote mountain town because the unfriendly priest recognizes in the emblem on Sean's chest an old holy insignia . . ."

— The two adventurers in the story encounter a lone bandit. In the film, they encounter a group of bandits whom Peachy tricks by spitting bullets into a fire when they aren't looking. The bullets explode, distracting the bandits, and Peachy and Daniel take them by surprise. No such incident occurs in the story.

— In the story, Daniel is not shot with an arrow. In the film, the scene is crucial. Unknown to the natives, the arrow lodges in Daniel's ammunition pack. When they see that he is not injured, they think he is a god, and he begins to carry a golden arrow around as a symbol of his godliness. It is this challenge to immortality and the gods that Huston examines. Daniel, in the film, is rational and in control when he is king. It is only when he assumes the role of a god that his fate, like Ahab's, is sealed. Daniel believes he can deal with and trust the priests and understand their religion. As in so many Huston films, religious figures are dangerous, removed from normal relationships and understandings. The priests in *The Man Who Would Be King,* like the priests in *A Walk with Love and Death* and the church in *The Night of the Iguana,* tell the protagonist to abstain from love and human relationships. Daniel refuses to refrain, moved by sexual desire in the Kipling story, and both sexual desire and the wish to challenge the gods in the film.

— In the story, Daniel shares his crown with Peachy and tells the priests that Peachy is his younger brother. Huston separates the two men completely. Peachy remains the loyal pragmatist, like Howard in *The Treasure of the Sierra Madre,* and Daniel, like Dobbs, becomes obsessed with gold and power and suffers for it.

— In the Kipling story, the priests select the potential wife for Daniel so she can bite him. In the Huston film, Daniel seals his own doom by selecting her himself. He becomes for Huston a victim of his own romance and confidence in his ability to control the woman.

— In Huston's film, Peachy, crucified and humbled, limps away into the night, leaving Kipling with Daniel's crowned skull. In the story, Kipling makes it clear that Peachy survives only a few days longer and is considered mad. For Huston, the character of Peachy is a worldly-wise and protected individual. For Kipling, he is a poor romantic soul, not much different from Daniel.

— In Kipling's story, Billy Fish is not someone the two men knew from the past but one of the chiefs who joins them. In the film, Billy Fish dies in a heroic lone sword charge at the hundreds of attacking priests. In the story, his throat is cut. For Huston, Billy Fish becomes a necessary member of the male group, a figure of courage from the past who must be given his moment of glory.

— The girl chosen for Daniel in the Kipling story is described as "white as death." Huston selected Michael Caine's Indian wife, Shakira, for the role, explaining that it was one thing for Kipling to give her a pale façade in a story, but when they tried to cast a blond in the role, it looked foolish. Of course, Kipling never specified a blond. It is possible that Huston's interest in thin, dark women who lead the protagonist into danger and possible death had prevailed over Kipling's minimal description.

When most directors his age were making small films in easy locations, Huston at sixty-eight took on a huge film in a difficult, inaccessible part of a little-known country. His cast was enormous and included thousands of Moroccan extras, all in costume.

"In *The Man Who Would Be King,*" said Edith Head, "we had 15,000 people. Some of the larger scenes involved several thousand warriors, soldiers, etc., and Huston surveyed them just as critically as he would a star in costume. He's a super perfectionist."

In addition to costuming thousands of extras for each day's shooting, Huston's crew had to see to it that the more than 1,000 actors playing priests had their heads properly shaved each day for their scenes.

In his casting of unknown actors or nonactors in key roles, Huston as usual extracted striking performances. Saeed Joffrey, who plays Billy Fish, and Doghmi Larbi, who plays Ootah, join a distinguished list of those who gave their most memorable or only performances in Huston films. Some of these actors and their roles were Ernest Anderson, who played the wrongly accused black man in *In This Our Life;* Alfonso Bedoya, who played Gold Hat in *The Treasure of the Sierra Madre;* Bill Mauldin, who played Tom Wilson in *The Red Badge of Courage;* Ivor Barnard, who played the mad major in *Beat the Devil;* Friedrich Ledebur, who played Queequeg in *Moby Dick* and Qvist in *The Roots of Heaven;* Fernand Ledoux, who played Charcot in *Freud;* Grayson Hall, who played Miss Fellowes in *The Night of the Iguana;* Ulla Bergryd, who played Eve in *The Bible;* Zorro David, who played Anacleto in *Reflections in a Golden Eye;* Assaf Dayan, who played Heron in *A Walk with Love and Death;* and Curtis Cokes, who played Earl in *Fat City.*

Huston has always said that he had not made a practice of directing actors, of telling them what to do. When reviewers praised Caine's and Connery's performances Huston explained in an NBC-

TV interview, "Occasionally, there's an actor who likes to talk about his role, so I'll talk with him. But that doesn't happen very often. In fact, with Sean Connery and Michael Caine, there was not one conversation between us. They just did it themselves."

When shooting was finished, Allied Artists put on the biggest publicity campaign for a Huston film since *The Bible*. Huge ads were taken in the daily papers, and double-page spreads featuring excellent reviews and full-page pictures of John Huston were printed in several issues of the *Hollywood Reporter*. Each ad gave a new set of quotations from reviewers praising Huston, Connery, Caine, and the film.

In addition, *The Man Who Would Be King* became a substantial moneymaker soon after its release. Huston and Gladys Hill were nominated for an Academy Award for their screenplay but lost in the final voting to *One Flew over the Cuckoo's Nest*.

While the film was doing well around the world, the government of Afghanistan refused to allow it to be shown in their theaters because of the childlike presentation of the natives. An examination of Huston's films makes it clear that this treatment is usual. Huston has traditionally viewed animals and natives as amoral, entertaining creatures who need to be taken care of, admired, amused, and used but never trusted or treated as equals. To a certain degree, this is also the director's attitude toward women. Huston's world is men on horses with guns, in battle with uniforms, with memories, men who give their trust infrequently to other men but in doing so expect the friendship guaranteed by that trust to outlast even the threat of death.

More than half the films Huston has directed have been set in a past whose values he cherishes. That past is doomed in these films, but Huston nonetheless admires it. His move to Ireland was a move to the past, and his interest in aristocracy and the ancient sport of fox hunting reflects a past where simple, brave scoundrels and rogues can sometimes triumph over masked pretenders to civilization and religion.

After finishing *The Man Who Would Be King*, Gladys Hill and Huston went to Mexico to work on the screenplay of Ernest Hemingway's 1950 novel, *Across the River and into the Trees*.

"I want my pictures to have moments that are so immediate audiences come into a personal experience," he told Vernon Scott in a 1975 UPI interview. "In that way people no longer are an audience. They become protagonists. Hemingway did this in literature."

While continuing to write the script, Huston accepted several acting roles, one as Sherlock Holmes's adversary Moriarty in a made-for-television film with Roger Moore as the detective, one in *Jocasta,* starring Sophia Loren, and one as a reporter in *Tentacles.*

The Hemingway story deals with an old army colonel who is dying and knows it. He takes one last trip back to Venice, where he participated in World War I battles. He visits his old comrades and a recent female friend who loves him and knows he is dying, and he goes duck hunting one last time. The colonel dies in the back seat of his car on the way back to his army post, having known in advance that the strain of his visit to Venice would kill him.

Hemingway's novel, like Huston's films, is a search for values by a man of the past, a man who remembers the thrill of battle, male friendships, and hunting, and bravely faces his own death.

The Hemingway project was temporarily put aside in 1977 while Huston directed Charles Bronson and Jill Ireland in *Love and Bullets, Charlie.* Writer Wendell Mayes worked with Huston on the film, Pancho Kohner produced it, and the production designer was Stephen B. Grimes.

"At my advanced age," said Huston to Watters, "I'm becoming aware of the intransigencies of this life. So I told the architect who's building a new home for me in Puerto Vallarta to build something that doesn't last too long, something that'll go back into the mountain, say in five years."

In the winter of 1977, Huston and his fifth wife, Celeste, were divorced.

Huston talks less about films than he used to. "We never talk movies around here," Gladys Hill said. "It's art or literature."

However, when asked by Charles Champlin of the Los Angeles *Times* to comment on his present view of the movies, Huston said, "The only interesting thing is magic. What you try to become is a bringer of magic. For magic and truth are closely allied and movies are sheer magic. When they are misused, it's a debasement of magic. But when they work, it is glorious."

John Huston has produced much glorious magic.

FILMOGRAPHY
BIBLIOGRAPHY
INDEX

Filmography

THE FILMS directed by John Huston, those in which he acted and those for which he has a writing credit, are included.

WRITER

1938   *Jezebel*   Warner Brothers

PRODUCER: Henry Blanke
DIRECTOR: William Wyler
SCREENPLAY: Clements Ripley, Abem Finkel, and John Huston, from the play by Owen Davis
CINEMATOGRAPHER: Ernest Hailer
EDITOR: Warren Low
MUSIC: Max Steiner
ART DIRECTOR: Robert Haas
CAST: Bette Davis (Julie Morrison), Henry Fonda (Preston Dillard), George Brent (Buck Cantrell), Margaret Lindsay (Amy Bradford Dillard), Fay Bainter (Aunt Belle Massey), Richard Cromwell (Ted Dillard), Donald Crisp (Dr. Livingstone), Henry O'Neill (General Bogardus), John Litel (Jean La Cour), Gordon Oliver (Dick Allen), Janet Shaw (Molly Allen), Theresa Harris (Zette)

1938   *The Amazing Dr. Clitterhouse*   Warner Brothers

PRODUCER: Anatole Litvak
DIRECTOR: Anatole Litvak
SCREENPLAY: John Huston and John Wexley, from the play by Barre Lyndon
CINEMATOGRAPHER: Tony Gaudio
EDITOR: Warren Low
CAST: Edward G. Robinson (Dr. Clitterhouse), Claire Trevor (Jo Keller), Humphrey Bogart (Rocks Valentine), Allen Jenkins (Okay), Donald Crisp (Inspector Lane), Gale Page (Nurse Randolph), Henry O'Neill (Judge), Thurston Hall (Grant), Maxie Rosenbloom (Butch), Burt Hanlon (Pal), Curt Bois (Rabbit), Vladimir Sokoloff (Popus), Billy Wayne (Candy), Robert Homans (Lt. Johnson), Irving Bacon (jury foreman)

1939   *Juarez*   Warner Brothers

PRODUCER: Hal Wallis
DIRECTOR: William Dieterle
SCREENPLAY: John Huston, Wolfgang Reinhardt, and Aeneas Mackenzie, based on *Maximilian and Carlotta* by Franz Werfel and *The Phantom Crown* by Bertita Harding
CINEMATOGRAPHER: Tony Gaudio
EDITOR: Warren Low
MUSIC: Erich Wolfgang Korngold
ART DIRECTOR: Anton Grot
CAST: Paul Muni (Benito Pablo Juarez), Bette Davis (Empress Carlotta von Hapsburg), Brian Aherne (Emperor Maximilian von Hapsburg), Claude Rains (Louis Napoleon), John Garfield (Porfirio Diaz), Donald Crisp (Marechale Bazaine), Gale Sondergaard (Empress Eugenie), Joseph Calleia (Alejandro Uradi), Gilbert Roland (Col. Miguel Lopez), Henry O'Neill (Miguel de Miramon)

1940   *Dr. Ehrlich's Magic Bullet*   Warner Brothers

PRODUCER: Hall Wallis
DIRECTOR: William Dieterle
SCREENPLAY: John Huston, Heinz Herald, and Norman Burnside, from an idea by Burnside; based on biographical material in possession of the Ehrlich family
CINEMATOGRAPHER: James Wong Howe
EDITOR: Warren Low
MUSIC: Max Steiner
ART DIRECTOR: Carl Jules Weyl
CAST: Edward G. Robinson (Dr. Paul Ehrlich), Ruth Gordon (Mrs. Ehrlich), Otto Kruger (Dr. Emil von Behring), Donald Crisp (Minister Althoff), Maria Ouspenskaya (Franziska Speyer), Montagu Love (Professor Hartmann), Sig Rumann (Dr. Hans Wolfert), Donald Meek (Mittelmeyer), Henry O'Neill (Dr. Lentz), Albert Basserman (Dr. Robert Koch), Edward Norris (Dr. Morgenroth), Louis Calhern (Dr. Brockdorf), Louis Jean Heydt (Dr. Kunze)

1941   *High Sierra*   Warner Brothers

PRODUCER: Jack Warner, Hal Wallis
DIRECTOR: Raoul Walsh
SCREENPLAY: John Huston and W. R. Burnett, from the novel by Burnett
CINEMATOGRAPHER: Tony Gaudio
EDITOR: Jack Killifer
MUSIC: Adolph Deutsch
CAST: Humphrey Bogart (Roy Earle), Ida Lupino (Marie), Alan Curtis (Babe), Arthur Kennedy (Red), Joan Leslie (Velma), Henry Hull ("Doc" Banton), Elizabeth Risdon (Ma), Cornell Wilde (Louis Mendoza), Minna Gombel (Mrs. Baugham), Paul Harvey (Mr. Baugham)

1941   *Sergeant York*   Warner Brothers

Producer: Jesse Lasky, Hall Wallis
DIRECTOR: Howard Hawks
SCREENPLAY: Abem Finkel, Harry Chandler, John Huston, and Howard Koch,

from *War Diary of Sgt. York* by Sam K. Cowan, *Sgt. York and his People* by Sam K. Cowan, and *Sergeant York — Last of the Long Hunters* by Tom Skeyhill
CINEMATOGRAPHER: Sol Polito (Arthur Edeson)
EDITOR: William Holmes
MUSIC: Max Steiner
CAST: Gary Cooper (Alvin York), Walter Brennan (Pastor Rosier Pile), Joan Leslie (Gracie Williams), George Tobias ("Pusher" Ross), David Bruce (Bert Thomas), Stanley Ridges (Major Buxton), Margaret Wycherly (Ma York), Dickie Moore (George York), Ward Bond (Ike Botkin), Noah Beery, Jr. (Buck Lipscomb), Harvey Stephens (Capt. Danforth), Charles Trowbridge (Cordell Hull), Howard da Silva (Clem), June Lockhart (Rosie York), Elisha Cook, Jr. (The pianist)

1946   *The Killers*   Universal

PRODUCER: Mark Hellinger
DIRECTOR: Robert Siodmak
SCREENPLAY: Anthony Veiller (Huston actually wrote the script, according to Siodmak, but was not credited as he was under contract to Warner Brothers)
EDITOR: Arthur Hilton
MUSIC: Miklos Rosza
ART DIRECTOR: Jack Otterson, Martin Obzina
CAST: Burt Lancaster (Swede Lunn), Edmund O'Brien (James Reardon), Ava Gardner (Kitty Collins), Albert Dekker (Jim Colfax), Sam Levene (Sam Lubinsky), Charles McGraw, William Conrad (the killers)

1946   *The Stranger*   RKO, International

PRODUCER: S. P. Eagle (pseudonym for Sam Spiegel)
DIRECTOR: Orson Welles
SCREENPLAY: Anthony Veiller, from a story by Victor Trivas and Decla Dunning; John Huston and Orson Welles uncredited
CINEMATOGRAPHER: Russell Metty
EDITOR: Ernest Nims
MUSIC: Bronislaw Kaper
ART DIRECTOR: Perry Ferguson
CAST: Orson Welles (Franz Kindler, alias Prof. Rankin), Edward G. Robinson (Inspector Wilson), Loretta Young (Mary Longstreet), Philip Merivale (Judge Longstreet), Richard Long (Noah Longstreet), Brian Keith (Dr. Lawrence), Billy Horse (Mr. Potter), Martha Wentworth (Sarah).

1946   *Three Strangers*   Warner Brothers

PRODUCER: Wolfgang Reinhardt
DIRECTOR: Jean Negulesco
SCREENPLAY: John Huston and Howard Koch, from a 1936 story by Huston
CINEMATOGRAPHER: Arthur Edeson
EDITOR: George Amy
MUSIC: Adolphe Deutsch
ART DIRECTOR: Ted Smith
CAST: Geraldine Fitzgerald (Crystal), Sydney Greenstreet (Arbutny), Peter Lorre (Johnny West), Peter Whitney (Gabby), Rosalind Ivan (Lady Rhae), Robert Shayne (Fallon), Clifford Brooke (Sr. Clerk), John Alvin (Jr. Clerk), Arthur

Shields (Prosecuter), Marjorie Riordan (Janet), Stanley Logan (Major Beach), Alan Napier (Shackleford), Joan Loring (Icy)

DIRECTOR

1941 *The Maltese Falcon* Warner Brothers

PRODUCER: Hal Wallis
DIRECTOR: John Huston
SCREENPLAY: John Huston, from the novel by Dashiell Hammett
CINEMATOGRAPHER: Arthur Edeson
EDITOR: Thomas Richards
MUSIC: Adolph Deutsch
ART DIRECTOR: Robert Haas
CAST: Humphrey Bogart (Sam Spade), Mary Astor (Brigid O'Shaughnessy), Gladys George (Iva Archer), Peter Lorre (Joel Cairo), Barton MacLane (Lt. Dundy), Lee Patrick (Effie Perrine), Sydney Greenstreet (Kaspar Gutman), Ward Bond (Det. Polhaus), Jerome Cowan (Archer), Elisha Cook, Jr. (Wilmer), Murray Alper (Frank Richman), John Hamilton (Bryan), James Burke (Luke), Walter Huston (Capt. Jacobi)

1942 *In This Our Life* Warner Brothers

PRODUCER: Hal Wallis
DIRECTOR: John Huston
SCREENPLAY: Howard Koch (Huston uncredited), from the novel by Ellen Glasgow
CINEMATOGRAPHER: Ernest Haller
EDITOR: William Holmes
MUSIC: Max Steiner
ART DIRECTOR: Robert Haas
CAST: Bette Davis (Stanley Timberlake), Olivia de Havilland (Roy Timberlake), George Brent (Craig Fleming), Dennis Morgan (Peter Kingsmill), Charles Coburn (William Fitzroy), Frank Craven (Asa Timberlake), Billie Burke (Lavinia Timberlake), Hattie McDaniel (Minerva Clay), Lee Patrick (Betty Wilmoth), Ernest Anderson (Passy Clay), Walter Huston (bartender)

1942 *Across the Pacific* Warner Brothers

PRODUCER: Jerry Wald, Jack Saper
DIRECTOR: John Huston (finished by Vincent Sherman)
SCREENPLAY: Richard Macaulay, from the serial "Aloha Means Goodbye" by Robert Carson
CINEMATOGRAPHER: Arthur Edeson
EDITOR: Frank Magee (montage by Don Seigel)
MUSIC: Adolph Deutsch
ART DIRECTOR: Robert Haas
CAST: Humphrey Bogart (Rick Leland), Mary Astor (Alberta Marlow), Sydney Greenstreet (Dr. Lorenz), Charles Halton (A. V. Smith), Victor Sen Yung (Joe Totsuiko), Roland Got (Sugi), Lee Tung Foo (Sam Wing)

1943   *Report from the Aleutians* (Documentary)   U.S. Signal Corps
(*Why We Fight* series)

DIRECTOR: (Captain) John Huston
SCREENPLAY: John Huston
NARRATOR: Walter Huston
CINEMATOGRAPHER: Jules Buck, Ray Scott
MUSIC: Dmitri Tiomkin

1945   *(Battle of) San Pietro* (Documentary)   U.S. Army Pictorial Service

DIRECTOR: (Major) John Huston
SCREENPLAY: John Huston
NARRATOR: John Huston
CINEMATOGRAPHER: John Huston, Jules Buck, and others
MUSIC: Dmitri Tiomkin

1946   *Let There Be Light* (Documentary)   U.S. Army

(Unreleased)

DIRECTOR: John Huston
SCREENPLAY: Charles Kaufman, John Huston
NARRATOR: Walter Huston
CINEMATOGRAPHER: Stanley Cortez, John Huston
MUSIC: Dmitri Tiomkin

1948   *The Treasure of the Sierra Madre*   Warner Brothers

PRODUCER: Henry Blanke
DIRECTOR: John Huston
SCREENPLAY: John Huston, from the novel by B. Traven
CINEMATOGRAPHER: Ted McCord
EDITOR: Owen Marks
MUSIC: Max Steiner
MUSIC DIRECTOR: Leo Forbstein
ART DIRECTOR: John Hughes
CAST: Humphrey Bogart (Dobbs), Walter Huston (Howard), Tim Holt (Curtin), Bruce Bennett (Cody), Barton MacLane (McCormick), Alfonso Bedoya (Gold Hat), Arthur Soto Rangel (The Presidente), Manuel Donde (El Jefe), José Torvay (Pablo), Margarito Luna (Pancho), Bobby Blake (Lottery Boy), Jacqueline Dalya (Ciquita), *John Huston* (American tourist)

1948   *Key Largo*   Warner Brothers

PRODUCER: Jerry Wald
DIRECTOR: John Huston
SCREENPLAY: Huston and Richard Brooks, from the play by Maxwell Anderson
CINEMATOGRAPHER: Karl Freund
EDITOR: Rudi Fuhr
MUSIC: Max Steiner
ART DIRECTOR: Leo Kuter

CAST: Humphrey Bogart (Frank McCloud), Lauren Bacall (Nora Temple), Lionel Barrymore (James Temple), Edward G. Robinson (Johnny Rocco), Claire Trevor (Gaye Dawn), Thomas Gomez (Curly), Harry Lewis ("Toots" Bass), John Rodney (Clyde Sawyer), Marc Lawrence (Ziggy), Monte Blue (Ben Wade), Dan Seymour ("Angel" Garcia), Jay Silverheels (Johnny), Rodric Redwing (Tom)

1949   *We Were Strangers*   Columbia, Horizon

PRODUCER: S. P. Eagle (pseudonym for Sam Spiegel)
DIRECTOR: John Huston
SCREENPLAY: John Huston and Peter Viertel, from a segment in *Rough Sketch* by Robert Sylvester
CINEMATOGRAPHER: Russell Metty
EDITOR: Al Clark
MUSIC: George Antheil
ART DIRECTOR: Gary Odell
CAST: John Garfield (Tony Fenner), Jennifer Jones (China Valdes), Pedro Armendariz (Armando Ariete), Gilbert Roland (Guillermo), Wally Cassel (Miguel), Ramon Novarro (leader of the revolutionaries), David Bond (Ramon)

1950   *The Asphalt Jungle*   MGM

PRODUCER: Arthur Hornblow, Jr.
DIRECTOR: John Huston
SCREENPLAY: John Huston and Ben Maddow, from the novel by W. R. Burnett
CINEMATOGRAPHER: Harold Rosson
EDITOR: George Boemler
MUSIC: Miklos Rosza
ART DIRECTOR: Cedric Gibbons
CAST: Sterling Hayden (Dix Handley), Louis Calhern (Alonzo D. Emmerich), Jean Hagen (Doll Conovan), Sam Jaffe ("Doc" Erwin Riedenschneider), James Whitmore (Gus Minissi), Marc Lawrence (Cobby), John McIntire (Hardy), Anthony Caruso (Louis Ciavelli), Teresa Celli (Maria Ciavelli), Marilyn Monroe (Angela Phinlay), Barry Kelley (Dietrich), William Davis (Timmons), Dorothy Tree (May Emmerich), Brad Dexter (Bob Brannen), John Maxwell (Swanson)

1951   *The Red Badge of Courage*   MGM

PRODUCER: Gottfried Reinhardt
DIRECTOR: John Huston
SCREENPLAY: John Huston, from the novel by Stephen Crane
CINEMATOGRAPHER: Harold Rosson
EDITOR: Ben Lewis, supervised by Marguerite Booth
MUSIC: Bronislaw Kaper
ART DIRECTOR: Cedric Gibbons
CAST: Audie Murphy (Henry Fleming, "The Youth"), Bill Mauldin (Tom Wilson, "The Loud Soldier"), John Dierkes (Jim Conklin, "The Tall Soldier"), Royal Dano ("The Tattered Soldier"), Arthur Hunnicutt (Bill Porter), Tim Durant (The General), Douglas Dick (The Lieutenant), Robert Easton Burke (Thompson), Andy Devine ("The Fat Soldier"), Smith Bellow (The Captain), Dixon Porter (a Veteran). Added commentary spoken by James Whitmore

1952   *The African Queen*   United Artists, Horizon,
                                                          Romulus

PRODUCER: S. P. Eagle (pseudonym for Sam Spiegel)
DIRECTOR: John Huston
SCREENPLAY: John Huston and James Agee, from the novel by C. S. Forester
CINEMATOGRAPHER: Jack Cardiff (Technicolor)
EDITOR: Ralph Kemplen
MUSIC: Allan Gray
ART DIRECTOR: Wilfred Singleton
CAST: Humphrey Bogart (Charlie Allnutt), Katharine Hepburn (Rose Sayer), Robert Morley (Samuel Sayer), Peter Bull (Captain of the *Luisa*)

1953   *Moulin Rouge*   United Artists, Romulus

PRODUCER: John Huston
DIRECTOR: John Huston
SCREENPLAY: Anthony Veiller, John Huston, from the book by Pierre La Mure
CINEMATOGRAPHER: Oswald Morris (Technicolor)
EDITOR: Ralph Kemplen
MUSIC: Georges Auric
ART DIRECTOR: Paul Sheriff, Marcel Vertés
CAST: José Ferrer (Toulouse-Lautrec), Colette Marchand (Marie Charlet), Suzanne Flon (Myriamme Hayen), Zsa Zsa Gabor (Jane Avril), Katherine Kath (la Goulue), Claude Nollier (Countess Toulouse-Lautrec), Muriel Smith (Aicha), George Lannes (Patov), Rupert John (Chocolate), Tutti Lemkov (Aicha's partner), Eric Pohlmann (bar owner), Walter Crisham (Valentin le Désossé), Mary Clare (Mme. Loubet), Lee Montague (Maurice Joyant), Christopher Lee (Paul Gaugin)

1954   *Beat the Devil*   United Artists, Santana,
                                                          Romulus

PRODUCER: John Huston (in association with Humphrey Bogart)
DIRECTOR: John Huston
SCREENPLAY: John Huston and Truman Capote, from the novel by James Helvick, also Anthony Veiller and Peter Viertel
CINEMATOGRAPHER: Oswald Morris
EDITOR: Ralph Kemplen
MUSIC: Franco Mannino
ART DIRECTOR: Wilfred Singleton
CAST: Humphrey Bogart, (Billy Dannreuther), Gina Lollobrigida (Maria Dannreuther), Jennifer Jones (Gwendolyn Chelm), Robert Morley (Peterson), Peter Lorre (O'Hara), Edward Underdown (Harry Chelm), Ivor Barnard (Major Ross), Marco Tulli (Ravello)

1956   *Moby Dick*   Warner Brothers, Moulin

PRODUCER: John Huston, Vaughan Dean
DIRECTOR: John Huston
SCREENPLAY: John Huston, Ray Bradbury, from the novel by Herman Melville
CINEMATOGRAPHER: Oswald Morris (Technicolor)

EDITOR: Russell Lloyd
MUSIC: Philip Stanton
ART DIRECTOR: Ralph Brinton
CAST: Gregory Peck (Ahab), Richard Basehart (Ishmael), Orson Welles (Father
   Mapple), Leo Genn (Starbuck), Harry Andrews (Stubb), Bernard Miles (Manx-
   man), Mervyn Johns (Peleg), Noel Purcell (Carpenter), Friedrich Ledebur (Quee-
   queg), James Robertson Justice (Captain Boomer), Edric Conner (Daggoo),
   Seamus Kelly (Flask), Royal Dano (Elijah), Francis de Wolff (Captain Gardiner),
   Philip Stainton (Bildad), Joseph Tornelty (Peter Coffin), Tamba Alleney (Pip),
   Ted Howard (blacksmith), Tom Clegg (Tashtego)

1957   *Heaven Knows, Mr. Allison*   Twentieth Century-Fox

PRODUCER: Buddy Adler, Eugene Frenke
DIRECTOR: John Huston
SCREENPLAY: John Huston and John Lee Mahin, from the novel by Charles Shaw
   (Ring Lardner, Jr., not credited)
CINEMATOGRAPHER: Oswald Morris (DeLuxe color)
EDITOR: Russell Lloyd
MUSIC: Georges Auric
CAST: Robert Mitchum (Allison), Deborah Kerr (Sister Angela)

1958   *The Barbarian and the Geisha*   Twentieth Century-Fox

PRODUCER: Eugene Frenke
DIRECTOR: John Huston
SCREENPLAY: Charles Grayson, story by Ellis St. Joseph
CINEMATOGRAPHER: Charles G. Clarke (DeLuxe, Cinemascope)
EDITOR: Stuart Gilmore
MUSIC: Hugo Friedhofer
ART DIRECTOR: Lyle Wheeler, Jack Martin Smith, Walter M. Scott, and Don B.
   Greenwood (sets)
CAST: John Wayne (Townsend Harris), Eiko Ando (Okichi), Sam Jaffe (Henry
   Heusken), So Yamamamura (Tamuro), Norman Thomson (Captain), James Rob-
   bins (Lt. Fisher), Morika (Prime Minister), Kodaya Ichikawa (Daimyo), Hiroshi
   Yamato (the Shogun), Tokujiro Iketaniuchi (Harusha), Fuji Kasai (Lord Hotta),
   Takeshi Kumagai (Chamberlain)

1958   *The Roots of Heaven*   Twentieth Century-Fox

PRODUCER: Darryl Zanuck
DIRECTOR: John Huston
SCREENPLAY: Romain Gary, Patrick Leigh-Fermor, from the novel by Gary
CINEMATOGRAPHER: Oswald Morris (DeLuxe, Cinemascope)
EDITOR: Russell Lloyd
MUSIC: Malcolm Arnold
ART DIRECTOR: Stephen Grimes
CAST: Errol Flynn (Forsythe), Trevor Howard (Morel), Juliette Greco (Minna),
   Eddie Albert (Abe Fields), Orson Welles (Cy Sedgewick), Paul Lukas (Saint
   Denis), Herbert Lom (Orsini), Gregoire Aslan (Habib), Friedrich Ledebur (Peter
   Qvist), Edric Connor (Waitari), André Luguet (governor), Olivier Hussenot (the
   Baron), Pierre Dudan (Major Sholscher), Marc Doelnitz (De Vries), Dan Jackson

(Madjumba), Maurice Cannon (Haas), Jacques Marin (Cerisot), Bachir Touré (Yussef), Habib Benglia, Alain Savvy, Roscoe Stallworth, Assane Fall, Francis De Wolff

1960   *The Unforgiven*   United Artists, Continental
                                                          Hecht/Hill/Lancaster

PRODUCER: James Hill
DIRECTOR: John Huston
SCREENPLAY: Ben Maddow, from the novel by Alan LeMay
CINEMATOGRAPHER: Franz Planer (Technicolor, Panavision)
EDITOR: Hugh Russell Lloyd
MUSIC: Dmitri Tiomkin
ART DIRECTOR: Stephen Grimes
CAST: Burt Lancaster (Ben Zachary), Audrey Hepburn (Rachel), Lillian Gish (Mattilda Zachary), John Saxon (Johnny Portugal), Charles Bickford (Zeb Rawlins), Albert Salmi (Charlie Rawlins), Audie Murphy (Cash), Joseph Wiseman (Abe Kelsey), Doug McClure (Andy Zachary), Kipp Hamilton, Arnold Merritt, June Walker, Carlos Rivas

1961   *The Misfits*   United Artists, Seven Arts

PRODUCER: Frank Taylor
DIRECTOR: John Huston
SCREENPLAY: Arthur Miller
CINEMATOGRAPHER: Russell Metty
EDITOR: George Tomasini
MUSIC: Alex North
ART DIRECTOR: William Newberry, Stephen Grimes
CAST: Marilyn Monroe (Roslyn Taber), Clark Gable (Gay Langland), Montgomery Clift (Perce Howland), Eli Wallach (Guido Dellini), James Barton (old man in bar), Kevin McCarthy (Roslyn's husband), Dennis Shaw (young man in bar), Philip Mitchell (Charles Steers), Walter Ramage (old groom), Peggy Barton (fiancée), Estelle Winwood, J. Lewis Smith, Marietta Tree, Bobby Lasalle, Ryall Bowker, Ralph Roberts

1963   *Freud*   Universal

PRODUCER: Wolfgang Reinhardt
DIRECTOR: John Huston
SCREENPLAY: Wolfgang Reinhardt, Charles Kaufman
CINEMATOGRAPHER: Douglas Slocombe
EDITOR: Ralph Kemplen
MUSIC: Jerry Goldsmith
ART DIRECTOR: Stephen Grimes
CAST: Montgomery Clift (Sigmund Freud), Susannah York (Cecily Koertner), Larry Parks (Dr. Joseph Breuer), Susan Kohner (Martha Freud), Eileen Herlie (Frau Ida Koertner), Fernand Ledoux (Professor Charcot), David McCallum (Carl von Schlosser), Rosalie Crutchley (Frau Freud), David Kossof (Jacob Freud), Joseph Furst (Jacob Koertner), Eric Portman (Dr. Theodore Meynert)

1963   *The List of Adrian Messenger*   Universal

PRODUCER: Edward Lewis
DIRECTOR: John Huston
SCREENPLAY: Anthony Veiller, from the novel by Phillip MacDonald
CINEMATOGRAPHER: Joseph McDonald (Ted Scaife in Europe)
EDITOR: Terry Morse
MUSIC: Jerry Goldsmith
ART DIRECTOR: Stephen Grimes, George Webb
CAST: Kirk Douglas (George Bruttenholm), George C. Scott (Anthony Gethryn), Dana Wynter (Lady Jocelyn Bruttenholm), Clive Brook (Marquis of Gleneyre), Herbert Marshall (Sir Wilfred Lucas), Gladys Cooper (Mrs. Karoudjian), Jacques Roux (Raoul LeBorg), John Merivale (Adrian Messenger), Marcel Dalio (Max Karoudjian), Walter Anthony Huston (Derek Bruttenholm), Bernard Archard (Inspector Pike), Roland D. Long (Carstairs), *John Huston* (Lord Acton), Tony Curtis (organ grinder), Burt Lancaster (old woman), Frank Sinatra (gypsy), Robert Mitchum (J. Slattery)

1964   *The Night of the Iguana*   MGM, Seven Arts

PRODUCER: Ray Stark, John Huston
DIRECTOR: John Huston
SCREENPLAY: John Huston, Anthony Veiller, from the play by Tennessee Williams
CINEMATOGRAPHER: Gabriel Figueroa (Cinemascope)
EDITOR: Ralph Kemplen
MUSIC: Benjamin Frankel
ART DIRECTOR: Stephen Grimes
CAST: Richard Burton (Reverend T. Lawrence Shannon), Ava Gardner (Maxine Faulk), Deborah Kerr (Hannah Jelkes), Sue Lyon (Charlotte Goodall), James Ward (Hank Prosner), Grayson Hall (Judith Fellowes), Cyril Delevanti (Nonno), Mary Boylan (Miss Peebles), Gladys Hill (Miss Dexter), Billie Matticks (Miss Throxton), Emilio Fernandes (barkeeper), Fidelmar Duran (Pepe), Roberto Leyra (Pedro), C. G. Kim (Chang), Eloise Hardt, Thelda Victor, Betty Proctor, Dorthy Vance, Liz Rubey, Bernice Starr, Barbara Joyce (teachers)

1965   *The Bible*   De Laurentiis

PRODUCER: Dino De Laurentiis
DIRECTOR: John Huston
SCREENPLAY: Christopher Fry (Dialogue by Mario Soldati)
CINEMATOGRAPHER: Guiseppe Potunno (Technicolor)
EDITOR: Alberto Galliti
MUSIC: Toshiro Mayuzumi
ART DIRECTOR: Stephen Grimes
CAST: Michael Parks (Adam), Ulla Bergryd (Eve), Richard Harris (Cain), Franco Nero (Abel), Stephen Boyd (Nimrod), *John Huston* (Noah), George C. Scott (Abraham), Ava Gardner (Sarah), Peter O'Toole (the Messenger), Gabriele Ferzetti (Lot), Eleonora Rossi Drago (Lot's wife), Pupella Maggio (Noah's wife), Grazia Maria Spina and Adriana Ambesi (Lot's daughters), Zoe Sallis (Hagar), Gabriella Pallotta, Rosanna Di Rocco, Anna Maria Orso, Peter Henze, Erik Leuzinjer, Angelo Boscanol, Alberto Lucantoni, Luciano Conversi, Robert Rietti, Flavio Bennati, Amru Sani, Marie-Catherine Pratt

1967   *Casino Royale*   Columbia

PRODUCER: Charles K. Feldman, Jerry Bresler
DIRECTOR: John Huston, Ken Hughes, Val Guest, Robert Parrish, and Joseph McGrath
SCREENPLAY: Wolf Mankowitz, John Law, Michael Sayers, suggested by the novel by Ian Fleming
CINEMATOGRAPHER: Jack Hildyard
EDITOR: Bill Lenny
MUSIC: Burt Bacharach
ART DIRECTOR: John Howell, Ivor Beddoes, Lionel Couch
CAST: Peter Sellers (Evelyn Tremble), Ursula Andress (Vesper Lynd), David Niven (Sir James Bond), Orson Welles (le Chiffre), Joanna Pettit (Mata Bond), Daliah Lavi (the Detainer), Woody Allen (Jimmy Bond), Deborah Kerr (Agent Mimi), William Holden (Ransom), Charles Boyer (le Grand), *John Huston* (McTarry), Kurt Kasznar (Smernov), George Raft (himself), Jean-Paul Belmondo (French Legionnaire), Terence Cooper (Cooper), Barbara Bouchet (Moneypenny), Angela Scoular (Buttercup), Gabriella Licudi (Eliza), Tracy Crisp (Heather), Elaine Taylor (Peg), Jacqueline Bisset (Miss Goodthighs)

1967   *Reflections in a Golden Eye*   Warner Brothers, Seven Arts

PRODUCER: Ray Stark
DIRECTOR: John Huston
SCREENPLAY: Chapman Mortimer, Gladys Hill, based on the novel by Carson McCullers
CINEMATOGRAPHER: Aldo Tonti (Technicolor)
EDITOR: Russell Lloyd
MUSIC: Toshiro Mayuzumi
ART DIRECTOR: Bruno Avesani
CAST: Elizabeth Taylor (Leonora Penderton), Marlon Brando (Major Weldon Penderton), Brian Keith (Lt. Col. Morris Langdon), Julie Harris (Alison Langdon), Robert Forster (Pvt. Williams), Zorro David (Anacleto), Gordon Mitchell (Stables Sergeant), Irvin Dugan (Capt. Weincheck), Fay Sparks (Susie)

1969   *Sinful Davey*   United Artists

PRODUCER: William N. Grof, Walter Mirisch (Executive Producer)
DIRECTOR: John Huston
SCREENPLAY: James R. Webb, based on the book *The Life of David Haggert,* by David Haggert
CINEMATOGRAPHER: Freddie Young, Edward (Ted) Scaife (DeLuxe, Panavision)
EDITOR: Russell Lloyd
MUSIC: Ken Thorne
ART DIRECTOR: Carmen Dillon
CAST: John Hurt (Davey), Pamela Franklin (Annie), Nigel Davenport (Constable), Ronald Fraser (McNab), Robert Morley (Duke of Argyll), Fidelma Murphy (Jean), Maxine Audley (Duchess of Argyll), Fionnuala Flanagan (Penelope), Donal McCann (Sir James), Allan Cuthbertson (Capt. Douglas), Eddie Byrne (Bill), Niall MacGinnis (Boots), Noell Purcell (Jock), Judith Furse (Mary), Francis De Wolff (Andrew), Paul Farrell (Bailiff), Geoffrey Golden (Warden), Leo Collins (Dr. Gresham), Mickser Reid (Billy the Goat), Derek Young (Bobby), John Franklyn (George), Eileen Murphy (Mary Kidd)

1969   *A Walk with Love and Death*   Twentieth Century-Fox

PRODUCER: Carter De Haven
DIRECTOR: John Huston
SCREENPLAY: Dale Wasserman; adapted by Hans Koningsberger from his novel
CINEMATOGRAPHER: Ted Scaife (DeLuxe)
EDITOR: Russell Lloyd
MUSIC: Georges Delerue
ART DIRECTOR: Wolf Witzemann
CAST: Anjelica Huston (Claudia), Assaf Dayan (Heron), Anthony Corlan (Robert),
    John Hallam (Sir Meles), Robert Lang (Pilgrim Leader), Guy Deghy (priest),
    Michael Gough (mad monk), George Murcell (captain), Eileen Murphy (gypsy),
    Anthony Nicholls (Father Superior), Joseph O'Conner (St. Jean), *John Huston*
    (Robert the Elder), John Franklin (whoremaster), Francis Heim (knight), Melvin
    Hayes, Barry Keegan, Nicholas Smith

1970   *The Kremlin Letter*   Twentieth Century-Fox

PRODUCER: Carter De Haven, Sam Wiesenthal
DIRECTOR: John Huston
SCREENPLAY: John Huston, Gladys Hill, from the novel by Noel Behn
CINEMATOGRAPHER: Ted Scaife (Panavision, DeLuxe)
EDITOR: Russell Lloyd
MUSIC: Robert Drasnin, composed by Toshiro Mayuzumi
ART DIRECTOR: Elven Webb
CAST: Bibi Andersson (Erika), Richard Boone (Ward), Nigel Green (Whore), Dean
    Jagger (highwayman), Lila Kedrova (Sophie), Michael MacLiammoir (Sweet
    Alice), Patrick O'Neal (Rone), Barbara Parkins (B.A.), Ronald Radd (Pot-
    kin), George Sanders (Warlock), Raf Vallone (puppetmaker), Max Von Sydow
    (Kosnov), Orson Welles (Bresnavitch), Sandor Eles (Grodin), Niall MacGin-
    nis (Erector Set), Anthony Chinn (Kitai), Guy Degny (professor), *John Huston*
    (Admiral), Fulvia Ketoff (Sonia), Vonetta McGee (Negress), Marc Lawrence
    (priest), Cyril Shaps (police doctor), Christopher Sanford (Rudolph), Anna-Maria
    Pravda (Mrs. Kazar), George Pravda (Kazar), Ludmilla Dutarova (Mrs.
    Potkin), Dimitri Tamarov (Ilya), Pehr-Olof Siren (receptionist), Daniel Smid
    (waiter)

1972   *Fat City*   Columbia

PRODUCER: Ray Stark (John Huston — Rastar) for Columbia
DIRECTOR: John Huston
SCREENPLAY: Leonard Gardner, from his novel
CINEMATOGRAPHER: Conrad Hall (Eastman Color)
EDITOR: Marguerite Booth
MUSIC (Supervision): Marvin Hamlisch
PRODUCTION DESIGNER: Richard Sylbert (no Art Director credit)
CAST: Stacy Keach (Tully), Jeff Bridges (Ernie Munger), Candy Clark (Faye),
    Susan Tyrell (Oma), Nicholas Colosanto (Ruben), Art Aragon (Babe), Curtis
    Cokes (Earl), Sixto Rodriguez (Lucero), Billy Walker (Wes), Wayne Mahan
    (Buford), Ruben Navarro (Fuentes)

1972   *The Life and Times of Judge Roy Bean*   National, General

PRODUCER: John Foreman
DIRECTOR: John Huston
SCREENPLAY: John Milius
CINEMATOGRAPHER: Richard Moore
EDITOR: Hugh S. Fowler
MUSIC: Maurice Jarre
ART DIRECTOR: Tambi Larsen
CAST: Paul Newman (Judge Roy Bean), Ava Gardner (Lillie Langtry), Victoria Principal (Marie Elena), Anthony Perkins (Reverend LaSalle), Tab Hunter (Sam Dodd), *John Huston* (Grizzly Adams), Stacy Keach (Bad Bob), Roddy McDowell (Frank Gass), Jacqueline Bisset (Rose Bean), Ned Beatty (Tector Crites), Jim Buck (Bart Jackson), Matt Clark (Nick the Grub), Steve Kanaly (Whorehouse Lucky Jim), Bill McKinney (Fermil Parlee), Billy Pearson

1973   *The Mackintosh Man*   Warner Brothers

PRODUCER: John Foreman (William Hill, Associate Producer)
DIRECTOR: John Huston
SCREENPLAY: Walter Hill, from *The Freedom Trap,* by Desmond Bagley
CINEMATOGRAPHER: Oswald Morris (Technicolor)
EDITOR: Russell Lloyd
MUSIC: Maurice Jarre
ART DIRECTOR: Alan Tomkins
DESIGNER: Terry Marsh
CAST: Paul Newman (Reardon), Dominique Sanda (Mrs. Smith), James Mason (Sir George Wheeler), Harry Andrews (Mackintosh), Ian Bannen (Slade), Michael Hordern (Brown), Nigel Patrick (Soames — Trevelyan), Peter Vaughan (Brunskill), Roland Culver (Judge), Percy Herbert (Taafe), Robert Lang (Jack Summers), Jenny Runacre (Gerda), John Bindon (Buster), Hugh Manning (prosecutor), Wolfe Morris (Malta police commissioner), Noel Purcell (O'Donovan), Donald Webster (Tervis), Keith Bell (Palmer), Niall MacGinnis (Warder)

1975   *The Man Who Would Be King*   Associated Artists

PRODUCER: John Foreman (James Arnett, Associate Producer)
DIRECTOR: John Huston
SCREENPLAY: Gladys Hill, John Huston, from the story by Rudyard Kipling
CINEMATOGRAPHER: Oswald Morris
EDITOR: Russell Lloyd
PRODUCTION SUPERVISOR: Ted Lloyd
PRODUCTION DESIGN: Alex Trainer
COSTUMES: Edith Head
ART DIRECTOR: Tony Inglis
MUSIC: Maurice Jarre
CAST: Sean Connery (Daniel Dravot), Michael Caine (Peachy Carnehan), Christopher Plummer (Rudyard Kipling), Saeed Joffrey (Billy Fish), Karrovin Ben Bouih (Kafu-Selim), Jack May (district commissioner), Doghmi Larbi (Ootah), Shakira Caine (Roxanne), Mohammed Shamsi (Babu), Paul Antrim (Mulvaney), Albert Moses (Ghulam)

ACTOR IN MAJOR ROLES

1977   *Love and Bullets, Charlie*   I.T.C.

PRODUCER: Pancho Kohner
DIRECTOR: John Huston
SCREENPLAY: Wendell Mayes
PRODUCTION DESIGN: Stephen B. Grimes
CAST: Charles Bronson, Jill Ireland

1929   *Shakedown*   Universal

DIRECTOR: William Wyler
CAST: James Murray, Barbara Kent, George Kotsonaros
Huston had a small role
No production credit available (AFI Index)

1929   *Hell's Heroes*   (listed 1930 in AFI Index)   Universal

DIRECTOR: William Wyler
PRODUCER: Carl Laemmle
CAST: Charles Bickford, Raymond Hatton, Fred Kohler
Huston had a small role

1930   *The Storm*   Universal

DIRECTOR: William Wyler
PRODUCER: Carl Laemmle
CAST: Lupe Velez, Paul Cavanaugh, William Boyd
Huston had a small role

1963   *The Cardinal*   Columbia

DIRECTOR: Otto Preminger
PRODUCER: Otto Preminger
CAST: Tom Tryon, Romy Schneider, John Saxon, Carol Lynley, Raf Vallone, Burgess Meredith
Huston as Cardinal Glennon

1968   *Candy*   Cinerama

DIRECTOR: Christian Marquand
PRODUCER: Robert Haggiag
CAST: Marlon Brando, Ringo Starr
Huston played Dr. Dunlap

1969   *De Sade*   A.I.P.

DIRECTOR: Cy Enfield
PRODUCER: Samuel Z. Arkoff, James H. Nicholson
CAST: Keir Dullea, Senta Berger, Lilli Palmer
Huston played The Abbé

1970   *Myra Breckenridge*   Twentieth Century-Fox

DIRECTOR: Michael Sarne
PRODUCER: Robert Fryer
CAST: Raquel Welch, Mae West, Rex Reed
Huston played Buck Loner (given second bill)

1971   *The Bridge in the Jungle*   United Artists

DIRECTOR: Pancho Kohner
PRODUCER: Pancho Kohner
SCREENPLAY: Pancho Kohner, based on the novel by B. Traven
CAST: Charles Robinson, Katy Jurado
Huston played Sleigh (given top bill)

1971   *The Deserter*   Paramount

DIRECTOR: Burt Kennedy
PRODUCER: Norman Baer, Ralph Serpe
CAST: Bekim Fehmiu, Richard Crenna, Chuck Connors, Ricardo Montalban, Ian
   Bannen, Brandon de Wilde, Slim Pickens
Huston played General Miles (given second bill)

1971   *Man in the Wilderness*   Warner Brothers

DIRECTOR: Richard Sarafian
PRODUCER: Sanford Howard
CAST: Richard Harris, John Bindon, Ben Carruthers, Percy Herbert, Henry Wil-
   coxón
Huston played Captain Henry (given second bill)

1974   *Battle for the Planet of the Apes*   Twentieth Century-Fox

DIRECTOR: J. Lee Thompson
PRODUCER: Arthur P. Jacobs
CAST: Roddy McDowell, Claude Akins, Natalie Trundy
Huston played Lawgiver (given third bill)

1974   *Chinatown*   Paramount

DIRECTOR: Roman Polanski (Howard Koch, Jr., Assistant Director)
PRODUCER: Robert Evans
CAST: Jack Nicholson, Faye Dunaway
Huston played Noah Cross (given third bill)

1975   *Breakout*   Columbia

DIRECTOR: Tom Gries
CAST: Charles Bronson, Robert Duvall, Jill Ireland, Randy Quaid
Huston played Harris (listed as guest star)

1975   *The Wind and The Lion*   United Artists

DIRECTOR: John Milius
PRODUCER: Herb Jaffe

CAST: Sean Connery, Candice Bergen, Brian Keith
Huston played John Hay (given fourth bill)

1976   *Sherlock Holmes in New York*

DIRECTOR: Boris Sagal
CAST: Roger Moore, Charlotte Rampling, Gig Young
Huston played Professor Moriarty (given second bill)

1977   *Tentacles*   A.I.P.

DIRECTOR: Oliver Hellman (Ouidio Assonitis)
PRODUCER: E. F. Doria
CAST: Shelley Winters, Henry Fonda, Bo Hopkins
Huston played Ned Turner (given top bill)

Bibliography

THIS BIBLIOGRAPHY includes only key books and articles that the author found particularly valuable. It is by no means a complete list of publications dealing with John Huston.

Reviews, which number in the thousands, are not included. For a guide to reviews of Huston's films see *Index to Critical Film Reviews,* compiled and edited by Stephen E. Bowles (New York: Burt Franklin & Co., Inc., 1974).

Books on or dealing with John Huston
(A selected list)

Agee, James. *Agee On Film.* Beacon Press, 1964.

Agee, James. *Agee On Film: Five Film Scripts.* Foreword by John Huston. Beacon Press, 1965.

Allais, Jean-Claude. *John Huston* (in French). Premier Plan, 1960.

Astor, Mary. *A Life On Film.* Dell, 1972.

Benayoun, Robert. *John Huston* (in French). Seghers, 1966.

Carey, Gary. *Brando!* Pocket Books, 1973. (Section on *Reflections in a Golden Eye.*)

Cecchini, Riccardo. *John Huston* (in Italian). Viridiana, 1969.

Crowther, Bosley. *The Lion's Share.* E. P. Dutton, 1957. (Scattered information on *The Red Badge of Courage.*)

Davay, Paul. *John Huston* (in French). Club du live de Cinema, 1957.

Flynn, Errol. *My Wicked, Wicked Ways.* G. P. Putnam's Sons, 1959. (Section on *The Roots of Heaven.*)

Frischauer, Willi. *Behind the Scenes of Otto Preminger.* William Morrow, 1974.

Fry, Christopher. *The Bible.* Pocket Books, 1966. (A screenplay with a preface by Fry.)

Gilles, Jacob. *Le Cinema Moderne* (in French). Serdoc, 1964. (Pp. 93–100.)

Godley, John. *Living Like a Lord.* Houghton Mifflin, 1956. (On *Moby Dick.*)

Goode, James. *The Story of the Misfits.* Bobbs-Merrill, 1963.

Goodman, Ezra. *The Fifty-Year Decline and Fall of Hollywood.* Simon and Schuster, 1961.

Guiles, Fred Lawrence. *Norma Jean: The Life of Marilyn Monroe.* Bantam, 1973.

Gussow, Mel. *Zanuck: Don't Say Yes Until I Finish Talking.* Doubleday, 1971.

Hamblett, Charles. *The Crazy Kill* (novel). Sedgewick and Jackson, 1956.

Hayden, Sterling. *Wanderer.* Knopf, 1963.

Higham, Charles. *Ava.* Delacorte Press, 1974.

Hughes, Robert, ed. *Film Book 2: Films of Peace and War.* Grove Press, 1962. (Interview with Huston and script of *Let There Be Light.*)

Huston, John. *Frankie and Johnny* (a play and versions of the legend). Boni and Liveright, 1930.

Hyams, Joe. *Bogie.* New American Library, 1966.

Morley, Robert, and Stokes, Sewel. *Robert Morley,* Simon and Schuster, 1966.

Nolan, William. *John Huston: King Rebel.* Sherbourne Press, 1965.

Niven, David. *Bring on the Empty Horses.* Putnam, 1975. (Pp. 337–38 on *The African Queen.*)

Rivkin, Allen, and Kerr, Laura. *Hello, Hollywood: A Book about the Movies by the People Who Make Them.* Doubleday, 1962. (See pp. 129–30 and pp. 305–9 on *The Barbarian and the Geisha.*)

Ross, Lillian. *Picture.* Rinehart & Co., 1952. (From *The Red Badge of Courage.*)

Selznick, David O. *Memo From: David O. Selznick.* Selected and edited by Rudy Behlmer. Viking Press, 1972.

Shepard, Dick. *Elizabeth.* Doubleday, 1974. (See pp. 411–13, 435.)

Swindell, Larry. *Body and Soul: The Story of John Garfield.* William Morrow, 1975.

Viertel, Peter. *White Hunter, Black Heart* (novel). Doubleday, 1953.

Articles on or dealing with John Huston
(A selected list)

Aba, Marika. "Huston Back in Stream with Kremlin." Los Angeles *Times,* May 11, 1969, pp. 24–25.

American Film Institute *Dialogue on Film.* "Cinematographer Conrad Hall," October 1973, pp. 1–24.

Archer, Eugene. "John Huston — The Hemingway Tradition in American Film," *Film Culture* #19, 1959, pp. 66–101.

Bachmann, Gideon. "How I Make Films." *Film Quarterly,* Fall 1965, pp. 3–13. (An interview with John Huston.)

————. "Watching Huston." *Film Comment,* January-February 1976, pp. 21–22.

Barnes, Peter. "The Director on Horseback." *Film Quarterly,* Spring 1956, pp. 281–87.

Bester, Alfred. "John Huston's Unsentimental Journey." *Holiday,* May 1959, pp. 111–18.

Blume, Mary. "Huston Directing Daughter in 'Walk,' " Los Angeles *Times,* February 2, 1969, p. 15.

Boyle, Hal. "Free Soul Huston." Los Angeles *Times,* June 18, 1969.

Cahiers du Cinema in English. "John Huston, *The Bible* and James Bond," No. 5, 1966, pp. 7–8.

Champlin, Charles. "Huston Before, Behind Camera," *Calendar,* Los Angeles *Times,* August 4, 1974, pp. 1–2.

Close-Up. "Huston, Madman, Myth or Magician," November 6, 1958, pp. 3–4.

Ebert, Roger. "Caine and Connery on Films, Booze, Pubs and Sex." *Show,* Chicago *Sun-Times,* February 8, 1976, pp. 1–2.

Eng, Frank. "Frank Eng's Column." Los Angeles *Daily News,* July 23, 1948, p. 36.

Ford, Dan. "Legend Tackles Legend: Huston, Judge Roy Bean." Los Angeles *Times,* May 28, 1972, p. 1.

Fowler, Dan. "Walter Huston's Bad Boy John." *Look,* November 3, 1948, pp. 40–44.

Francine, Renee. "Ham, Genius." *The American Weekly,* June 26, 1960.

Gilder, Rosamond. "Time and the Rivals." *Theatre Arts,* March 3, 1942, pp. 149–50.

Gilmore, Eddy. Interview. Associated Press, Summer, 1969.

Graham, Sheilah. "John Huston Wants Hepburn for Film." Hollywood *Citizen-News,* September 5, 1967.

Grencer, Cynthia. "Huston at Fontainbleau." *Sight and Sound,* Autumn 1958, pp. 280–85.

Griffith, Richard. "Wyler, Wellman and Huston." *Films in Review,* February 1950, pp. 1–5.

Hawkins, Robert F. "The Bible." *New York Times,* February 21, 1965.

Hine, Al. "Paris in the 90's." *Holiday,* April 1953, pp. 26–27.

Hopper, Hedda. "Director Says 'Iguana' Stars Adored Themselves, Each Other." Los Angeles *Times,* December 12, 1963.

––––––. "John Huston Weds Screen Newcomer." Los Angeles *Times,* March 20, 1950.

Huston, John. "The African Queen." *Theatre Arts,* February 1952, pp. 42–49, 92.

––––––. "Figures of Fighting Men." *The American Mercury,* May 1931.

––––––. "Fool" (a short story). *The American Mercury,* March 1929.

––––––. "Home is Where the Heart is — and So Are Films." *Screen Producers Guild Journal,* March 1963, p. 3.

––––––. "Humphrey Bogart Died Monday Morning" (in French). *Positif,* Numero 21.

––––––. "Monkeys I Have Known." *Pageant,* August 1965.

Kennedy, Paul. "John Huston's Iguana." *New York Times,* December 1, 1963.

Knight, Arthur. "The Director." *Saturday Review,* June 9, 1956, pp. 29–30.

Koningsberger, Hans. "From Book to Film — via John Huston." *Film Quarterly,* Spring 1969.

Kunert, Arnold R. "Ray Bradbury on Hitchcock, Huston and other Magic of the Screen." *Take One,* September 1973, pp. 15–23.

Kurnitz, Harry. "Captain Huston Takes Moby Dick." *Holiday,* July 1956, pp. 78–79.

Laurot, Edouard. "An Encounter with John Huston." *Film Culture,* No. 8, 1956, pp. 1–4.

Lennon, Peter. "Huston in Focus on Film Industry." Los Angeles *Times,* September 16, 1967.

Life. "The Ark that John Built." August 13, 1965, pp. 43–44.

––––––"John Cardinal Huston." November 22, 1963.

Look. "John Huston Hits a Double." November 1958, pp. 106–108.

Lord, Rosemary. "John Huston." *Transatlantic Review,* No. 50, Autumn–Winter 1974, pp. 140–45.

Mage, David A. "The Way John Huston Works." *Films in Review,* October 1952, pp. 393–98.

McClay, Howard. "Huston Concocting Another." Los Angeles *Daily News,* April 13, 1954.

McIntyre, Alice. "Making the Misfits." *Esquire,* March 1961, pp. 74–78.

Minetree, Harry. "In Marrakech Old Master John Huston Makes His Dream Movie." *People,* April 21, 1975, pp. 63–65.

Nason, Richard W. "Huston Hits High with Heaven and Geisha." *New York Times,* September 28, 1958.

Newsweek. "Director John Huston." January 9, 1956, pp. 67–70.

————. "John Huston, Actor." March 18, 1963, p. 102.

————. "John Huston's Big Stage." July 21, 1958, p. 87.

————. "Remarkable Man and the Movies in '56." January 9, 1956, pp. 67–70.

The New Yorker. "Questions." June 4, 1949, p. 21.

————. "Tales." June 14, 1969, pp. 31–32.

Oulahan, Richard. "Stars Fell on Mismaloya." *Life,* December 20, 1963.

Parsons, Louella O. "Louella O. Parsons" (column). Pictorial Living, Los Angeles *Examiner,* October 16, 1955.

Phillips, Gene D. "Talking with John Huston." *Film Comment,* May-June 1973, pp. 15–19.

Réalités. "A Home in Ireland." October 1973, pp. 25–27.

Reisz, Karel. "Interview with Huston." *Sight and Sound,* January-March 1952, pp. 130–32.

Ross, Lillian. "The Bible in Dinocitta." *The New Yorker,* September 25, 1965, pp. 185–212.

St. Pierre, Brian. "John Huston: As He Was, Is and Probably Always Will Be." *New York Times,* September 25, 1966, p. 130.

Scheuer, Philip K. "Huston Aided on Location by Army Life." Los Angeles *Times,* June 29, 1947, p. 1.

Scott, Vernon. "Interview with John Huston." United Press International, Winter 1975.

Smith, Cecil. "Back from Japan, Hustling Huston Flies to Africa." Los Angeles *Times,* February 16, 1958, p. 1.

Taylor, Curtice, and O'Brien, Glenn. "Interview with John Huston." *Interview,* September 1972, pp. 42–25.

Taylor, John Russell. "John Huston and the Figure in the Carpet." *Sight and Sound,* Spring 1969, pp. 70–73.

Thomas, Bob. "Huston Recalls Gable's Last." Associated Press, January 16, 1961.

Tozzi, Romano. *John Huston: A Pictorial Treasury of His Films.* Crescent Books, 1971.

Watters, Jim, "Huston: The Man Who Would be Kipling." Chicago *Daily News,* March 6–7, 1976, pp. 17–18.

Williams, Dick, "John Huston Tells Tales of Irish Fox Hunting." *Mirror-News,* November 21, 1955.

Wolf, Warren, "Goodbye Patriotism: Hello Sex, Money and Corruption." *Cue,* June 28, 1969, pp. 10–11.

Index

Aba, Marika, 184

Abarran, Pablo, *see* Huston, Pablo

Abe Lincoln in Illinois, JH's acting role in, 15

Across the Pacific (directed by JH), 89, 99; discussion of, 31–35; mask motif in, 195

Across the River and into the Trees (written by JH), 202–3

Adler, Renata, 151

African Queen, The (directed by JH), 80, 91–92, 97, 118, 173, 182; discussion of, 83–90; success of, 90; compared with *Heaven Knows, Mr. Allison,* 112

Agee, James, 11; *Life* magazine article by, on JH, 3, 5; Henry Blanke on JH to, 16; on *The Battle of San Pietro,* 40–41, 42–43; on withholding of *Let There Be Light,* 43; on *The Treasure of the Sierra Madre,* 57; on *Key Largo,* 60, 62; and *The African Queen,* 80, 84, 90; JH on, 84, 90

Agony and the Ecstasy, The, 161

Albert, Eddie, *The Roots of Heaven,* 120, 121

Albright, Lola, *Champion,* 71

Allen, Woody, *Casino Royale,* 171

Allied Artists, 198, 202

Alpert, Hollis, 113

Amazing Dr. Clitterhouse, The (written by JH), 16

Ambler, Eric, 39, 40; *The Mask of Dimitrios,* 39; *Journey Into Fear,* 39

American Film Institute, *Dialogue on Film* of, 189

American Mercury, The, JH's stories in, 9, 12

Anderson, Ernest, *In This Our Life,* 28, 29, 201

Anderson, Maxwell, *Key Largo,* 59

Anderson, Sherwood, *The Triumph of the Egg,* 8

Aragon, Art, *Fat City,* 188

Archer, Eugene, 29; on *Across the Pacific,* 33

Aristophanes, *Lysistrata,* 108

Armendariz, Pedro, 64

Asphalt Jungle, The (directed by JH), 55, 67, 79, 117, 126, 182, 185; Sam Jaffe's role in, 8; discussion of, 69–73; reviews of, 72; Academy Award nominations for, 72; Marilyn Monroe's role in, 129

Astor, Mary, 47; *The Maltese Falcon,* 20, 22–23; *A Life on Film,* 22; *The Great Lie,* 22; *Across the Pacific,* 31–34

Aumont, Jean-Pierre, 186

Aumont, Tina, 186

Ayres, Lew, 63

Bacall, Lauren, 26, 58; *Key Largo,* 59–61; and House Un-American Activities Committee, 63; and filming of *The African Queen,* 85, 86

Bachmann, Gideon, 5–6, 16, 197, 199; and *Moby Dick,* 103

Bagley, Desmond, *The Freedom Trap,* 194

Barabbas, 161, 162

Barbarian and the Geisha, The (directed by JH), 8, 34, 119; discussion of, 115–18

Barnard, Ivor, 201

Barnes, Howard, on *The Maltese Falcon,* 24

Barrymore, John, 48

Barrymore, Lionel, *Key Largo,* 59–60

Basehart, Richard, *Moby Dick,* 104, 105

Battle for the Planet of the Apes, JH's acting role in, 152

Battle of San Pietro, The (documentary directed by JH), 62, 81; discussion of, 39–43

Beat the Devil (directed by JH), 55, 182, 198, 201; discussion of, 97–99; reception given to, 99–100

Bedoya, Alfonso, *The Treasure of the Sierra Madre,* 201

Behn, Noel, *The Kremlin Letter,* 183

Ben Hur, 8, 123, 162
Bergryd, Ulla, *The Bible*, 166, 201
Bester, Alfred, 122
Biberman, Herbert J., 63
Bible, The (directed by JH), 42, 171, 186, 201, 202; JH's role in, 79, 106, 152, 153, 164–65; discussion of, 162–70; cost of making, 163; JH's narration of, 167; reviews of, 167–68; success of, 169–70, 176
Bickford, Charles, 11; *The Unforgiven*, 126–27
Black, Leslie: JH's proposal to, 15; her marriage to JH, 16; her divorce from JH, 45
Black Narcissus, 111
Blanke, Henry, 21, 56, 58; on JH at 31 years old, 15–16; and *The Treasure of the Sierra Madre*, 48; and *The African Queen*, 83
Bogart, Humphrey, 47, 197; JH's first meeting with, 16; *Key Largo*, 16, 59–61; *The Amazing Dr. Clitterhouse*, 16–17; *High Sierra*, 18, 21; *The Maltese Falcon*, 20–26 *passim*, 30; JH on, 23–24; *Across the Pacific*, 31–35 *passim; All Through the Night*, 32; and Sam Spiegel, 48; *The Treasure of the Sierra Madre*, 56–57, 89; and House Un-American Activities Committee, 63; *The African Queen*, 83–90 *passim;* his Oscar for *The African Queen*, 83, 87, 90; *Beat the Devil*, 97–99
Boni and Liveright, 11
Boone, Richard, *The Kremlin Letter*, 184
Boyer, Charles, *Casino Royale*, 172
Boyle, Hal, 177
Bradbury, Ray: and *Moby Dick*, 101–2, 103–4, 108; *The Martian Chronicles*, 102
Brando, Marlon, 188; *Reflections in a Golden Eye*, 173–74, 176
Breakout, JH's acting role in, 152
Brennan, Walter, *The Westerner*, 192
Brent, George, *In This Our Life*, 27, 28, 30
Bresson, Robert, 163
Breuer, Joseph, 139. *See also Freud*
Bridge in the Jungle, The, JH's acting role in, 151
Bridges, Jeff, *Fat City*, 188
Bronson, Charles, 153; *Love and Bullets, Charlie*, 203
Brook, Clive, *The List of Adrian Messenger*, 143
Brooks, Richard, *Key Largo*, 59, 60
Brouillet (artist), 141–42
Brown, Paddy, 182
Brute Force, 59
Buchwald, Art, 92
Buck, Jules, 37, 39, 40; and *The Battle of San Pietro*, 41; founding of Horizon Films by, with Sam Spiegel and JH, 62
Burks, Robert, 61

Burnett, W. R., 10; *Little Caesar*, 13, 69; and *High Sierra*, 18, 69; *The Asphalt Jungle*, 69
Burton, Richard, 170, 174, 198; *Cleopatra*, 156; *The Night of the Iguana*, 156–59
Butch Cassidy and the Sundance Kid, 188, 198

Cagli, Corrado, 164
Cahiers du Cinema, 168, 172
Cahn, Edward, 13
Caine, Michael, *The Man Who Would Be King*, 198, 201–2
Caine, Shakira, *The Man Who Would Be King*, 201
Calhern, Louis, *The Asphalt Jungle*, 69, 71
Candy, JH's acting role in, 151, 152
Capa, Robert, 108
Capote, Truman, and *Beat the Devil*, 97, 98–99
Capra, Frank, 37, 38
Captains Courageous, 111
Cardinal, The: JH's acting role in, 149–50, 153; reviews of, 150–51
Carey, Gary, *Brando!*, 174
Carson, Robert, "Aloha Means Goodbye," 31
Caruso, Anthony, *The Asphalt Jungle*, 71
Casino Royale (directed by JH): JH's role in, 79, 152, 171–72; success of, 170, 173, 176; discussion of, 171–73; cost of, 171
Champion, 71
Champlin, Charles, 203
Chaplain, Charlie, 164
Charcot, Jean Martin, 125, 141. *See also Freud*
Chennault, General Claire, 38
Chennault, Jack, 38
Chiari, Marco, 164, 165
Chicago *Daily News*, 197
Chicago *Tribune*, 15
Chinatown, JH's acting role in, 152
Clark, General Mark, 39, 41
Clarke, Charles G., 117
Cleopatra, 156
Clift, Montgomery, 77; *The Misfits*, 129, 132, 134, 136; automobile accident of, 135, 140; *Freud*, 139–40; death of, 174
Close-Up magazine, 7
Clymer, John B., 13
Coburn, Charles, *In This Our Life*, 27, 28, 29
Cohen, Benjamin, 66
Cokes, Curtis, *Fat City*, 188, 201
Collins, Charles, 15
Columbia Pictures, 64, 66
Commodore Marries, The, 9
Communist Daily Worker, 64
Connery, Sean, *The Man Who Would Be King*, 199, 201–2
Conrad, Barnaby, *Matador*, 96
Cook, Elisha, Jr., 25

Cooper, Gary: *Sergeant York,* 18; *High Noon,* 96; *The Westerner,* 192
Copland, Aaron, 134
Corbett, Jim, 34
Cortez, Ricardo, 20, 43
Cortez, Stanley, 43
Corwin, Norman, 63, 66
Covarrubias, Miguel, 9
Crane, Stephen, *The Red Badge of Courage,* 76–77
Craven, Frank, *In This Our Life,* 27, 28
Crawford, Joan, 48
Crazy Kill, The, 84
Crist, Judith, 150
Crossfire, 59
Croves, H., 50
Crowther, Bosley, 57; *The Lion's Share,* 76; on JH's role in *The Cardinal,* 150–51; on *The Bible,* 168
Cue, 183
Curtis, Tony, 126; *The List of Adrian Messenger,* 144, 146

Dam Busters, The, 106
Daniels, Bebe, 20
Dano, Royal: *The Red Badge of Courage,* 79; *Moby Dick,* 128
Davenport, Nigel, *Sinful Davey,* 176
David, Zorro, *Reflections in a Golden Eye,* 175, 201
Davis, Bette, 26, 83; and *Jezebel,* 16; *Satan Met a Lady,* 21; *In This Our Life,* 27, 28; *The Night of the Iguana,* 155, 156
Dayan, Assaf, *A Walk with Love and Death,* 179, 180, 181, 201
Dayan, Moshe, 179
Death of a Salesman, 134
DeCarl, Lennard, 45
De Haven, Carter, 186
De Laurentiis, Dino, 161, 170, 185; *The Bible,* 162–64, 167, 169
Del Ruth, Roy, 12
De Mille, Cecil B.: *The Greatest Show on Earth,* 96; *The Ten Commandments,* 167
De Sade, JH's acting role in, 151
Deserter, The, JH's acting role in, 151
Desire Under the Elms, 7
Devil and Daniel Webster, The, 108
Devine, Andy, *The Red Badge of Courage,* 78
Dexter, Brad, *The Asphalt Jungle,* 71
Dierkes, John, *The Red Badge of Courage,* 79
Dieterle, William: *Juarez,* 16; *Satan Met a Lady,* 21
Digges, Dudley, 20
Dillinger, 192
Dirty Harry, 32
Dodsworth, 23

Dortu, M. G., *Lautrec by Lautrec* (with P. Huisman), 91
Douglas, Kirk, *The List of Adrian Messenger,* 143, 144, 145
Douglas, Melvyn, *Hud,* 151
Dunham, Katherine, 166
Dunne, Philip, 63

Eastwood, Clint, 153
Easy Mark, The, 7
Edens, Olive, "Heart and Hand," 13
Eiko Ando, 116
Elisofon, Eliot, 94
Elmer the Great, 9
Endfield, Cy, 151
Esquire, 129

Fairlie, Gerard, 72–73
Farewell to Arms, A, 114, 119
Fat City (directed by JH), 10, 193, 201; discussion of, 187–91; success of, 191
Faulkner, William, *Intruder in the Dust,* 69
Feldman, Charlie, 172
Fellini, Federico, 163, 167
Fernandez, Emilio, 157
Ferrer, José, 172; *Moulin Rouge,* 92–93, 95, 96
"Figures of Fighting Men" (written by JH), 12
Film Comment, 19, 197
Film Culture, 29, 125
Film Daily, 57
Film Quarterly, 5, 16, 179
Films in Review, 118
Fitzgerald, Geraldine, *No Exit,* 47
Flaherty, Robert, 14; *Man of Aran,* 104
Fleischer, Richard, 186
Fleming, Ian, *Casino Royale,* 171
Florey, Robert, 13
Flynn, Errol: *Gentleman Jim,* 34; brawl between JH and, 34, 120; *The Roots of Heaven,* 34, 120–23; *My Wicked, Wicked Ways,* 121; fall taken by, while filming *The Roots of Heaven,* 121, 123
Fonda, Henry, 63
"Fool" (written by JH), 9–10
Forbes, Bryan, 183
Ford, Dan, 193, 194
Ford, John, *The Quiet Man,* 96
Foreman, John, 192, 198
Forester, C. S., *The African Queen,* 83
Forster, Robert, *Reflections in a Golden Eye,* 173
Fountain, The, 9
Fowler, Dan, 7, 48, 58, 65
Francher, Hampton, III, 157
Francine, Renee, 101

Frankie and Johnny (book by JH), 11, 12
Frankie and Johnny (play written by JH), 9, 10–11
Franklin, Pamela, *Sinful Davey,* 176
Freud (directed by JH), 42, 127, 128, 201; discussion of, 139–43; reviews of, 143; protagonist in, 190
Freud, Sigmund, 44, 132, 146; JH's film on, 125, 139. *See also Freud*
Freund, Karl, 61
Fry, Christopher, and *The Bible,* 162, 163
Fuller, Buckminster, 158

Gable, Clark, 197; *The Misfits,* 129–31, 134–35; *It Happened in Naples,* 130; death of, 134, 135
Gabor, Zsa Zsa, *Moulin Rouge,* 94
Gardner, Ava, 63, 108; *The Killers,* 47; *The Night of the Iguana,* 156, 157, 158, 159; *The Life and Times of Judge Roy Bean,* 192
Gardner, Leonard, *Fat City,* 187
Garfield, John, 56, 63, 80; *We Were Strangers,* 64, 70
Gary, Romain, *The Roots of Heaven,* 119, 120
Gate of Hell, 115, 118
Genn, Leo, *Moby Dick,* 105–6
Gentleman Jim, 34
George, Gladys, 24
Gershwin, Ira, 63
Gigi, 114
Gilmore, Eddy, 161
Giradoux, Jean, *The Madwoman of Chaillot,* 183
Gish, Lillian, *The Unforgiven,* 126–27
Glasgow, Ellen, *In This Our Life,* 27
Goddard, Paulette, 57, 63
Golden Boy, 189
Goldwyn, Samuel, 83
Goldwyn Studios, 12, 13
Gomez, Thomas, *Key Largo,* 59
Gone With The Wind, 76
Goode, James, 131, 134
Good Earth, The, 61
Goodman, Benny, 63
Grayson, Charles, 115, 117
Greatest Show on Earth, The, 96
Great Lie, The, 22
Great White Hope, The, 189
Greco, Juliette: *The Roots of Heaven,* 120–24 *passim;* blood disease contracted by, 122, 123
Green, Nigel, *The Kremlin Letter,* 184
Greenstreet, Sydney, 47; *The Maltese Falcon,* 20–23 *passim; Across the Pacific,* 31–35 *passim; Three Strangers,* 31; *The Mask of Dimitrios,* 31; *The Verdict,* 31; *No Exit,* 47
Grencer, Cynthia, 123, 124

Gries, Tom, 152
Griffith, D. W., *Abraham Lincoln,* 15
Grimes, Stephen B.: and *The Unforgiven,* 126; and *The Misfits,* 130; and *The Night of the Iguana,* 156; and *Reflections in a Golden Eye,* 173; and *Love and Bullets, Charlie,* 203
Gris, Juan, 109
Guest, Val, 171
Guiles, Fred Lawrence, 70; *Norma Jean: The Life of Marilyn Monroe,* 133
Guinness, Alec, 164
Gunga Din, 7
Gusson, Mel, *Don't Say Yes Until I Finish Talking,* 121

Haas, Ernst, 166
Hagen, Jean: *The Asphalt Jungle,* 69–70; *Singin' in the Rain,* 70
Hall, Conrad, 188–89
Hall, Grayson, *The Night of the Iguana,* 201
Hamilton, Kipp, *The Unforgiven,* 126
Hammett, Dashiel, *The Maltese Falcon,* 19–20, 21
Harding, Warren G., 18
Harris, Julie, *Reflections in a Golden Eye,* 173, 176
Harris, Richard, *The Bible,* 166
Harris, Townsend, 115–18
Harvey, Dorothy, JH's first marriage to, 8
Havilland, Olivia de, 45; *In This Our Life,* 27, 28, 45
Hawkins, Robert F., 96, 100; and *The Bible,* 164, 165, 166
Hawks, Howard, 18
Hayden, Sterling, 63; *The Asphalt Jungle,* 69–70; *Wanderer,* 70; *The Killing,* 72
Head, Edith, 195, 201
Heaven Knows, Mr. Allison (directed by JH), 115, 157, 172, 173, 182, 198; discussion of, 111–14; reviews of, 114
Hecht, Ben, 114
Hecht-Hill-Lancaster, 126
Heflin, Van, 63
Hell's Heroes, JH's acting role in, 11
Helvick, James, *Beat the Devil,* 97, 98
Hemingway, Ernest, 10, 12, 51, 135–36; *The Killers,* 47; *A Farewell to Arms,* 114; *Across the River and into the Trees,* 202–3
Hepburn, Audrey, *The Unforgiven,* 126–27, 181
Hepburn, Katharine, 63; *The African Queen,* 84, 86–88; *The Madwoman of Chaillot,* 183
Heston, Charlton, *The Ten Commandments,* 167
Higham, Charles, 86, 156, 159
High Noon, 96

High Sierra (written by JH), 18, 21, 69
Hill, Gladys, 118, 132, 174, 203; and *The Man Who Would Be King,* 198, 202; and *Across the River and into the Trees,* 202
Hine, Al, 93
Hitchcock, Alfred, 61; *Saboteur,* 35
Hitler, Adolf, 41, 62
Holden, William, 120, 121; *Casino Royale,* 172
Holiday magazine, 93, 122
Hollywood Reporter, The, 64, 202
Holt, Tim, 57; *The Treasure of the Sierra Madre,* 56, 89
Hopper, Hedda, 158–59
Horizon Films, 64, 65, 67; founding of, by JH, Sam Spiegel, and Jules Buck, 62, 118; and *The African Queen,* 87
Hornblow, Arthur, Jr., 69, 72
Houghston, Elizabeth (McGibbon), 1–2
Houghston, Robert, 1–2
House Beautiful, 65
House Divided, A (written by JH), 13
Houseman, John, 63
House Un-American Activities Committee (HUAC), 62–64, 69, 140; Committee for the First Amendment to combat, 63
Howard, Trevor, *The Roots of Heaven,* 120, 122, 123
Hud, 151
Hughes, Ken, 171
Hughes, Matcher, *Ruint,* 8
Hughes, Robert, 38, 39, 40; ed., *Film: Book 2: Films of Peace and War,* 44
Huisman, Philippe, *Lautrec by Lautrec* (with M. G. Dortu), 91
Hurt, John, *Sinful Davey,* 176
Huston, Anjelica (daughter of JH), 102, 109, 176, 185; birth of, 84; JH's portrait of, 177; *A Walk with Love and Death,* 179, 180, 182; death of mother of, 183
Huston, John Marcellus: birth of, 1; becomes Irish citizen, 2, 161; early years of, 3–6; his interest in horses, 4, 8; boxing career of, 5–6, 7, 10; joins father in New York, 6–7; and Sam Jaffe, 7–8; his interest in art, 8; first marriage of, to Dorothy Harvey, 8; enlists in Mexican army, 8–9; his gambling, 11; early writing of, in Hollywood, 13–14; his adventures in London and Paris, 14–15; return of, to Hollywood, 15; second marriage of, to Leslie Black, 16; becomes writer for Warner Brothers, 16–18; becomes director, 19; on Humphrey Bogart, 23–24; nicknames for, 26, 27, 48; brawl between Errol Flynn and, 34, 120; WWII army films of, 37–45; his divorce from Leslie Black, 45; third marriage of, to Evelyn Keyes, 45; his role in *The Treasure of the Sierra Madre,* 53, 78–79; his Academy Award for best director, 57; Oscar celebration held by, 57–58; founding of Horizon Films by, with Sam Spiegel and Jules Buck, 62, 118; and House Un-American Activities Committee, 62–64; his divorce from Evelyn Keyes, 66; fourth marriage of, to Enrica Soma, 66; death of his father, 73; his role in *The Red Badge of Courage,* 79; birth of his son, 79–80; on James Agee, 84, 90; birth of his daughter, 84; move to Ireland by, 97; on Robert Mitchum, 114; his narration of *Freud,* 142; his cameo in *The List of Adrian Messenger,* 144; acting roles of, 149–53, 203; likes and dislikes of, 177; return of, to serious painting, 177; death of his fourth wife, 183; fifth marriage of, to Celeste Shane, 193; selling of Irish estate of, 196; his divorce from Celeste Shane, 203. *See also* individual films and plays throughout index
Huston, Mrs. John, first (Dorothy Harvey), 8
Huston, Mrs. John, second (Leslie Black), 15, 16, 45
Huston, Mrs. John, third (Evelyn Keyes), 63, 101; marriage of, to JH, 45; and Pablo Abarran Huston, 56; and Paulette Goddard, 57–58; JH's design of home for, 65; her divorce from JH, 66
Huston, Mrs. John, fourth (Enrica Soma): JH's fourth marriage to, 66; birth of her son, 79–80; birth of her daughter, 84; JH's letter to, from Africa, 85; move to Ireland by, 97; riding accident of, 102; death of, 183
Huston, Mrs. John, fifth (Celeste Shane), 193, 203
Huston, Pablo (Abarran), 56, 79
Huston, Rhea (Gore), 1, 2–3, 4, 6, 11, 15; death of, 16
Huston (formerly Houghston), Walter (father of JH), 11, 69, 146–47; marriage of, to Rhea Gore, 1, 2–3; birth and early years of, 1–2; marriage of, to Bayonne Whipple, 3–4; theatrical career of, 6–7, 9, 13, 15; marriage of, to Nan Sunderland, 16; in *A Passenger to Bali,* 17–18; and *The Maltese Falcon,* 22–23, 116–17; "good luck" roles played by, 22, 28; in *In This Our Life,* 28, 30; his narration of war documentaries, 37, 43; and Evelyn Keyes, 45; in *The Treasure of the Sierra Madre,* 53, 56, 57, 89, 116–17; Academy Award for *The Treasure of the Sierra Madre* for, 57; on JH, 58; death of, 73
Huston, Walter Anthony (son of JH), 102, 109; birth of, 80; screen debut of, in *The List of Adrian Messenger,* 143–44, 147; death of mother of, 183

Hyams, Joe, 56; *Bogie*, 83, 98
Hyman, Elliot, 125; and *The Misfits*, 129–30

In Cold Blood, 59
In Convict Stripes, 2
Indiscretion of an American Wife, 97
Interview, 176, 187, 188, 191
In This Our Life (directed by JH), 45, 201; discussion of, 27–30
In Time to Come (written by JH), 18, 149
Ireland, Jill, *Love and Bullets, Charlie*, 203
Ireland, JH's move to, 97
It Happened in Naples, 130
Ives, Burl, 99, 132

Jacks, Bobby, 121
Jaffe, Sam, 7–8; and JH's *Frankie and Johnny*, 11; *The Asphalt Jungle*, 69; *The Barbarian and the Geisha*, 115, 117
Jagger, Dean, *The Kremlin Letter*, 184
Jenny (JH's fox terrier), 58
Jezebel (written by JH), 16, 26
Joanna, 151
Jocasta, JH's acting role in, 203
Joffrey, Saeed, *The Man Who Would Be King*, 201
Johnny Belinda, 59
Johnny O'Clock, 56
Jolson Sings Again, 139
Jolson Story, The, 56, 139
Jones, Jennifer, 58; *We Were Strangers*, 64–65, 98; *Indiscretion of an American Wife*, 97; *Beat the Devil*, 97, 98, 99
Juarez (written by JH), 16
Julius Caesar, 2

Kael, Pauline, 151, 183
Kanin, Gar, 18
Kasznar, Kurt, *Casino Royale*, 172
Kaufman, Charles, 139
Kaye, Danny, 63
Keach, Stacy: *Fat City*, 10, 188, 191; *The Life and Times of Judge Roy Bean*, 192
Kedrova, Lila, *The Kremlin Letter*, 184
Keith, Brian, *Reflections in a Golden Eye*, 173, 176
Kelly, Gene, 63, 64, 92
Kelly, Seamus, *Moby Dick*, 104
Kennedy, Burt, 151
Kennedy, Paul, 158
Kerr, Deborah: *Black Narcissus*, 111; *Heaven Knows, Mr. Allison*, 111, 113; *The Night of the Iguana*, 156, 157, 158; *Casino Royale*, 172
Keyes, Evelyn, 63, 101; her marriage to JH, 45; and Pablo Abarran Huston, 56; and Paulette Goddard, 57–58; JH's design of

home for, 65; her divorce from JH, 66
Key Largo (directed by JH), 16, 69, 72, 173, 190; discussion of, 59–62
Kilbracken, John, 104, 107; *Living like a Lord*, 104–5
Killers, The, JH's role in, 47, 92
Killing, The, 72
King, Henry, *The Sun Also Rises*, 120
Kipling, Rudyard, "The Man Who Would Be King," 49, 197, 198; story and film compared, 199–201
Knight, Arthur, 103, 104, 107, 160
Koch, Howard, 18; *The Manchurian Candidate*, 15; *The Odd Couple*, 15; *In This Our Life*, 27; *Three Strangers*, 47
Kohner, Pancho, 151, 203
Kohner, Paul, 78, 125, 133
Kongo, 9
Koningsberger, Hans, *A Walk with Love and Death*, 179–81
Kremlin Letter, The (directed by JH), 55, 152, 187; JH's role in, 79, 185; discussion of, 183–86; reviews of, 186; compared with *The Mackintosh Man*, 195–96
Kubrick, Stanley: *The Killing*, 72; *Lolita*, 156
Kukan, 37
Kunert, Arnold R., 103

La Farge, Oliver, *Laughing Boy*, 14
La Mure, Pierre, *Moulin Rouge*, 91
Lancaster, Burt: *The Killers*, 47; *The Unforgiven*, 126–27; *The List of Adrian Messenger*, 144
Landau, Ely, 183
Lang, Fritz, *Spies*, 35
Larbi, Doghmi, *The Man Who Would Be King*, 201
Lardner, Ring, 9, 10
Lark, The, 108
Lasky, Jesse, 66
Last Laugh, The, 61
Last Picture Show, The, 188
Last Run, The, 186, 187
Laurot, Edouard, 125
Law and Order (written by JH), 13
Lawrence, Marc: *Key Largo*, 59; *The Asphalt Jungle*, 69, 71
Ledebur, Count Friedrich, 132; *The Roots of Heaven*, 120, 122, 201; *Moby Dick*, 201
Ledoux, Fernand, *Freud*, 141, 201
Lee, Christopher, 95
Leigh-Fermor, Patrick, 120
Leighton, Margaret, *The Night of the Iguana*, 155
LeMay, Alan, *The Unforgiven*, 126
Lerner, Alan Jay, *Gigi*, 114
Let's Make Love, 130, 134

Let There Be Light (documentary directed by JH), 55, 78, 139; discussion of, 43–45

Liberty (JH's monkey), 57, 58

Life and Times of Judge Roy Bean, The (directed by JH), 127, 195, 198; discussion of, 191–94; JH's role in, 193; cost of making, 194; success of, 194

Life magazine, 3, 5, 94

List of Adrian Messenger, The (directed by JH), 42, 127, 149, 181, 186; discussion of, 143–47; JH's cameo in, 144; reviews of, 147; mask motif in, 195–96

Litvak, Anatole, 16, 37, 38, 92

Loew's Consolidated Enterprises, 76

Lolita, 156

Lollobrigida, Gina, *Beat the Devil,* 98, 99

Lonely Man, JH's acting role in, 15

Look magazine, 7, 48, 58

Lord, Rosemary, 10, 106, 114, 135

Lord Jim, 59

Loren, Sophia, 130; *Jocasta,* 203

Lorre, Peter: *The Maltese Falcon,* 23, 25; *Three Strangers,* 31; *The Mask of Dimitrios,* 31; *The Verdict,* 31; *Background to Danger,* 33; *No Exit,* 47; *Beat the Devil,* 98

Los Angeles *Herald-Examiner,* 179, 180, 181

Los Angeles *Times,* 115, 125, 184, 193, 203

Lost Horizon, 8

Love and Bullets, Charlie (originally to be directed by JH), 203

Loy, Myrna, 63

Luciano, Lucky, 62

Lugosi, Bela, 13

Lukas, Paul, *The Roots of Heaven,* 120, 123

Lupino, Ida, 58

Lyon, Sue: *Lolita,* 156; *The Night of the Iguana,* 156, 157, 158

Macaulay, Richard, 31

McCallum, David, *Freud,* 141

McCarten, John, 57; on *We Were Strangers,* 64

McClure, Doug, *The Unforgiven,* 126–27

McCullers, Carson, *Reflections in a Golden Eye,* 173–74, 175

MacDonald, Phillip, *The List of Adrian Messenger,* 143

McDowell, Roddy, *The Life and Times of Judge Roy Bean,* 194

Macgowan, Kenneth, 8

McGrath, Joe, 171

Mackintosh Man, The (directed by JH), 190, 198; discussion of, 194–96; reviews of, 196

Maddow, Ben, 69, 126

Madsen, Axel, 14

Madwoman of Chaillot, The, 183, 187

Mage, David A., 93, 95

Mahin, John Lee, 111, 114

Maltese Falcon, The (directed by JH), 15, 27, 31, 72, 190; discussion of, 19–26; reception of, 26; Academy Award nomination for, 26; compared with *In This Our Life,* 30; compared with *Across the Pacific,* 33; compared with *The Treasure of the Sierra Madre,* 55; John Wayne on, 116–17; cost of making, 126; protagonist in, 190; mask motif in, 195

Manchurian Candidate, The, 15

Mangano, Silvana, 93

Man in the Wilderness, JH's acting role in, 151

Mankowitz, Wolf, 171

Man of Aran, 104

Mansfield, Richard, 2

Mantz, Paul, 45

Man Who Would Be King, The (directed by JH), 42, 49, 55, 153; Freemasonry in, 34; JH's lifelong wish to make, 91, 109, 135, 170; discussion of, 197–99; film and Kipling's story compared, 199–201; casting of, 201–2; success of, 202

Manzu (artist), 164

Marchand, Colette, *Moulin Rouge,* 94–95

Marquand, Christian, 151

Marshall, General George C., 41

Marton, Andrew, 77

Marty, 126

Marvin, Lee, 174

Mason, James, *The Mackintosh Man,* 195

Mauldin, Bill, *The Red Badge of Courage,* 78, 89, 201

Mayer, Louis B., 75–76; and *The Red Badge of Courage,* 76–77, 78

Mayes, Wendell, 203

Melville, Herman, 106; *Moby Dick,* 101, 103, 107–8; *Typee,* 108

Mencken, H. L., 9

Meredith, Burgess, 63

Merritt, Arnold, *The Unforgiven,* 126

Metropolis, 61

Meyer, Nicholas, *The Seven Per-Cent Solution,* 139

MGM, 64, 65, 69; *The Asphalt Jungle,* 67, 70; *The Red Badge of Courage,* 75, 82, 83; power struggle at, 75–76

Mid-Week Pictorial magazine, 15

Mildred Pierce, 59

Milestone, Lewis, 48

Milius, John, 152, 192

Miller, Arthur: *The Misfits,* 129–36 *passim;* *Death of a Salesman,* 134

Minnelli, Vincent, 160

Mirisch, Walter, 176

Mirko (artist), 164

Misfits, The (directed by JH), 84, 139, 140, 182, 190; discussion of, 129–37; critical response to, 137

Mister Pitt, 6

Mitchum, Robert: *Heaven Knows, Mr. Allison,* 112, 113–14; JH on, 114; *The List of Adrian Messenger,* 144, 146

Moby Dick (directed by JH), 84, 91, 100, 120, 128, 152, 201; relation of color to subject in, 95; discussion of, 101–7; whales built for, 105, 106–7, 126; novel and film compared, 107–8; awards for, 108; JH on, 108–9; JH's injury during, 132; religious subject matter of, 159, 168; compared with *The Bible,* 168–69; categorizing of, 182, 190; protagonist in, 190; Oswald Morris and, 198

Monet, Claude, 109

Monroe, Marilyn, 108; *The Asphalt Jungle,* 69, 70–71, 129; marriage of, to Arthur Miller, 129; *The Misfits,* 129–35 *passim;* *Let's Make Love,* 130, 134; end of her marriage to Miller, 133; death of, 135

Montand, Yves, 130, 133

Montez, Maria, 186

Montezuma and Cortez, JH's wish to make film about, 125

Moore, Brian, *The Lonely Passion of Judith Hearne,* 183

Moore, Roger, 152, 203

Morgan, Dennis, *In This Our Life,* 27, 28

Morley, Robert, 172; *The African Queen,* 88; *Beat the Devil,* 98, 99; *Sinful Davey,* 176

Morris, Oswald, 94, 107, 112, 120, 198

Morris, R. F., Jr., 15

Mortimer, Chapman, 174

Motion Picture National Board of Review, 108

Moulin Rouge (directed by JH), 8, 107, 140, 181, 198; discussion of, 91–97; success of, 96, 101

Muni, Paul, 59; and *Juarez,* 16

Murders in the Rue Morgue (written by JH), 13

Murphy, Audie: *The Red Badge of Courage,* 78, 79, 89; *The Unforgiven,* 126–27

Myra Breckinridge, JH's acting role in, 151, 152

Nason, Richard W., 119

Nation, The, 40, 42, 43, 60

Negulesco, Jean, 47

Newman, Paul: *The Life and Times of Judge Roy Bean,* 192, 193, 194; *The Mackintosh Man,* 194, 195

Newsweek, 4, 11, 123; on *The Treasure of the Sierra Madre,* 57; on *In This Our Life,* 29; on *The Red Badge of Courage,* 80

New York *Daily News,* 77

New York Drama Critics Circle award, 18, 47, 155

New Yorker, The, 57, 64, 67, 151, 162, 179; on *The Asphalt Jungle,* 72; and *The Red Badge of Courage,* 75

New York Film Critics award, 57, 108

New York *Graphic,* 11

New York *Herald Tribune,* 24, 150

New York Post, 44

New York Times, 27, 37, 96, 118, 119, 158, 164; on *Report from the Aleutians,* 38; on *The Treasure of the Sierra Madre,* 57; on JH's role in *The Cardinal,* 150–51; on JH's role in *Candy,* 151; on *The Bible,* 168

Night of the Iguana, The (directed by JH), 42, 161, 168, 174, 200, 201; discussion of, 155–60; success of, 160

Niven, David: *Bring on the Empty Horses,* 83; *Casino Royale,* 172

No Exit (directed by JH), 47–48

Nolan, William, 11, 14

North, Alex, 134

O'Brien, Glenn, 176

Odd Couple, The, 15

Olivier, Laurence, *Hamlet,* 57

O'Neal, Patrick: *The Night of the Iguana,* 155, 174; *The Kremlin Letter,* 185

One Flew over the Cuckoo's Nest, 202

O'Neill, Eugene, *Desire Under the Elms,* 7

One World Committee, 65–66, 67

Other Side of the Wind, The, JH's acting role in, 152

O'Toole, Peter, 170, 198; *The Bible,* 166

Paramount Pictures, 66

Parish, James Robert, 45

Parker, Freddy, 131

Parkins, Barbara, *The Kremlin Letter,* 184

Parks, Larry, *Freud,* 139–40

Parrish, Robert, 171

Parsons, Louella, 102, 108

Passenger to Bali, A (directed by JH), 17–18

Patrick, Lee, 30

Paulette (JH's German shepherd), 57

Pearson, Billy, 92, 108, 132, 133, 194

Peck, Gregory, 63, 69, 109; *Moby Dick,* 101, 105, 107, 108

Peckinpah, Sam, *The Wild Bunch,* 157

Pemberton, Brock, 6

Phillips, Gene, 17, 18, 48; and *The Maltese Falcon,* 19, 21; and *The Battle of San Pietro,* 41; and *Let There Be Light,* 44; and *The Treasure of the Sierra Madre,* 56; and *The Red Badge of Courage,* 75, 82; and *Heaven Knows, Mr. Allison,* 111; and *The Barbarian and the Geisha,* 118; and *Freud,* 139, 140, 142; and *Reflections in a Golden Eye,* 175–76

Picasso, Pablo, 93

Picture (Lillian Ross), 4, 75, 84

Plummer, Christopher, 153; *The Man Who Would Be King,* 199

Polanski, Roman, 152

Polonsky, Abraham, 63

Powell, Dick, 56

Preminger, Ingo, 149

Preminger, Otto, 112; *In Time to Come,* 18, 149; *The Cardinal,* 149–50

Quiet Man, The, 96

Quo Vadis?, 65, 67, 69

Raft, George, 20; *Background to Danger,* 33

Rashomon, 115

Ray, Nicholas, 112

Réalités, 173, 182

Red Badge of Courage, The (directed by JH), 42, 89, 91, 130, 201; and conflict at MGM, 75–76, 83; discussion of, 76–82; reviews of, 80; Billy Pearson's role in, 92; categorizing of, 182

Red Dust, 111

Reed, Tom, 13

Reflections in a Golden Eye (directed by JH), 51, 95, 181, 185, 186, 201; discussion of, 173–76; response to, 176; assessment of, 187; protagonist in, 190

Reinhardt, Gottfried, 76, 77, 79, 80

Reinhardt, Wolfgang, 133, 139

Reminiscences of a Cowboy, 65, 67

Report from the Aleutians (documentary directed by JH), 39; discussion of, 37–38

Reuss, Antoinette, *A Walk with Love and Death,* 179

Richardson, Tony, *Tom Jones,* 176

Ritter, Thelma, 132, 135

Rivkin, Allen, 14; *Hello, Hollywood,* 14; *The Maltese Falcon,* 19, 20

Roberts Company, 63

Robinson, Edward G., 80; *Key Largo,* 16, 59–60; *The Amazing Dr. Clitterhouse,* 16–17

Romanoff, Mike, 45

Roosevelt, Franklin D., 15, 38

Roots of Heaven, The (directed by JH), 34, 129, 132, 152, 198, 201; discussion of, 119–25; reviews of, 125; categorizing of, 182

Ross, Lillian, 8, 76, 80, 162; *Picture,* 4, 75, 84; and *The Red Badge of Courage,* 78, 79; and *The Bible,* 163

Rotunno, Giuseppe, 166

Roux, Jacques, *The List of Adrian Messenger,* 144

Ryman, Lucille, 70

Sahl, Mort, 132

St. Joseph, Ellis, 17

St. Pierre, Brian, 125

Salmi, Albert, *The Unforgiven,* 126–27

Sanda, Dominique, *The Mackintosh Man,* 195

Sanders, George, 98; *The Kremlin Letter,* 184

Sarafian, Richard, 151

Sarne, Michael, 151

Sarris, Andrew, 174

Sartre, Jean Paul, 139, 182; *No Exit,* 47–48

Satan Met a Lady, 21

Saturday Evening Post, 31

Saturday Review, 47, 103, 104, 113, 160

Scarlet Express, The, 7–8

Schary, Dore, 75–76; and *The Red Badge of Courage,* 78, 79

Schenck, Nicholas, 76

Scheuer, Philip K., 49

Schulberg, Budd, 59

Scott, George C.: *The List of Adrian Messenger,* 143, 146, 186; *The Last Run,* 186

Scott, Ray, 37

Scott, Vernon, 202–3

Screen Directors Guild award, 72

Screen Producer's Guild Journal, The, 143

Screen Writers' Guild, 103

Sellers, Peter, *Casino Royale,* 171, 172

Selznick, David O., 66, 76, 97, 98; and *A Farewell to Arms,* 114, 119

Sen Yung, Victor, *Across the Pacific,* 33, 34

Sergeant York (written by JH), 18

Seven Arts Company, 155

Seven Arts Production, 125

Seymour, Dan, 61

Shades of Grey, 45

Shadows Pursuing (written by JH), 15

Shakedown, JH's acting role in, 11

Shane, Celeste, 196; JH's fifth marriage to, 193; JH's divorce from, 203

Sharpe, Alan, 186

Shaw, Charles, *Heaven Knows, Mr. Allison,* 111

Sheriff, Paul, 92

Sherlock Holmes in New York, JH's acting role in, 152, 203

Sherman, Vincent, 32

Shingelton, Wilfred, 87

Shootist, The, 32

Siegel, Don, 32, 33

Sight and Sound, 147, 185, 191

Sinatra, Frank, *The List of Adrian Messenger,* 144

Sinful Davey (directed by JH), 181, 182, 183, 186, 187; discussion of, 176

Singin' in the Rain, 70
Siodmak, Robert, 47
Sleeping Prince, The, 108
Smith, Cecil, 115, 116
Socrates (JH's burro), 58
Soma, Anthony, 66
Soma, Enrica (Rica): JH's fourth marriage to, 66; birth of her son, 79–80; birth of her daughter, 84; JH's letter to, from Africa, 85; move to Ireland by, 97; riding accident of, 102; death of, 183
Southern, Terry, 151, 171
Spiegel, Sam, 48, 66, 70; founding of Horizon Films by JH, Jules Buck, and, 62, 118; and *The African Queen,* 84, 87–88, 118
Stark, Ray, 155
Starr, Ringo, 151
Stars and Stripes (military newspaper), 78
Steinbeck, John, 92; *The Moon is Down,* 18
Steiner, Max, 57
Stevens, George, *A Place in the Sun,* 90
Storm, The, JH's acting role in, 11
Storm Child (written by JH), 15
Strada, La, 161
Sturges, Preston, 18
Sullivan, Barry, 63
Sun Also Rises, The, 120
Sunderland, Nan, Walter Huston's marriage to, 16
Sylvester, Robert, *Rough Sketch,* 64

Tanaka, I., 118
Taylor, Curtice, 176
Taylor, Elizabeth, 69, 156, 157–58, 170; *Reflections in a Golden Eye,* 173–74, 176
Taylor, Frank, and *The Misfits,* 129, 130–31, 134
Taylor, John Russell, 147, 185, 191
Taylor, Robert, 69
Ten Commandments, The, 167
Tentacles, JH's acting role in, 151, 203
Theatre Arts, 85, 86
Theatre Magazine, 6
Thomas, Bob, 135
Thomas, J. Parnell, 63
Thompson, J. Lee, 152
Three Strangers (written by JH), 47
Time, 60, 62; on *In Time to Come,* 18; on *The Battle of San Pietro,* 43; on *No Exit,* 47; on *The Treasure of the Sierra Madre,* 57; on JH in *The Cardinal,* 151; on *A Walk with Love and Death,* 183
Tiomkin, Dmitri, 37, 41, 43
Tom Jones, 176
Toshiro Mayuzumi, 166
Toulouse-Lautrec, Henri de, 8, 91, 109, 172,

181; and *Moulin Rouge,* 91–94, 96–97
Tracy, Spencer, 79
Transatlantic Review, 10, 114
Traveling Executioner, The, 188
Travern, B.: *The Treasure of the Sierra Madre,* film and novel compared, 48–54, 151; *The Bridge in the Jungle,* 151
Treacher, Arthur, 21
Treasure of the Sierra Madre, The (directed by JH), 15–16, 61, 91, 151, 200, 201; novel and film compared, 48–55; JH's role in, 53, 78–79; discussion of, 55–57; reviews of, 57; Academy Awards for John and Walter Huston for, 57, 59; releasing of, without mention of JH, 62; failure of, to turn a profit, 64; absence of women in, 77; placement of characters in, 89; John Wayne on, 116–17; categorizing of, 182; protagonists in, 190
Tree, Marietta, *The Misfits,* 131
Trevor, Claire: *The Amazing Dr. Clitterhouse,* 16; *Key Largo,* 16, 59–61
Triumph of the Egg, The, JH's acting role in, 8
Trumbo, Dalton, 63
Twentieth Century-Fox, 83; JH's three-picture contract with, 109, 114, 115; and *Heaven Knows, Mr. Allison,* 111; and *The Barbarian and the Geisha,* 116; and *The Roots of Heaven,* 119; and *The Bible,* 167
Two Americans, JH's acting role in, 11
Tyrell, Susan, *Fat City,* 188

Underdown, Edward, *Beat the Devil,* 98, 99
Unforgiven, The (directed by JH), 130, 181, 191; cost of making, 126; discussion of, 126–28; reviews of, 128
United Artists, 125
Universal Studios, 13, 14; and *Freud,* 140, 142; and *The List of Adrian Messenger,* 143
Utrillo, Maurice, 109

Vallone, Raf, 150
Van Devere, Trish, 186
Van Every, Dale, 13
Variety, 150, 160; on *The Bible,* 167–68, 170
Veiller, Anthony: and *Moulin Rouge,* 92; and *Beat the Devil,* 97; and *The List of Adrian Messenger,* 143; and *The Night of the Iguana,* 155
Venice Film Festival award, 57
Vertes, Marcel, 92
Vidal, Gore, 151
Vidor, Charles, 45, 115
Viertel, Peter, 96, 157; *We Were Strangers,* 64; *White Hunter, Black Heart,* 84–85, 157; and *The African Queen,* 88; and *Beat the*

Devil, 97; and *The Man Who Would Be King,* 109
Village Voice, 174
Visconti, Luchino, 163, 166
Von Sydow, Max, *The Kremlin Letter,* 184

Wald, Jerry, and *Key Largo,* 59
Walker, June, *The Unforgiven,* 126, 128
Walk with Love and Death, A (directed by JH), 51, 186, 187, 200, 201; JH's role in, 79, 179; discussion of, 179–83
Wallace, Henry, 63
Wallach, Eli, *The Misfits,* 129, 132, 134
Wallis, Hal, 16
Walpole, Hugh, 15
Walsh, Raoul, 18; *Background to Danger,* 33
War Department, JH's army films made for, 37–43 *passim*
Warner, Jack, 104; and *The Maltese Falcon,* 19, 24; and *The Treasure of the Sierra Madre,* 56; and *Key Largo,* 61
Warner Brothers, 1, 63, 72; JH becomes contract writer for, 16–18; and *The Maltese Falcon,* 22, 24, 26; and *In This Our Life,* 27; and *Across the Pacific,* 31, 32; and *The Treasure of the Sierra Madre,* 48, 55–56, 57; JH's departure from, 62; and *The African Queen,* 83; and *Moby Dick,* 104; and *Reflections in a Golden Eye,* 175
Wasserman, Dale, 179
Watters, Jim, 118, 197, 203
Wayne, John, *The Barbarian and the Geisha,* 34, 115–18
Weldon, Hattie, 8
Welles, Orson, 163; *Moby Dick,* 106, 152; *The Roots of Heaven,* 120, 156; *The Other Side of the Wind,* 156; *The Kremlin Letter,* 156, 184
West, Bobby, 6
Westerner, The, 192
Westmore, Bud, 144

We Were Strangers (directed by JH), 66, 70, 84, 98, 182; discussion of, 64–65
Wexley, John, 16
What Makes Sammy Run?, 59
Whipple, Bayonne (Mrs. Walter Huston), 3–4
Whitmore, James: *The Asphalt Jungle,* 69, 71, 79; his narration of *The Red Badge of Courage,* 79
Why We Fight (documentary series), 37
Wild Bunch, The, 157
Wilde, Cornel, 63
Wilder, Billy, 63
William, Warren, 21
Williams, Dick, 103
Williams, Tennessee, *The Night of the Iguana,* 155, 156, 160
Wilson, Marie, 21
Wilson, Woodrow, 18
Wind and the Lion, The, JH's acting role in, 152, 192
Winston, Archer, 44–45
Wiseman, Joseph, *The Unforgiven,* 127
Wolfson, P. J. "Pinky," 14
WPA Federal Theater Project, 15
Wright, Frank Lloyd, 65
Wyatt, Jane, 63
Wyler, William, 26, 29, 80, 162; his influence on JH, 11, 30; JH's work with, 13–14; and *Jezebel,* 16; and Hollywood blacklist, 63; on *The Red Badge of Courage,* 79; and *Heaven Knows, Mr. Allison,* 111; and *The Westerner,* 192
Wynter, Dana, *The List of Adrian Messenger,* 144

York, Susannah, *Freud,* 140

Zanuck, Darryl, and *The Roots of Heaven,* 119–25 *passim*
Zolotow, Maurice, *Shooting Star,* 116